Historic Dinosaurs

Historic Dinosaurs
Evidence that dragons are not mythological beasts®

revised edition

Russel Tingley

Copyright © 2015. Russel Tingley. All rights reserved.
Registered U.S. Copyright # TSu 1-985-481. October 12, 2015.
No part of this publication may be reproduced or transmitted in any form or by any means electronic or mechanical, including photocopy, recording, or any information storage and retrieval system available, without permission in writing from the author. Quoting brief passages for personal use is allowed as long as they are in their proper context and correct credit references used. All illustrations to be copied must have written permission from the illustrator before use and must be correctly credited. All photos to be copied must have permission from their respective sources. Photo credits are given where applicable. None of the photographers and referenced authors have endorsed this book unless indicated otherwise. Due to the dynamic nature of the internet, web addresses may have changed since publication.

ISBN: 978-0-9968404-0-8

Printed in the United States of America.
Revised first edition.   January 2019 / January 2023 / January 2025

Written and illustrated by Russel Tingley.
Edited by Dr. Jeff Vore.
Dr. Vore kindly gave of his limited time to review and edit the major textual mistakes in the initial version of this book. It is entirely my fault if any errors remain or have been added upon revision.

Cover painting: *Nine Dragons handscroll* (section). By Chen Rong.
1244 AD. Chinese Song Dynasty.
Francis Gardner Curtis Fund, 17.1697. Photograph © 2015. Museum of Fine Arts, Boston.

Fonts: Times New Roman, University Ornate, Adobe Ming.
Biblical references are from the New American Standard Bible unless indicated otherwise.

Another book by this author: "Chinese Dictionary of Individual Characters - Comparing Simplified, Traditional, Small Seal, and Large Seal Scripts".

Russel Tingley
16600 Monterey St. #308
Morgan Hill, CA 95038

For family, friends, and fellow believers

Table of Contents

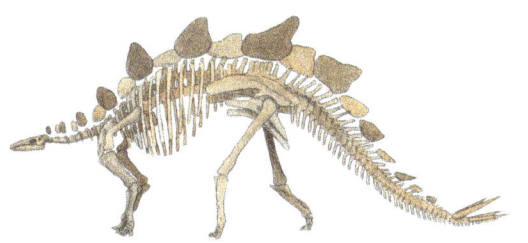

Preface — x

Introduction — xi

Arguments:

1: Opposing views (theological perspective) — 1

2: Geologic Evidence of a Catastrophe (scientific perspective) — 17

Evidence:

3: Eastern Historic Dragons — 29

4: Western Historic Dragons — 67

5: Flying Fiery Serpents and Thunderbirds — 100

6: Monsters of the Deep — 113

7: Modern Accounts — 142

8: Dragon Art — 164

Afterward — 183

Appendices:

A: Living Fossils — 185

B: Toxins & Bioluminescence — 198

C: Biblical Dragons — 201

D: Corrections and Notes — 206

References — 211

Graphic references — 230

Index — 231

Preface

This book is perhaps the largest compilation of evidences in a single volume (some never before presented) supporting the view that mankind and dinosaurs (aka: dragons, behemoths, etc.) were contemporaries. It was born out of the desire to present a more thorough argument than what is generally given on this particular topic. The ultimate goal is to affirm that the Bible, particularly the creation account in Genesis, can be trusted and taken literally.

Divided into two sections, this book first gives a brief overview of the theological and scientific arguments supporting a young earth history and a single global catastrophic flood as described in creation accounts in virtually every major culture on the planet. The second section describes often overlooked evidences found throughout the earth that indicate man and dinosaurs lived side-by-side throughout much of recorded history. Effort was made to provide correct and precise manuscript sources. If the source text was not in English, the best authoritative translation was used.

These two sections go hand in hand. If the earth is young, and a global flood is responsible for nearly all fossils we see, then it is not difficult to determine that man and dinosaurs were contemporaries at some point. *Please note that the evidence provided in the second section is not contingent upon the arguments in the first section. In other words, if you prefer to avoid such theological and scientific argumentation, simply skip this first section.* Nevertheless, each section strengthens the other and the entire book should be seen as a single argument.

Great care has been taken to attain a high level of integrity in this work to support such an unconventional (and often ridiculed) view. It is written with hope that the reader is honored by the evidence gathered and will find it compelling as well.

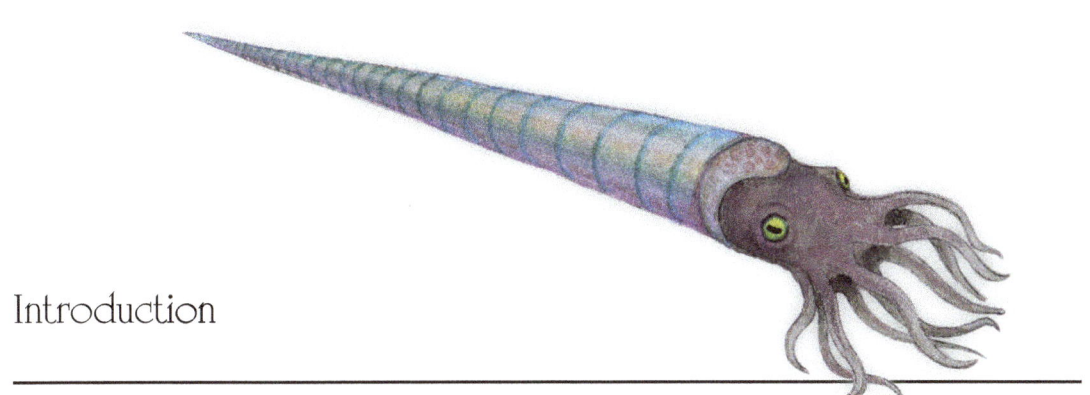

Introduction

Contrary to popular belief, Western techniques of the modern scientific method were borne out of the Christian world view.[1] The assumption was that if the God described in the Bible was a being of logical order, we should be able to study His creation to find out how it worked. Also, due to the creation account described in the book of Genesis, it was naturally believed by the early church that the universe was relatively young. An estimated six (to as much as twelve) thousand years have been calculated since the universe was created by God in six literal days. Various philosophies throughout history challenged this view however, by arguing that the universe is very old. Despite these philosophical arguments, the church upheld the traditional understanding that the universe is indeed young as described in the Bible.

Many centuries later, on November 24, 1859, Charles Darwin published his revolutionary book "On the Origin of the Species...". On several expeditions he recognized various creatures adapting to their environment by means of slight modifications from one generation to the next. He then extrapolated that in the course of time simple organisms would eventually mutate into more advanced organisms. As history has shown, this placed a serious challenge against the young-earth view since the theory required many millions of years to develop all the life forms we see today while offering a reason to ignore the "God problem". In light of the scientific method, Darwin's observations were so compelling that the church began to question their traditional views of Biblical interpretation and ultimately compromised with the Darwinian view.

In the course of time, science began to separate itself from religion to the point that though it claimed to seek the truth wherever it may lead, it denied any evidence that indicated that a metaphysical being existed. It eventually became completely

---

1. Rodney Stark, *For the Glory of God*. See chapter 2; "God's Handiwork: The Religious Origins of Science".

founded in Naturalism; a belief that only the observable universe exists and there is nothing outside of it, including God. Thus (in light of cosmological argumentation of similar nature throughout church history) two essential opposing paradigms came into being, which we will refer to as "Young Earth" and "Old Earth" views.

One of the reasons why these opposing views are important (in regards to this book) is how one interprets the historical evidence regarding dinosaurs and man as possible contemporaries. If the young earth view is believed, the evidence for the co-existence of dinosaurs and man is considered reasonable and is no threat to that point of view. God must have created the dinosaurs along with all the other animals in the same week he created mankind. On the other hand, if the old earth view is believed, then the presented evidence may not be very convincing, though it is problematic, since that paradigm insists that dinosaurs became extinct before mankind evolved from the apes (or mankind was created afterwards, depending on which cosmological view one holds).

Just prior to the time when Darwin made his theories public, Sir Richard Owen, an anatomist and paleontologist, coined the word "dinosaur", meaning 'terrible lizard,' in 1842. This means that the word 'dinosaur' was only used for the past 170+ years. What did people call dinosaurs before then – dragons? Were these beasts merely overgrown reptiles, or did some of them have mammalian or other unexpected characteristics and features? Did they breath fire or spit some kind of acid? Did they go extinct from a comet impact millions of years ago, or were they hunted down by man for various reasons, like tigers and dodo birds? Who knows? Paleontologists are still arguing if dinosaurs were warm or cold blooded, or which had feathers instead of scales, and so forth. There is still much we don't know about these creatures or what they actually looked like since mainstream science only examines the fossil record in regards to this issue. A record that unfortunately reveals little other than what we can surmise from the bones and scant tissue samples. On the rare occasion that a "living fossil" is found, like the Coelacanth fish or the Okapi, scientists are amazed and quickly state that such creatures were "lucky" to survive after millions of years and not succumb to evolutionary forces.

The cross-cultural evidence spread throughout our history indicates that dinosaurs did not evolve into other creatures that we see today, or become altogether extinct for that matter, with only a few "lucky" surviving specimens. To the contrary, there may even be a few living fossils that remain hidden in various sparsely populated areas throughout the world. Though this remains to be seen, this is not mere speculation or fantasy since the evidence is compelling enough to cause many expensive explorations to search for such creatures.

Historians use various documented eyewitness accounts as evidence for actual historical events; why not the same for dragons? There are more documented accounts of dragons throughout the world than just about any other single topic in ancient times. Such documentation should cause us to reconsider our view of (Darwinian) evolutionary history.

Throughout our entire lives we are told by scientists, teachers, and the media that dinosaurs and mankind never coexisted since dinosaurs became extinct over 65 million years ago. Anyone who believes otherwise would be considered a lunatic since the *only* evidence we have is the fossil record. This common belief does not consider all the physical and historical facts however. There is a great deal of consistent evidence that speaks to the contrary indicating that the mainstream idea of non-coexistence between man and dinosaurs is actually misleading if not downright false. This book seeks to remedy that common misconception.

	Pre — 1842 A.D. — Post	
General:	"Dragons"	"Dinosaurs"
Specific:	Aždaja	Apatosaur
	Behemoth	Allosaurus
	Ch'i Lung	Brachiosaur
	Emela Ntuoka	Dimetrodon
	Grendel	Stegosaur
	Mokele Mbembe	Triceratops
	Sirrush	Tyrannosaurus rex
		Tsintaosaurus spinorhinus
	Gwiber (*"flying snake"*)	Velociraptor
	Iaculus	
	Serpent Seraphim	Dimorphodon
	Thunderbird	Pteranodon
		Quetzalcoatlus
	Con rit	Ramphorinchus
	Leviathan	
	Naga	Ichthyosaur
	Sea Serpent	Plesiosaur
	Water Panther	Tylosaur
	(*etc.*)	(*etc.*)

In the beginning God created the heavens and the earth.
– Genesis 1:1

But from the beginning of creation, God made them male and female.
– Mark 10:6

1: Opposing Views

Setting the Stage

Before we look at the evidence for historical dinosaurs, a little background is necessary to help the reader understand the position being presented and why the notion of dinosaurs being contemporary with mankind is a reasonable case to consider. "Contemporary" meaning at least for a fair portion of mankind's known history; not necessarily living today (though a few may still be!).

Throughout the Bible, it would seem a number of extraordinary claims have been made. Because of these incredible statements, believers and skeptics alike are divided over literal and figurative interpretations, particularly regarding the creation account in the book of Genesis. Understandably, our interpretations can be biased partly due to external influences like philosophical and scientific world views. The Bible remains steadfast in its claim however, as being God's inspired word, unchanging and true, and that it would remain forever.[1] Supporting this claim, fulfilled specific prophecies prove the Bible is divinely inspired.[2] The prophetic accuracy of the Bible is far beyond any other so-called prophetic book or prognosticator. There is no comparison!

According to Jesus, every word of scripture was divinely inspired and He warned against altering it in the book of Revelation.[3] If this is true, that the Bible is the inspired word of God, we need to be careful in our interpretation of the scriptures, since to misinterpret them will cause a misunderstanding of historical reality as well as the potential of being under God's judgment. If the Bible is God's word and accurate in its descriptions, it forces us to either compromise with the mainstream scientific

---
1. Prov. 30:5-6; II Cor. 4:2; II Tim. 3:16-17.
2. See: Josh McDowell, *The New Evidence that Demands a Verdict.* Thomas Nelson Publishers.
3. Matthew 5:18, Revelation 22:18,19.

perspective that by default presupposes that if God does not exist, the universe must be very old, or we must believe the Bible at face value which indicates that the universe is only several thousand years old.

Contemplating the pluralistic ideas of his day, Pontius Pilate asked Jesus, "What is truth?"[4] That philosophical question of whether truth is relative or absolute is still asked today in our post-modern society. Put simply, postmodernism is a result of society turning away from God and believing that the universe is all there is. Man ultimately came from star dust. If the universe is all there is and it is eternal, then there is no need for a metaphysical being. Darwinian evolution and uniformitarian principles play a strong part in supporting this popular paradigm. However, scientists have recently discovered (confirmed) what the Bible has stated all along, that the universe indeed had a beginning and is therefore not eternal. This conclusion indicates there had to be a *Cause* outside of time and space to bring the universe into being.

Pilate's question about truth is also often applied to the Bible itself. Some would argue that God's Word is relatively true and can be interpreted to match whatever personal views one may hold. Specifically regarding the age of the earth, the Jews in the Old Testament as well as the early church, up to the 19th century, generally held to the view that the earth was relatively young as described at face value in the book of Genesis.[5] Today, the creation account is no longer interpreted from the traditional hermeneutical[6] perspective and is considered highly questionable or at least allegorical in light of recent scientific discovery.

Theologians wrestle with how to interpret the Bible accurately while comparing it to the latest scientific data. The traditional view holds that God created the universe in six literal days, yet the mainstream scientific community indicates that the universe came about after billions of years of evolutionary development. Which view is correct? Some would argue that God may have inspired the scriptures to support both views simultaneously so that it could be interpreted to match the prevailing view at a given time. This cannot be the case however, since it is a form of deception of the actual reality of what happened. Historical events only happen once and are unrepeatable in the technical sense. Therefore God must have intended His word about the creation account to be interpreted one way. Either God created the universe in a week's time and plainly stated so in Genesis[7], or He took billions of years and didn't expect believers to fully understand that fact until the discovery of various evidences that support the Big Bang theory or other scientific evidence founded on uniformitarian principles (as taught today). There is no middle ground of interpretation in this case —the universe is either young or old.

Furthermore, arguments between Bible believers regarding the interpretation

---

4. John 18:38.
5. Dr. Terry Mortenson, *The Great Turning Point*. See also *Coming to Grips with Genesis,* chapters 1 - 3.
6. Hermeneutics: the study of the principles of interpretation regarding the books of the Bible.
7. ... and Exodus 20:11.

of the creation account in Genesis can be broken down into two general positions, the young-earth (**YE**) traditional view and the old-earth (**OE**) view. Two prominent OE views (among many) that will be focused on in this chapter are Theistic Evolution and to a larger degree Progressive Creation.

No Compromise

Wanting to appeal to both sides of the coin, some Bible believers have compromised the traditional reading of scripture with the latest scientific findings that are ultimately based on some form of evolutionary or uniformitarian theory. We can determine that scripture has indeed been compromised due to the fact that the post-modern scientific view is contrary to the Biblical text. Nowhere in scripture does it indicate or even hint at that the universe was created over a long period of time or that God utilized evolutionary-type processes to accomplish the task. Nor is there any indication in the Genesis creation account, or in the New Testament, that God intended His words regarding creation to be a poetic allusion to historical reality and that the truth of the matter would only be discovered later in the age of scientific discovery. It must also be stated here that a person's stance on how God created the universe is not a salvation issue, though the stance one takes will influence their understanding of the gospel message.

The Demands of Naturalism

The mainstream scientific perspective is currently based on Naturalism and uniformitarian principles. Simplistically, naturalism essentially denies that God exists, and uniformitarianism states that the way things are today is the way it has always been. This mainstream perspective demands that the universe be billions of years old. It is therefore a slippery slope for religious proponents to hold to an Old Earth view since that particular view is inconsistent with the (traditional) Biblical view of creation. Furthermore, the OE perspective has substantially gained popular acceptance only relatively recently; one that the church at large did not consider as being reasonable until the 1800's, during the advent and popular rise of Darwinism.[8]

Uniformity vs. Uniformitarianism

The early church argued against the secular philosophical views that ultimately indicated that the universe was eternal. 2 Peter 3:4 states that people will eventually ask, "Where is the promise of His coming? For ever since the fathers fell asleep, *all*

---

8. Mortenson, *The Great Turning Point*, pp. 11-54. See also *Coming to Grips with Genesis,* primarily chapter 1.

continues just as it was from the beginning of creation."[9] Since this verse contextually speaks against uniformitarianism, we can reasonably conclude (if the Bible is true) that creation as we know it today did not 'behave' in the same manner as it is now (this will be discussed in more detail momentarily). In opposition, some would argue that Jeremiah 31:35,36[10] indicates uniformitarian principles were decreed by God Himself. Though it is true that the seasons are impossible for mankind to change, the argument implies that it was always this way for billions of years, thus supporting the OE view. It is interesting to note, however, that God made that particular promise *after* the flood occurred. Nevertheless, the passages in Jeremiah support the main point in that due to the uniformity of the seasons since the flood, mankind is under the impression that it has *always* been this way. Even if the seasons were the same from the first creation week, these verses do not necessarily support an OE view. They support uniformity in creation, not uniformitarianism.

> The Bible teaches uniformity. But this does not mean that *conditions* in the core of Jupiter will be the same as on Earth… The Bible does not teach *uniformitarianism* – the notion that present rates and processes are constant over time or space.
>
> God's consistent power does not imply that conditions or rates have always been identical. In fact, the Bible specifically denies this. Genesis 1:31 teaches that the world was once very good, but now it is under a bondage of corruption due to Adam's sin (Rom. 8:20-22). The world was once totally under water (Gen. 7:19-23), but now it isn't…. God has made a universe in which conditions and rates can change quite drastically, and yet God Himself does not change. He upholds the universe in a consistent way. So the Bible teaches uniformity but denies uniformitarianism.[11]

When science presents evidence that conflict with scripture, many (understandably) believe we must conform scripture to the evidence. The problem lies in the fact that nearly all scientific observations can be interpreted differently depending on a person's point of view. Furthermore, science has changed its view many times throughout history. For example, scriptural geologists prior to the twentieth century perceived the geological evidence as indicating a young earth.[12] As Darwinian theories began to be accepted, the preconceived perspectives regarding the 'problem' of a young earth were thrown out for the new paradigm which perceived the geological evidence as indicating a very old earth. Though the scriptural geologists presented much evidence to refute the encroaching OE view, they were ultimately shunned and their evidence disregarded by those who rejected the traditional Biblical creationist view.

---

9. Italics added for emphasis.
10. Jer. 31:35,36 - "Thus says the LORD, Who gives the sun for light by day and the fixed order of the moon and the stars for light by night … If this fixed order departs from before Me," declares the LORD, "Then the offspring of Israel also will cease from being a nation before Me forever."
11. Dr. Jason Lisle, *The Ultimate Proof of Creation resolving the origins debate*, p. 151.
12. Mortenson, *The Great Turning Point*.

Yom: the Context Demands a Literal Day

It has also been argued to a large degree that the days indicated in Genesis 1 represent large periods of time instead of 24 hour days. Many discussions on the correct interpretation of the Hebrew word "yom" (meaning "day") have not arrived at a solid answer regarding its appropriate meaning. Both YE and OE proponents hold fast to their opposing views as to the proper interpretation of God's Word. In fact, "yom" *by itself* can be interpreted either way. So in this sense, both sides are correct! However, how the word is correctly interpreted depends entirely on its specific context. Therefore, only one view can be correct. The scriptural evidence weighs heavily towards a literal meaning – a 24 hour day. This can be determined hermeneutically, since scripture validates scripture.[13] Not only are the days in the creation week defined numerically, but also delineated by phrases like "morning and evening." Also, to reinforce the understanding of a literal creation week, God Himself clarified the context in the Ten Commandments;[14] that the creation week was specifically done in such a manner so as to be an example for us to follow regarding the Sabbath day. Progressive creationists *must* reinterpret God's clarification of the literal six day scenario since it does not fit their cosmological paradigm. God was not deceitful to all previous generations; we can be confident that He meant a literal week by the specific context/comparison in which He explained the sabbath day.

Additionally, the Hebrew word "barasheet" in Genesis 1:1 reinforces the literal day perspective.

> ... the word "barasheet" – which means "in the beginning" – is a compound word made up of "ba" (meaning "in") and "sheet" (meaning "six"). "Bara" means "created" and "Elohim", of course, means "God", so that within the first half of the verse we can read, "In six God created..."[15]

There is no indication or hint in the Old Testament that God created the universe over billions of years. In opposition, some would point out the scripture passage that states that "a thousand years is like one day" to God[16]. The context of that verse is indicating that God is not under the rule of time. He is truly eternal and is the One who created time. The context is not indicating that the universe is older than traditionally believed. Unlike the OE view, a plain reading does not need to reinterpret the scriptures to match current personal and/or mainstream perspectives.

---

13. "Sacra Scriptura sui interpres" (see also: 2 Peter 1:20,21).
14. Exodus 20:1-17 (particular verses: Exodus 20: 9-11: *"Six days you shall labor and do all your work, but the seventh day is a sabbath to the Lord your God... For in six days the Lord made the heavens and the earth, the sea, and all that is in them, but he rested on the seventh day."*)
15. Mark Cadwallader, Creation Moments, *May 2015 Newsletter*.
    (Gen 1:1 Hebrew transliteration: *"Barasheet bara Elohim et ha'shamayim v'et ha'retz"*).
16. Psalm 90:4 (see also: 2 Peter 3:8).

Death

The Bible specifically states in Romans 5:12 that death entered the world through sin. If the scriptures are correct, then progressive creationism, theistic evolution, and Darwinian evolution cannot be true. This single statement in the Bible counters these theories of an old earth due to the very nature of the theories themselves requiring death and disease to occur before mankind was created.

The argument that death occurred before Adam and Eve sinned, states that death was occurring in the animal kingdom before the act of sin. Some consider this a reasonable interpretation of scripture for various reasons. One being that Jesus did not sacrifice himself for the animals but for mankind only (saving us from spiritual death). Another interpretation is that the verse only talks about death entering and affecting the world of mankind ("and so death spread to all men") and doesn't mention the animals. If this interpretational view is correct, then several issues arise in regards to Romans 8:19-23 which states (emphasis mine),

> The *creation waits* in eager expectation *for* the sons of God to be revealed. For the *creation was subjected to futility*, not willingly, but *because of Him who subjected it*, in hope that the ***creation itself also will be set free from its slavery to corruption*** into the freedom of the glory of the children of God. For we know that the whole creation groans and suffers the pains of childbirth together until now."

It is clear that the context is referring to *all* of creation – not just the "world of mankind" since creation is described as waiting "for" something – which is mankind. Therefore, the context of Romans 8:20-23 is consistent with the traditional view of Romans 5:12. Death entered all of creation (subjecting it to 'futility and corruption') upon the event of the sin of mankind. The context does not infer that futility and corruption occurred before the event of sin, since the context (with the remaining part of the chapter) indicates that all of creation is tied in with the situation of mankind's salvation and relationship with God. Furthermore, this verse states that God Himself was the one who subjected creation to the curse ("…but because of Him who subjected it…"), which is consistent with the Genesis account. Death was not in effect until mankind sinned in which God consequently carried out the pre-warned punishment.

Now some may object from a scientific standpoint, that death *had* to occur from the beginning to keep the cycle of life in motion. Yet the Bible does not ascribe plants with the status of "life" as we do today. Plants are described as withering and fading, not "dying".[17] This is partly due to plants not having souls (Hebrew = *nephesh*). Before the fall of man, both animals and humans were only vegetarian[18] so they were

---

17. Isaiah 40:6-8; James 1:10 (some Bible translations read "pass away" instead of "wither")
18. Genesis 1:29

not killing each other for food. Therefore death, in the Biblical sense, was not in effect before the fall since the ecology of plants did not seem to be part of the living and dying equation. After the fall and consequent change in the environment due to the curse, the plant kingdom was also altered in some manner. Genesis 3:18 indicates that the cursed ground would then cause plants to grow thorns and thistles. Even so, this is still admittedly problematic from our perceptions today. Some may object that this is a mere matter of semantics. What is certain is that the Bible indicates that the entire environment has seriously changed due to sin, and death for humans and animals was the consequent result.

Those who support the OE view claim that death must have occurred before sin since the evidence can be seen in the geologic strata. Fossil remains (the 'Cambrian Explosion' being a prime example) are said to indicate "proof positive" that death and disease occurred long before mankind was ever around. This is true if the strata were laid down over hundreds of millions of years, as the mainstream scientific community insists upon. It is false if the strata are indicative of a global catastrophic flood as described in the Bible.

If the flood caused the geologic strata and all that we see in the fossil record, then it is logical to understand that animals were eating and killing each other and being susceptible to disease before the flood occurred since the Bible states that the world was bent on doing evil at that time. Death would have occurred after the fall of man however, as already discussed in Romans – it is also consistent with the redemption story.

According to Genesis and Romans, death entered the (entire) world through sin. God prophetically indicated death's defeat as a 'crushing of the head', demonstrating that death is not "good" but an enemy of God. In contrast, God called His work "good" during each day of the creation. If death and disease were part of the natural order of things that God was creating, as the progressive creationist asserts, then God is hypocritical in proclaiming death and disease as "good" since everywhere else in the Bible God is opposed to it and deals with it in some manner. For instance, the resurrection of Jesus proclaimed victory over death, which will also be the last enemy of God to be destroyed.

God did not use natural selection as a means of creation either, nor would He consider it "good". The French biologist and Nobel laureate Jacques Monod stated that if God used it to create, then modern society was more ethical than God. He also said:

> [Natural] selection is the blindest and most cruel way of evolving new species, and more and more complex and refined organisms… The struggle for life and elimination of the weakest is a horrible process, against which our whole modern ethics revolts. An ideal society is a non-selective society, one where the weak is protected; which is exactly the reverse of the so-called natural law. I am surprised that a Christian would defend the idea that this is

the process which God, more or less, set up in order to have evolution.[19]

Some may also argue that God uses death throughout the Bible[20], asserting that death is "neutral" (neither good or bad) in the eyes of God. Though true, God may currently allow death as a means for judgment over nations and individuals, this only indicates God's sovereign power over His enemies. Despite this, He will eliminate death in the end since it was not intended to exist when He initially created all things. Death was a result of disobedience by angels and men, not as an incorporated device of God's own creation.

In regards to time frame, it appears that Adam and Eve were in the garden only for a brief period of time before that fateful day of disobedience and death entered the scene. Support for this is that though they were commanded to have offspring beforehand,[21] the fourth chapter of Genesis indicates that Eve did not have children until after they were expelled from the garden of Eden.

The Curse

When God cursed the ground as punishment for Adam's sin[22], this indicates that (at least a portion of) the creation was not associated with the consequences of sin prior to the fall. "Both thorns and thistles it shall grow for you;" is scriptural evidence that creation (at least the ground and plant kingdom in this specific verse) was different before the fall of man. Furthermore, we see the animal kingdom suffered similar consequences. Genesis 3:14 states that when God cursed the Serpent for deceiving Eve, He said, "Cursed are you *more* than the cattle..." This indicates that the animal kingdom is also under the curse that God proscribed on that day (though the serpent/Satan got the brunt of it). The point indicated in these economically written verses is clear in that the environment *and* animal kingdom (neither of which were morally culpable) had changed for the worse due to God's curse upon it *after* sin entered the (entire) world through man. God warned beforehand that on the specific day that mankind disobeys Him and eats of the forbidden tree that would be the day mankind would begin to die (i.e., death enters the scene and a separation from God occurs).

> It is true that Adam and Eve didn't die the exact day they ate, as some seem to think Genesis 2:17 implies. The Hebrew is die-die (muwth-muwth), which is often translated as "surely die" or literally as "dying you shall die," which indicates the beginning of dying (i.e. an ingressive sense). At that point, Adam and Eve began to die and would return to dust. If they were meant to have died right then, the text should have used muwth only once, as is used in the

---

19. Mortenson and Ury, *Coming to Grips with Genesis - Biblical Authority and the Age of the Earth*, p. 393.
20. The death (and subsequent resurrection) of Jesus is a good example here.
21. Genesis 1:28
22. Genesis 3:17-19.

Hebrew meaning "dead, died, or die" and not "beginning to die" or "surely die."[23]

What may have been unexpected by Adam and Eve was that their decision to disobey would affect all of creation as well since they were placed in authority over it! Therefore, the verses previously mentioned from the book of Romans are consistent with the Genesis account and describe the consequences of sin as infecting all of creation, not just mankind alone.

The Flood Covered the Entire Planet

In like manner, regarding the flood of Noah, when the Bible refers to the "world" it means the entire planet – not just the "world of mankind". Dr. Hugh Ross (a proponent for progressive creation) claims that Noah's flood was a tremendous local flood. This is ridiculous since that makes God deceitful because He promised that He would not destroy the "whole earth" again by means of flooding, and yet major deadly local flooding continues to occur. It also makes Jesus and Peter[24] foolish to believe in such a story. Therefore, based off of the promise of God and his covenant with Noah (mankind), the *entire* earth, mountains included, was flooded – not just a local area. Dr. Ross' theory doesn't even jive with the laws of physics. Water seeks the easiest path and levels itself out. Even if the epic flood started in the Middle Eastern area *and covered the mountains in the vast region*, it would have overflowed to the rest of the world by the time it rose to that height.

The question may be asked, "Where did all the water go?" Many are not aware that the volume of water is about ten times greater than all land above sea level. If the waters came from the "fountains of the deep" (in addition to the torrential rain), as the Bible indicates, then that would explain the buckling of mountain ranges and distortion of the landscape due to massive subterranean water loss and volcanism. "If the effects of compressing the continents and buckling up of mountains were reversed, the oceans would again flood the entire earth. Therefore, the earth has enough water to cover the smaller mountains that existed before the flood."[25]   Perhaps this may help explain the origin of the deep ocean trenches and the volcanic "ring of fire".

The problem OE proponents have with the global flood is that it cannot and will not be repeated due to God's promise. They must therefore force the geological evidence to match their presuppositional ideas that the earth is very old. Though Dr. Ross opposes atheistic evolution, his perspective of the evidence is ironically based on uniformitarian views that the geological strata has been laid down layer by layer over

---
23. *Biblically, Could Death Have Existed before Sin? Satan, the Fall, and a Look at Good and Evil*, by Bodie Hodge.
24. Matthew 24:37-39 / 2 Peter 3:6,7 / (see also: Isaiah 54:9; 1 Peter 3:20; 2 Peter 2:5; Hebrews 11:7) i.e., It would be foolish for Jesus to use a myth to support his point.
25. See: Walt Brown, *In the Beginning Compelling Evidence for Creation and the Flood.* Also consider: Psalm 104:6

hundreds of millions of years. Progressive creationists must therefore reject a truly global flood since that would lend strong support for the geologic evidence indicating that the stratum was deposited by incredible amounts of soil erosion, massive eruptions of subterranean water, not to mention volcanism and other geological catastrophic events reshaping the earth's surface at that time. If the entire surface of the earth was catastrophically flooded as the Bible states, this strongly suggests that the earth, if not the universe, may actually be (relatively) young as the Bible indicates from a traditional reading since the geologic strata does not necessarily indicate vast ages at all.

A global catastrophic flood can reasonably explain what we see in geology. On the other hand, mainstream geologists who disagree with the Biblical account of the flood cannot adequately explain numerous anomalies found in various sections of strata throughout the globe. The artifacts are either dismissed or ignored, or explained away by the mainstream scientific community. However, the evidence mounts in favor of a global flood as opposed to millions of years of soil layering. Chapter 2 presents several brief examples supporting this.

Micro vs. Macro (Adaptation vs. Transformation) – Genetic evidence

Scientists are prone to making assumptions on the long-term based off of observations of the short-term. Micro-evolution is factual because creatures adapt to their environments – but (Darwinian) macro-evolution (i.e., one thing eventually evolves into a totally different thing) is only conjectural since it has never been observed, and the latest scientific discoveries continue to erode support for that view. For one example, at the genetic level, Darwinian evolution cannot explain adequately how DNA (*the most complex item known*) attained the information from the primordial ooze in order to cause proteins to manufacture more intricately complex DNA. Nor can it explain the symbiotic relationship between DNA and the various proteins that make up its own structure or other molecular structures.[26] This single piece of evidence alone strongly rules out the plausibility of Darwinian evolution, which states that life came from non-life accidentally, and was simple in composition.

There is additional genetic evidence that conflicts with the progressive creationist and Darwinian evolutionary models. Both claim that it took millions of years for animals to develop, either through means of natural selection or by God's intervention over vast periods of time. However, scientists have been able to approximate how long an organism has existed in history through mutations in mitochondrial DNA.

These biological facts create a new venue in which to compare the young-earth creation timescale to the secular timescale head to head. The

---
26. See the DVD *Unlocking the Mystery of Life* by Illustra Media.

true age of any given kind will be reflected in the amount of mitochondrial DNA diversity among its modern descendants. If kinds have existed on this planet for millions of years, then they should be quite genetically diverse. In contrast, if their origins trace back only 6,000 years, then they should be more genetically homogeneous.

These qualitative statements can be related with mathematical rigor. Predicting mitochondrial DNA diversity with precision is a straightforward calculation...

Secular scientists have measured the mitochondrial DNA mutation rate for four species—humans, fruit flies, roundworms, and water fleas. The Bible puts the origin of each of these about 6,000 years ago... However, the published evolutionary literature puts the origin of modern humans about 180,000 years ago; fruit flies, about 20 million years ago; roundworms, about 18 million years ago; and water fleas about 7.6 million years ago...

... On average, human mitochondrial DNA sequences differ at 10 positions. The biblical model predicts a range of diversity that accurately captures this value. In contrast, the evolutionary timescale... predicts levels of genetic diversity that are 12–29 *times off* the real DNA differences that we see today (124–290 mitochondrial DNA differences versus 10).

Similar calculations for fruit flies, roundworms, and water fleas depict the same result—evolutionary predictions that are *orders of magnitude off* from the real DNA differences we see today and creation predictions that either match actual diversity or are very close to it.[27]

Put simply, DNA itself indicates that life was complex from the beginning, that complex information was present, that complex symbiotic relationships occurred between DNA and proteins, and that life (both human and animal) arose approximately 6,000 to 10,000 years ago due to the amount of genetic differences we have today.

The Bible also speaks out against the macro-evolutionary paradigm in that all living things are to produce after their own kind.

Then God said, "Let the earth sprout vegetation, plants yielding seed, and fruit trees on the earth bearing fruit *after their kind* with seed in them"; and it was so. The earth brought forth vegetation, plants yielding seed *after their kind*, and trees bearing fruit with seed in them, *after their kind*; and God saw that it was good.   – Genesis 1:11, 12

But God gives it a body just as He wished, and to each of the seeds a body of its own. *All flesh is not the same flesh, but there is one flesh of men, and another flesh of beasts, and another flesh of birds, and another of fish.*"
– 1 Corinthians 15: 38, 39   [italics added for emphasis]

More recent findings continue to support the Biblical scenario. For instance, a 15-year study by The Rockefeller University found that each animal species, including humans, have the same amount of genetic variation (0.1%) despite how large or small

---

27. Nathaniel T. Jeanson, Ph.D., *New Genetic-clock Research Challenges Millions of Years*. Acts & Facts Magazine. April 2014.

the species population may be. Also, each species is an "island of sequence space", meaning that they are unique with no intermediates or transitions between them. The report also indicates (surprisingly) that each species (including humans) came into existence about the same time.

> Our paper strengthens the argument that the low variation in the mitochondrial DNA of modern humans also explains the similar low variation found in over 90% of living animal species—we all likely originated by similar processes and most animal species are likely young.
> ... Genetically, 'the world is not a blurry place.' It is hard to find 'intermediates' – the evolutionary stepping stones between species. The intermediates disappear.[28]

Since the evidence weighs heavily that macro-evolution did not occur at all, then theistic evolution is not true and one can logically arrive at the conclusion that God did not use that particular method to create anything. The progressive creationist view, on the other hand, is becoming increasingly popular since it denies Darwinian evolution, but ironically maintains an indirect hold on elements of uniformitarianism and macro-evolutionary principles, yet allows for God to be involved in miraculous steps along the way.[29] In this manner, progressive creation science is a type of esotericism, where scripture is reinterpreted by the scientific elite in order to unify (compromise) different beliefs into one belief.

It is also understood that the early church argued against OE philosophies and Jesus did not teach otherwise. The apostles even spoke out against uniformitarianism, suggesting that natural laws have not always behaved the same.[30] If the church today holds to a YE Creation perspective as traditionally taught, and not repeatedly compromise with secular theories that change over time, the world can respect that despite their disagreement with the YE view. The world has little toleration for those who ride the fence, however. God warns against doing so as well.

Scientific Cosmology is Not Science

Science has advanced much understanding on how the universe operates, but must depend on faith (not true science!) when it comes to the origin of the universe. Scientific cosmology states that the evidence can only lead to an old universe *if* some form of uniformitarian view is correct. The Bible speaks out against uniformitarianism however and consistently advocates a literal creation week. Many scientists are also considering the evidences for Intelligent Design over the Darwinian view since macro-

---
28. Online article. Accessed 1-12-2019. (https://phys.org/news/2018-05-special-humanity-tiny-dna-differences.html)
    Far from special: Humanity's tiny DNA differences are 'average' in animal kingdom. Science X. Rockefeller University. May 21, 2018. (Credit: Mark Cadwallader, *Creation Moments*, January 2019 newsletter)
29. Morris, *The Modern Creation Trilogy* - Volume One, p. 42.
30. See: Morton, Ury, *Coming to Grips with Genesis*, chapters 1, 11, 12.

evolution is not consistent with the latest findings.[31] Therefore, it is best to hold to a plain reading of scripture that states that God created the universe in a matter of 6 days.

In a similar manner with astronomy, the evidence is either being interpreted to match the mainstream paradigm, or the opposing evidence is considered "unscientific" and thrown out, depending on how it aligns with the accepted paradigm. The current widely-held view is the Big Bang theory, which Dr. Hugh Ross is outspoken in its support. Dr. Ross is banking on the assumption that the "Big Bang" will never be refuted. However, there are many opponents against the Big Bang theory in the secular scientific community that present much scientific evidence to indicate that the theory may not be *entirely* true. From their perspective, the universe is eternal and not created. Those who do not agree with the Big Bang theory are not necessarily OE supporters either. There is doubt about the compelling theory from both sides.

As the Director of the Center for Scientific Creation, Dr. Walt Brown (among others) has presented several scientific arguments against the Big Bang theory. He indicates that the theory was based upon three poorly understood observations: redshifting of stars, cosmic microwave background radiation (CMBR), and the amount of helium in the universe. Most scientists agree that redshifting indicates distance. Time is therefore inferred from redshifting measurements based on uniformitarian principles of the speed of light and how the universe was constructed via the big bang model. On the issue of redshifting, Dr. Brown states the following in an opposing argument:

> The redshift of starlight is usually interpreted as a Doppler effect; that is, stars and galaxies are moving away from Earth, stretching out (or reddening) the wavelengths of light they emit. Space itself supposedly expands – so the total potential energy of stars, galaxies, and other matter increases today with no corresponding loss of energy elsewhere. Thus, the big bang violates the law of conservation of energy…[which is also] violated in another important way. If a big bang happened, distant galaxies should not just be receding from us, they should be decelerating. Measurements show the opposite; they are accelerating from us.[32]

Added to these contentions is the observation that "many objects with high redshifts seem connected, or associated, with objects having low redshifts."[33] Also, there is evidence, confirmed by several astronomers, that redshifts from stars and galaxies vary only by a few fixed amounts. To clarify, if stars and galaxies are moving away from us, it appears that they can only travel at specific speeds. In other words, there are no intermediate speeds between them. Another study shows evidence that redshifting may be an atomic effect instead of a Doppler-like effect. Atoms emit small

---
31. Among many other sources, see *Science Finds God*, by Sharon Begley, Newsweek, July 20, 1998, and *Darwin's Black Box*, by M. J. Behe.
32. Walt Brown, *In the Beginning Compelling Evidence for Creation and the Flood*, p. 30.
33. Brown, p. 30.

bundles of energy called quanta. This energy is in fixed amounts with no intermediate amounts of energy between them. If the energy of light is slowly absorbed into space, it would be done in fixed increments. This would cause starlight to redshift the way it is observed – in generally fixed increments. This may be why some galaxies give two distinct redshifts.[34] Without going into various contentions with CMBR and the amounts of helium (among other issues), the point here is that the Big Bang theory that is supported largely by progressive creationists actually has many problems with it despite the popular perception that it is a solid case.

If the Big Bang theory is rejected by mainstream secular science in the distant future, what will the world think of Christians as a whole for holding to such an idea? Similar to the incidence with Galileo in the past, the secular community will not mock the individual for holding to an obsolete or 'politically correct' view, but will again mock the church for being wishy-washy (at best) for compromising and reinterpreting scripture to incorporate a theory based on an atheistic paradigm.

God performed a number of miracles that many take as true. (i.e., the walls of Jericho, the parting of the Red Sea, etc.) Yet when God states how he created the universe we doubt He did it that way. God has never asked us to do what He Himself has not done. The creation week was for our benefit in that God demonstrated beforehand that He worked six days and then rested. In the 10 commandments, He commands that we do the same that He has done. God always demonstrates the example first before expecting us to do the same. The life of Jesus is a prime example.

Another indication of compromise with secular scientific world-views and scripture can be found by reviewing early church history. Jesus stated in Mark 10:6 "But from the *beginning of creation*, God made them male and female." The traditional view that the church held was that the context of Jesus' words was the actual beginning of all creation (the initial first week of creation as introduced in Genesis 1:1, "*In the beginning*, God created..."),[35] but that context was changed in the past century or so by some to fit their progressive perspective to mean that Jesus must have been indicating 'the beginning of mankind' (billions of years after the initial creation event). They think that this *must* be the correct context since we now *know* that the universe must be old – because the evidence for the big bang is considered virtually irrefutable![36]

Science and Faith

The argument is not about how OE theories are in line with scientific Naturalism and YE theories are only religious views. YE Creationists use science as a method to support their findings, just like OE Creationists (i.e., progressive creationists).

---

34. Among other sources: *Doppler toppler?* by Halton Arp, and *Anisotropic Synchrony Convention*, by Jason Lisle.
35. Morton, Ury, *Coming to Grips with Genesis*, chapter 11 entitled: "Jesus' view of the age of the earth".
36. Sarcasm intended.

Secular OE theories are just as religious. The argument must stop being divided in this manner. All sides hold to some form of religious view on the origin of the universe. Instead, the argument should be what is the most probable. Since the Bible has proven itself to be the most reliable ancient historical text ever written, and has proven itself to be divinely inspired through accurate and fulfilled prophecy,[37] taking God at His Word may be the wisest choice of probabilities. God, after all, was a first-hand witness of the creation event.

As mentioned, due to the reliability of the Bible, it is precarious, if not dangerous to hold to an OE view because it forces a compromise with scripture to fit the latest scientific *perspectives*, despite God's warnings not to fool with His word.[38] Mainstream scientific views by default ultimately lean on the presupposition that God doesn't exist and/or an uniformitarian view. Yet many Christians compromise Biblical scriptures with these secular views by modifying them to include God's handiwork somehow.

Progressive creationists maintain that God's creation is His second witness – along with the Bible. However, they teach *through implication* that God's creation is the authority over scripture. They won't come straight out and state that, but by their arguments it is clear that *that* is the perspective they hold since scripture is constantly being reinterpreted to fit the latest findings.

If God plans to recreate the universe someday due to the fact that the current one is infected by sin's effects, while indicating that His word will never change, then it is precarious to put creation above scripture in regards to authority. Creation can only indicate God's creative power and is itself evidence that God exists, but it is unable to present the gospel of Jesus to someone who is unaware of the Biblical message. Therefore, it is reasonable to conclude that the Bible is the ultimate authority. Scientists holding to the progressive creationist view would have us believe otherwise, that the latest interpretation of the physical evidence supersedes the traditional scriptural claim. For additional reading on the problems and unfounded claims of the progressive creationist view the following books are recommended (see Reference section for publishing information):

Creation and Time: A Report on the Progressive Creationist Book by Hugh Ross.
Coming to Grips with Genesis - Biblical Authority and the Age of the Earth.
Old Earth Creationism on Trial - The Verdict is In.

Summary

All OE theories must adapt (to some degree) macro-evolutionary and uniformitarian principles into them which in turn dictate the reinterpretation of

---

37. Josh McDowell, *The New Evidence that Demands a Verdict*. Thomas Nelson Publishers.
38. Matthew 5:17-19, John 5:45-47, Proverbs 30:5,6.

scripture. Since macro-evolutionary theories are not supported by any significant scientific evidence, macro-evolutionary theories are without basis of significant truth and cannot be relied upon. To reiterate, Darwinian macro evolution is not supported by the latest scientific facts and can therefore be considered a type of historic dinosaur. The Bible also speaks out against uniformitarian principles and clarifies in various places in scripture that the creation account is indeed a literal week. It is therefore a precarious, if not dangerous position, in light of God's word, character, and authority, to compromise scripture with any theory that promotes an old universe paradigm that is based ultimately on secular and naturalistic views, since the Bible indicates otherwise.

Now what does all this have to do with dinosaurs and man? One can surmise that if the earth is less than 12,000 years old, then it is reasonable to figure that mankind and dinosaurs existed at the same time. Nevertheless, the Biblical text is not the only evidence that will be relied upon here. The next chapter will present some of the geological evidences that further indicate a young earth.

	Young Earth Creationism	Progressive Creationism	Theistic Evolution	Darwinian Evolution
"Each after their own kind" (1 Cor 15:38, 39)	■	■	☐	☐
Extreme genetic complexity from the beginning	■	■	☐	☐
Traditional interpretation of biblical timeline	■	☐	☐	
Man was made during beginning (lit. creation week)	■	☐		
Clarification of literal days in 10 commandments	■	☐		
Support by apostles and early church fathers	■	☐		
Bible stance on secular uniformitarian paradigm	■	☐		
Physical and spiritual death came after sin	■	☐		
Dragons (dinosaurs) and mankind coexisted	■			

Figure 1: Macro-evolutionary models are not compatible/consistent with scripture and do not match current scientific observations. Progressive creationism and theistic evolution compromise scripture with scientific cosmology. The early church fathers did not support such ideas until uniformitarian views controlled the scientific community in the mid 19th century.
■ = Consistent with   ☐ = Partially consistent with / reinterpretation of scripture or historical documents needed

2: Geologic Evidence of a Catastrophe

The Nonexistent Evolutionary Tree

Briefly discussed in the previous chapter, the genetic evidence supporting Darwinian macro-evolution is essentially nonexistent. The fossil record is no exception. Scientists have now concluded that there is practically no fossil evidence showing one creature evolving into another. "The known fossil record fails to document a single example of phyletic evolution accomplishing a major morphologic transition [a structural change relating to descent] and hence offers no evidence that the gradualistic model can be valid."[1] Furthermore, after 40 years of paleontological research, Professor Heribert Nilsson, director of the Botanical Institute at Lund University, Sweden, stated the following; "The fossil material is now so complete that...the lack of transitional series cannot be explained as due to the scarcity of the material. The deficiencies are real; they will never be filled... The true situation is that those fossils have not been found which were expected. Just where new branches are supposed to fork off from the main stem it has been impossible to find the connecting types."[2] In like manner, Robert Wesson declared, "The gaps in the fossil record are real... The absence of a record of any important branching is quite phenomenal. Species are usually static, or nearly so, for long periods; species seldom and genera never show evolution into new species or genera but replacement of one by another, and change is more or less abrupt."[3]

Regardless of these findings, some may still find it hard to believe that there are no transitional fossils and therefore fall back on the theory of "punctuated equilibrium". However, this particular theory (that is supposed to reasonably explain

---
1. Steven Stanley, Johns Hopkins University Professor, Department of Earth and Planetary Sciences.
2. Heribert Nilsson, *The Synthetic Origin of Species*, p. 1212.
3. Robert Wesson, *Beyond Natural Selection*, p. 45.

the gaps in the fossil record) doesn't have any hard evidence to support it either. In fact, it is even more difficult to substantiate than gradual evolution. Dr. William Lane Craig explains the situation in more detail;

> ... there is something of a crisis in origin of life studies today, as all the traditional scenarios of the origin of the first living cell in the primordial organic soup have broken down. Moreover, the gradualism of classical evolutionary theory based upon the mechanism of minor mutations and natural selection has been radically called into question by the proponents of "punctuated equilibrium," who argue that the transitional forms are absent from the fossil record because they never existed. Rather, they say evolution occurs by intermittent bursts from one form to another. Insofar as this new theory fails to account for these bursts and must appeal to "hopeful monsters"—massive mutations that produce new forms without transitional forms—the hypothesis of design becomes more plausible.[4]

Another theoretical proposal is that some dinosaurs evolved into birds. This popular theory has been rejected by scientists due to several factors.[5] One being that 'advanced' birds have been found in the fossil record that pre-date archaeopteryx![6] This fact indicates that a huge evolutionary gap remains between dinosaurs and birds. In other words, there are no intermediate fossils that have been found to substantiate any link between the two types of creatures. The discovery of these ancient birds, and various other fossils (as well as "living fossils"), are consistent with the young earth view however.

There are many other scientists not mentioned here that also conclude that there is little, if any, evidence showing prehistoric creatures evolving into more complex animals. This lack of transitional evidence in the fossil record is another indicator that Darwinian macro-evolution does not occur.

Rapid Burial

Paleontologists agree that most fossils all around the world show evidence of rapid burial by means of flooding. According to the Bible, the rapid burial of organisms are the result of a catastrophic global flood, yet mainstream paleontologists will not admit to a single specific global flood, but believe instead that multiple floods occurred over the course of millions of years. Throughout the world, there are many mass grave fossil sites indicating that the bodies were washed in place. Even sauropods, the largest land-dwelling creatures known, have been buried in this way.

In addition to land creatures being buried by means of flooding, approximately 90 percent of all fossils consist of marine organisms; which is what one would expect

---
4. William Lane Craig, *Reasonable Faith*, p. 91.
5. Jonathan Sarfati, *Refuting Evolution*. See chapter 4; "Bird Evolution?".
6. Marc Surtees, *Did Birds Evolve from Dinosaurs?*

from a global flood—not from localized flooding! For the vast amount of large to very small marine creatures to have been buried alive there must have been an unprecedented catastrophic event to cause massive amounts of soil debris to rapidly cover large sections of the ancient oceans. The furious avalanche of debris was epic in scope and too fast for fish and other swimming creatures to not be able to escape! Articulated fossils of marine animals are also found on top of mountain ranges and inland areas. They would not be found this way if the continents were covered with water that receded gradually over millions of years. Mainstream scientists would have us believe otherwise.

Despite the two opposing views on how rapid burial took place, agreement is made that fossil organisms were indeed buried quickly. This is seen in fossilized marine creatures giving birth at the time of burial[7], preserved soft tissues (i.e. insect wings, skin, organs, bone marrow, etc)[8], articulated skeletons (as opposed to dead creatures being torn apart by scavengers if left out in the open), bacteria and single-celled organisms, to name a few. Clam shells found on top of mountains in the closed position also offer strong support of a global flood and not millions of years of soil deposits. They must have not only been buried quickly, but also deep, since clams can dig their way through several feet of sand if necessary. When bivalves die, their muscles relax, opening the shell. When the hinge deteriorates, the bivalve separates in a matter of days. Due to rapid and deep burial, the weight of the sediment would keep their shells closed and intact, which is exactly what is frequently found in the fossil record.

Rapid Fossil Formation and the Ichthyosaur Dilemma

Not only is burial rapid, a fossil must form rapidly before the creature begins to decay (as in the bivalve example). This fact contradicts the common misperception that it takes millions of years for fossils to form. Tying this all together, an excellent example of both a lack of ancestral precursors in the so-called evolutionary tree and rapid burial and formation is the ichthyosaurus. Alfred Romer, a professor of paleontology, noted the following, "The peculiarities of ichthyosaur structure would seemingly have required a long time for their development and hence a very early origin for their group, but there are no known Permian reptiles antecedent to them."[9] Among the thousands of marine fossils showing creatures in the act of eating another (indicating rapid burial), at least a couple ichthyosaur fossils were also found showing the mother giving birth to live young. Furthermore, to dispel the notion that the ichthyosaurs evolved from land creatures that "went back to the sea", Romer also

---
7. Sarfati, Jonathan, *Refuting Evolution*, Green Forest: Master Books, 1999, p. 107.
8. Kelly Milner Halls, *Dinosaur Mummies Beyond Bare-Bone Fossils*, Darby Creek Publishing, 2003.
9. A.S. Romer, *Vertebrate Paleontology*, University of Chicago Press, 1966, p. 120.

indicated that the ichthyosaurs had eyes, ears, and flippers ("limbs") that were well adapted for the deep sea.[10] Since this is the case, and there are no precursors to the ichthyosaur in evolutionary terms, then this indicates that this particular creature came on the scene fully formed and created appropriately for life in the ocean. It did not evolve into that state in other words.

Even contemporary objects are occasionally fossilized when deposited rapidly in the right soil conditions. For example, a bowlers hat, among other items such as sandwiches and bags of flour, was found in the "buried village" of Te Wairoa in New Zealand, completely fossilized after 60 years of burial.[11] Capitalizing on another method of fossilization near that town by the natives is also described in the article entitled, "Tarawera's Night of Terror", which reads, "...some of the Maori folk who lived in the area made pocket money as a result of the tourist trade developing around the pink and white terraces. They placed various items, such as hats, into the water at the terraces so as to petrify them. Once petrified, they were sold as souvenirs."[12]

Quickly Carved Caves

Caves and caverns can also be created in a short period of time. A study indicated that one factor may be due to sulfuric acid (as opposed to carbonic acid) that cut out a fair percentage of a number of caverns.[13] Typically found in such underground places, speleothems (stalactites and stalagmites) can form faster than we are led to believe as well. This means millions of years are not needed to form these interesting features.

> A large number of reports concern the rapid growth of stalactites and stalagmites. Most of these observations have been made in tunnels, bridges, dams, mines, or other dated man-made structures which approximate cave conditions... [In summary], some of the early literature where stalactite growth averages about 1.25 centimeters (0.5 inch) yearly with some observed to grow over 7.6 centimeters (3 inches) yearly. Stalagmites observed by Fisher grew 0.6 centimeter (0.25 inch) in height and 0.9 centimeter (0.36 inch) in diameter at the base each year. At this rate of height increase the 1,900 centimeter tall stalagmite called "Great Dome" in Carlsbad Caverns might grow in less than 4,000 years.[14]

A more specific (and interesting) example of rapid speleothem growth is documented in *National Geographic* magazine on October, 1953. In the Carlsbad Caverns, New Mexico, a bat had fallen on a stalagmite formation. The stalagmite grew so fast that the bat not only became cemented on it, but the formation was able

---
10. Romer, p. 119.
11. Renton Maclachlan, *Tarawera's Night of Terror*, 1995.
12. Maclachlan, *Tarawera's Night of Terror*.
13. Michael Oard, *Rapid cave formation by sulfuric acid dissolution*.
14. Steven Austin, *Origin of Limestone Caves*. 1980. (brackets mine).

to preserve the dead bat before it decomposed. The evidence showing that caverns and speleothems can develop rapidly do not contradict, but reinforce, the Biblical flood scenario.

Misplaced Modern Bones

Speaking of caves, though it is beyond the scope of this book, a brief comment about cave men needs to be made. We are commonly told that men lived in caves in the ancient past. Yet all cave "dwellings" show temporary or ceremonial conditions only – not permanent residences, as we are led to believe. The evidence is overwhelming that human civilizations came on the historical scene abruptly and began roughly 5,000 years ago. Coincidentally, the global flood that is mentioned in the Bible also took place roughly 5,000 years ago. If a global flood did not occur, then we would not expect to find articulated human fossils in Cretaceous strata; however there are several cases where modern human fossil bones (and man-made artifacts) are indeed found in stratigraphic layers where they "should not be". Some human remains have even been found in Carboniferous layers estimated at being over three hundred million years old![15]

"Modern" human fossil bones have been found in "prehistoric" layers all over the earth. Paleontologists have explained away many of these findings as simple burial sites, yet have no adequate explanation when they are found within rock formations that have no evidence of artificial burial and that they are found too deep in the strata. Modern human bones have even been found in limestone several feet beneath ancient coral reefs![16] A well-known example is the discovery of "Malachite man".

> …skeletons of ten modern humans were buried under fifty-eight feet of Dakota Sandstone, in an area spanning about 50 by 100 feet. This rock formation is called the lower Cretaceous and is supposedly 140 million years old… Some of the bones are articulated. Some are not, appearing to have been washed into place… The bones are partially replaced with malachite and turquoise… Some insist this is a mass grave. Think about that! Who would dig a grave up to 54 feet deep through extremely hard sandstone layers? The modern mining operation was halted in the 1970's because the sandstone was so hard it was wearing out the bulldozers… It seems obvious that these 10 men, women and children, were buried rapidly by some catastrophe, like a flood.[17]

A Box of Tissues

As perplexing as fossilized human remains may be, soft-tissue 'fossil' remains

---

15. A "modern" human femur and skull cap/"calvarium" have been scientifically verified and found *in situ* in Carboniferous shale layers, approximately 300 mya by mainstream dating methods. Ed Conrad, discoverer. Found online at: http://wretchfossil.blogspot.com/2010/02/human-leg-bone-fossil-of-300-mya.html.
16. Bill Cooper, *Human Fossils from Noah's Flood*, Creation Ex Nihilo, 1:6, no. 3, 1983.
17. *Unlocking the Mysteries of Creation*, pp. 144,145. See also: www.bible.ca/tracks/malachite-man.htm.

of various organisms also have yet to be explained adequately in regards to the mainstream time-scale.[18] Paleontologists are puzzled how soft tissue and even proteins from dinosaur and other prehistoric creature remains could last for over 65 million years. If they perceived that the fossils were made roughly 5,000 years ago (approximate time of the flood), then there is little problem with the issue of time however. Predictably, paleontologists are quickly revising their theories to account for the new findings.

A recent and quite surprising find was unfossilized hemoglobin from a Tyrannosaur femur. Mary Schweitzer, assistant professor of paleontology at North Carolina State University who studied the soft tissues said, "We may not really know as much about how fossils are preserved as we think."[19] She also was challenged by her boss, "Dinosaur" Jack Horner, to prove that the material was not red blood cells. Six independent lines of evidence pointed to the existence of heme-containing compounds and/or hemoglobin breakdown products in extracts of trabecular tissues of the Tyrannosaur.[20] In other words, Schweitzer came to the conclusion that it was indeed dinosaur hemoglobin.[21]

Original and intact (non-fossilized) blood vessels of a duck-bill dinosaur have also been discovered.[22] The reason why this is noteworthy is that proteins with short-lived amino acids decay rapidly (in a matter of years depending on conditions). Yet the mainstream evolution paradigm states that dinosaurs went extinct sixty-five million years ago. Thus, non-fossilized blood vessels and hemoglobin defy this theory and are consistent with the Biblical account.

In 1961, a petroleum geologist discovered a large bone bed in Northwestern Alaska. Since the bones were not fossilized, he assumed, as did others, that they were from a herd of bison. About 20 years later, scientists realized that many of the unfossilized bones were indeed dinosaur bones of various types.[23] Another finding by a molecular paleontologist, Gerhard Muyzer, reported that organic osteocalcyn (a type of [noncollagenous] protein) was found in some dinosaur bones. There are over 40 reports of other "fresh" discoveries, like fragile protein found in dinosaur eggs.[24]

A final notable discovery was that of Precambrian worm casings. "Minerals have not replicated any part of the soft tissue and the carbonaceous material of the wall is primary [not replaced], preserving the original layering of the wall, its texture, and fabrics."[25] Note that according to the mainstream timeline, the Precambrian era occurred 540 million years ago (before the age of the dinosaurs), far too long for original tissues to survive.

---

18. http://creation.com/*dinosaur-soft-tissue-and-protein-even-more-confirmation*.
19. Discovery News, *T. Rex fossils yield soft tissue*, Mar 24, 2005.
20. Mary H. Schweitzer, Mark Marshall, Keith Carron, D. Scott Bohle, Scott C. Busse, Ernst V. Arnold, Darlene Barnard, J. R. Horner, and Jean R. Starkey, *Heme compounds in dinosaur trabecular bone*, PNAS June 10, 1997 vol. 94 no. 12 6291-6296.
21. M. Schweitzer and Staedter, T., *The Real Jurassic Park*, Earth, June 1997, pp. 55-57.
22. Brian Thomas, M.S., "Duck-Bill Dinosaur Blood Vessels". Acts & Facts, Feb 2016, p. 17.
23. Margaret Helder, *Fresh Dinosaur Bones Found*, Creation Ex Nihilo, vol. 14, p. 16.
24. Kenneth Carpenter, *Dinosaur Eggs and Babies*, Cambridge University Press, 1994, p. 3.
25. Cody, G. D. et al. 2011. *Geology.* 39 (3): 255-258. Cited in *Acts & Facts*, Aug. 2014. Vol 43, No 8. p. 9.

Trees that Cross the Line

Polystrate trees (fossil trees that project through multiple strata layers) are additional evidence that offer testimony of a global flood. Though they can be supported by both YE and OE arguments, these fossil trees indicate that rapid deposition must have taken place which does not conflict with a global flood. In fact, the evidence leans toward tremendous catastrophic flooding due (in part) to a mixing of both fresh and saltwater creatures in the fossil record. An excellent article about this that goes into greater detail and refutes the uniformitarian view can be found on the website of the Institute for Creation Research.[26]

Mount St. Helens

A modern example of how strata is often misunderstood as indicating long periods of time would be the after effects of the Mount St. Helens eruption on May 18, 1980. Shortly after the tremendous eruption, the trees from the local forest, which were blown down and scattered by the volcanic blast, were subsequently buried in the sediment at the bottom of Spirit Lake. Scientists discovered shortly afterwards that the trees at the bottom of the lake were being buried in the same fashion as fossilized polystrate tree trunks found all over the world. The implication was that polystrate trees were buried rapidly through catastrophic means, just as they were during the Mount St. Helens eruption. Furthermore, a one hundred foot deep canyon was cut in only a few days by a hot mud flow. The canyon exhibited many layers of strata, and a river runs through the bottom of it; just like the Grand Canyon. Put simply, Mount St. Helens accomplished in a matter of days what would normally have been interpreted as taking hundreds of millions of years.[27]

Conformities and Progradation

It is common knowledge that there are no major time breaks (unconformities) in the earth's sedimentary layers. Since unconformities are only localized to specific areas, possibly due to erosion, geologists can trace continuous paths from top to bottom in the stratigraphic record. The parallel layers in the earth's strata, also known as conformities, indicate not only rapid deposition, but that they were *deposited as a unit* throughout the earth. This is strong evidence for a global flood! In addition, several layers may contain fossils from vastly different time periods (according to the mainstream time line). Since the layers are conformable however, the creatures were

---

[26]. John D. Morris, Ph.D., *The Polystrate Trees and Coal Seams of Joggins Fossil Cliffs*.
[27]. See: Ken Ham's commentary, *Mount St. Helens—evidence for Genesis!*, May 17, 2000.

deposited at the same time.[28]

Furthermore, modern studies demonstrate that "lithologically similar sediments can develop one on top of another as materials are added to the front of a prograding delta. This is reflected in the horizontal "facies"... time is actually defined by the slope of the prograding surface and the diagonal stack of varying materials."[29] What this simply means is, the uniformitarian theory of superposition, which claims that the deeper the strata, the greater the age, is not necessarily true in all cases. In many areas around the world, the geologic evidence indicates a horizontal-type layering as opposed to vertical layering. Thus, an organism buried in lower strata is not necessarily older than an organism buried in upper strata. **Figure 2** demonstrates the horizontal deposition of progradation.

Progradation is not only found near lake and sea shores, but also far inland. The Navajo Sandstone formation, covering thousands of square miles in southwest United States, is one example. Modern studies indicate that it was formed by outward progradation by an unknown source (possibly the Appalachian Mountains) while the continent was submerged in the past.[30]

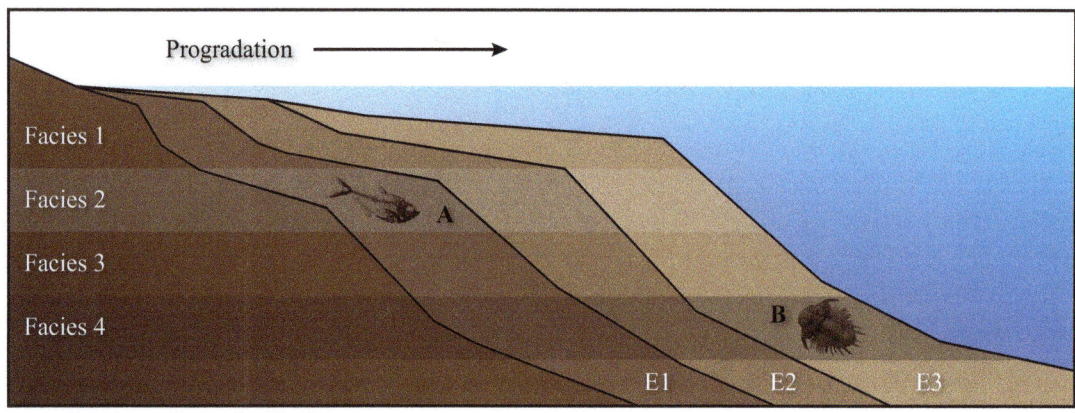

Figure 2: As sediment sorts itself according to mass vertically/diagonally via the effects of liquefaction, density, and other factors, layers of strata are formed. These layers make up facies, which are sections of rock layers that exhibit particular characteristics. Progradation occurs laterally over time due to water flow and/or various catastrophic events. In this simplified diagram, organism A is buried ("event" E1) before organism B, and is therefore older (even though it is found in higher strata/facies).[31]

Wrong Order Formations

In light of the evidence for global liquefaction and progradation, geologic strata, from the uniformitarian sense, do not necessarily indicate any consistent macro-evolutionary order. In many cases, fossils are found in layers that are unexpected in light of the theory. Walter E. Lammerts published several lists of approximately 200

---
28. Walt Brown, Ph.D., *In the Beginning - Compelling Evidence for Creation and the Flood*, pp. 36, 37.
29. Carl R. Froede Jr., *Geology by Design*, p. 18.
30. Froede, *Geology by Design*, pp. 18, 19.
31. See: Froede, *Geology by Design*, pp. 16-20 and http://noevolution.info (online video documentary of stratification).

wrong-order formations in the United States alone.[32] These findings do not contradict the global flood scenario however. Please consider the following examples of out-of-place fossils:

> ... In Uzbekistan, 86 consecutive hoofprints of horses were found in rocks dating back to the dinosaurs. Hoofprints of some other animal are alongside 1,000 dinosaur footprints in Virginia. ...Sometimes, land animals, flying animals, and marine animals are fossilized side-by-side in the same rock. Dinosaur, whale, elephant, horse, and other fossils, plus crude human tools, have reportedly been found in phosphate beds in South Carolina. Coal beds contain round, black lumps called coal balls, some of which contain flowering plants that allegedly evolved 100 million years after the coal bed was formed. In the Grand Canyon, in Venezuela, in Kashmir, and in Guyana, spores of ferns and pollen from flowering plants are found in Cambrian rocks – rocks supposedly deposited before flowering plants evolved. Pollen has also been found in Precambrian rocks deposited before life allegedly evolved.[33]

Earthquakes, wave action, and quicksand are all examples of liquefaction; which was a major factor during the global flood in sorting sediments and living organisms. "Liquefaction occurs whenever water is forced up through loose sediments with enough pressure to lift the topmost sedimentary particles."[34] Due to the variations in size, weight and density, sediments sort themselves as they fall back through the column of water, producing sharply defined layering. This is also indicative of local flooding, which occasionally produces horizontal strata. Liquefaction plumes, mounds, cyclothems, among other geologic formations, are further evidence of liquefaction processes and not indicative of millions of years of soil layering.[35]

A Simple Experiment

Mainstream theories of the principle of superposition (fossils found in the 'correct' sequence) were put in doubt through a simple repeatable experiment. In 2001, Dr. Karen Jensen personally discussed with Dr. Walt Brown an unpublished experiment at Loma Linda University. The experiment consisted of placing a bird, mammal, reptile, and amphibian in an open water tank. Their buoyancy shortly following death depended on their density when they were alive, among several other factors. The dead animals in the tank ultimately settled naturally in the following order from the bottom up: amphibian, reptile, mammal, and bird. "This order of relative buoyancy correlates closely with "the evolutionary order," but, of course, evolution did not cause it."[36]

---
32. Brown, *In the Beginning*, pp. 67, 68.
33. Brown, p. 12.
34. Froede, *Geology by Design*, p. 170.
35. Brown, *In the Beginning*, pp. 175 - 179.
36. Brown, p. 172. See also Mortenson and Ury, *Coming to Grips with Genesis*, (Paleontological Considerations), p. 279.

Unreliable Traces

Apparently, the mainstream uniformitarian theory that strata is formed over millions of years does not entirely match the geologic evidence. The mainstream view of the geologic column is not consistent with reality, in other words. Even circular reasoning is used when dating strata. The age of a particular strata layer is determined ultimately by what fossil types are found in it. In similar manner, the age of a fossil is determined by what layer of strata it is found in. This is not a reliable method of dating. Nor are trace fossils (tracks, trails, burrows; other secondary evidence) helpful in identifying turbidite facies (a layer of sediment or sedimentary rock that was deposited from a turbidity current). "We cannot overlook the possibility that some of the trace makers might have been displaced and so their traces may occur out of place compared to where they might have lived. As a result, caution must be exercised in using traces in any attempt to determine paleo-depth without additional evidence."[37]

Likewise, geologically measuring the depth of a body of water (bathymetry), through sediment particle sizes, bedding, and trace fossils, can also yield inaccurate results. "While many different types of traces have been found in association with turbidite deposits, ... there are still too many uncertainties to confidently predict the paleoenvironmental setting solely from trace fossils."[38]

Ancient Environments

There is universal agreement by scientists that the geologic record contains evidence of past storm events, called tempestites. Mainstream geologists believe that they represent local periodic events, though they could be viewed from a global flood scenario. As the world-wide flood began to subside, and the water began to run off the uplifted continents into the deepening oceans, "there is fossil evidence that marine life began to establish itself in some of the epeiric seas."[39] These shallow continental seas would have been influenced by passing storms, as can be seen in the tempestites and fossil record.

> If evolution were true, all sedimentary deposits would be found in small areas with few or no fossils. It really takes catastrophic, continent-covering flooding such as Noah's flood to produce vast horizontal sheets of fossil-rich layers; and that is what is found piled on top of the pre-Flood rocks at the Grand Canyon. Running underground, these layers of Flood rock stretch for thousands of square miles across much of North America![40]

---

37. Froede, *Geology by Design*, p. 124.
38. Froede, *Geology by Design*, p. 124.
39. Froede, p. 40 ["epeiric" - a shallow sea that extends over part of a continent].
40. Parker, Gary and Mary, *The Fossil Book*, p. 29.

Prehistoric environments are also taught from a uniformitarian perspective. Geologists examine the geologic materials and formations that make up the layers of sediment (i.e., sand, clay, carbonates, load features, cross-bedding, fossils). The ancient past is then assumed by relating it to the present environment. The problem is that all too often the uniformitarian perspective on past environments is given as the *only* possible conclusion, despite its inconsistencies with much of the evidence. We have all therefore been subject to uniformitarian and naturalist propaganda. Particularly regarding dinosaurs, due to the uniformitarian view, they became extinct about 65 million years ago—therefore, why look for evidence of dinosaurs outside of the fossil record? Yet that is precisely what this book intends to do!

To reiterate, uniformitarian scientists would have us believe that the many layers of geologic strata are indications of the passage of great lengths of time. If this were true, then we would expect to find a great number of paleosol layers as well. Paleosols are soils that formed in the ancient past ("ancient soil"). Currently, there are no standard methods used to identify a paleosol. In fact, the wide range of techniques in identification reveals that paleopedologists utilize subjective means of interpretation. Though there are a number of published works attempting to standardize the procedures in identifying a paleosol, paleopedologists cannot agree on a consistent method of identification and rely on their own world view. Nevertheless, "the time scale and conditions suggested by uniformitarian geoscientists regarding terrestrial conditions in the past are not supported by the sparse number of paleosols actually found in the rock record."[41]

To wrap this all up, during the past 50 years, "the truth of Genesis 1-11 has been increasingly vindicated, often by the work of evolutionists who scoffingly reject God's Word. [A growing number of geologists argue that] the rock record shows evidence of rapid catastrophic erosion or sedimentation, *drastically reducing the time involved in the formation of many geological deposits.*"[42] (emphasis mine) In other words, the uniformitarian view is beginning to be seen as inconsistent with the latest geological observations by atheists!

Cross Cultural Tales

Since it is beyond the scope of this book, the theological and geologic arguments for a young earth and global flood will need to rest at this point (though there is much more evidence). The Bible indicates that Noah took aboard the ark seven of each kind of clean animal and pairs of unclean animals.[43] Most likely any land-dwelling dinosaurs saved on the ark were considered unclean, but were saved nonetheless. As for having room on the ark for all the land animal kinds, Noah most likely took young

---
41. Froede, p. 62.
42. Mortenson and Ury, *Coming to Grips with Genesis - Biblical Authority and the Age of the Earth*, p. 101.
43. Genesis 7: 2,3.

adults only and had plenty of room left over for supplies and extra passengers.[44] In regards to land dwelling dinosaurs specifically, there are approximately 50 dinosaur kinds (or far less than 50 kinds, according to leading paleontologists[45]), whereas the average size of a full grown dinosaur (among all the different kinds) is the size of a bison, and those brought on the ark were most likely the size of a sheep on average.[46] In other words, the ark was definitely large enough to house hundreds of young dinosaurs along with the other "normal" animals.

In contrast to the geological record indicating a global flood, as mankind spread throughout the post-flood world, it is interesting to note that almost all cultures hold similar creation myths, including a flood. Naturally, the farther away from the Middle East one travels however, the more distorted those tales become from the direct and matter-of-fact Biblical account.[47] Needless to say, another cross-cultural concept is the dragon, which will be specifically focused on for the remainder of this book.

	Young Earth Creationism	Progressive Creationism	Theistic Evolution	Darwinian Evolution
Fossils indicate burial via flooding or cataclysm	■	■	■	■
Geologic forms indicate rapid burial and formation	■	■	■	■
Sedimentary layers formed as a global unit	■	■	■	■
Polystrate fossils indicate rapid strata formation	■	□	□	□
Unfossilized dinosaur remains	■	□	□	□
Ancient cultures describe a global (universal) flood	■	□	□	□
Fossils found in the wrong order/strata	■	□	□	□
Modern human remains are found in ancient strata	■	□	□	□
"Macro-evolutionary tree" does not exist at all	■	□		

Figure 3: Macro-evolutionary models are not completely compatible/consistent with current geologic observations. Since modern animals and human remains are found in the same strata as extinct animals (dinosaurs and prehistoric mammals), it is reasonable to conclude that dinosaurs ("dragons") lived contemporaneously with mankind at some point in history and have simply been rendered extinct along with other types of animals.
■ = Consistent with   □ = Partially consistent with / adjustment of proposed paradigm (theory) needed to explain.

---

44. See: John Woodmorappe, *Noah's Ark: A Feasibility Study*.
45. Jack Horner: Where are the baby dinosaurs? TEDxVancouver. November 2010.
46. Dr. Clarey, "Settling the Dinosaur Weight Debate", *Acts & Facts Magazine*, May 2015, p. 12. and Ken Ham, *The Great Dinosaur Mystery Solved!*, p. 65.
47. For example see: Kenneth Kitchen, *Ancient Orient and the Old Testament*, InterVarsity Press, 1966, p. 89, and/or *Did Genesis Borrow From Pagan Creation Myths?* by Kyle Pope.
    (found online at: http://ancientroadpublications.com/Studies/BiblicalStudies/DidGenesisBorrow.html).

3: Eastern Historic Dragons

Our modern understanding of what a typical dragon *should be* actually combines many features of what were originally *individual* dragons into a single mythical creature. Ancient documents do not support the idea of a single mythical beast but reveal to us that dragons appeared as different types of living creatures. The Chinese, for example, indicate that one type of dragon could fly while others could swim; some dragons had horns and some did not have horns; some were docile and some were dangerous; not to mention the various colors and behaviors that dragons possessed.

While reading through the evidence presented throughout this book, note also the consistencies and similar descriptions of the various kinds of dragons in the unrelated reports throughout the world and its history. For instance, many land-based dragons throughout Eurasia lived in caves and were killed by piercing the belly. Flying dragons had bat-like wings, were bright in color, and were considered as "weather forecasters". Dragons that lived in the water could breathe fire or were venomous, some had both hair and scales, and so forth. A main portion of this particular chapter will examine Chinese accounts, while being quite prolific, are too numerous to include them all.

Marco Polo

While travelling in Asia, Marco Polo gave the following account of an unknown serpent creature. In many respects, it sounds like a description of a species of dragon and not that of a large snake. Note the details of how the creature is killed by piercing its underside (a similar method is utilized in Europe), along with the attractive reasons for its demise. Consider other "normal" creatures in East Asia (i.e. various species of tigers, rhinos, and elephants) that were once quite numerous. Today they have nearly vanished or have become extinct altogether due to similar reasons of utilizing animal parts for food and medicinal purposes. Though this reasoning lends support for the serpent's extinction, some have proposed that the animal described may simply be a crocodile of some sort. However, the description of the three sharp claws on the forelimbs, that it lived in caves during the day, among other things, lead one to consider that it is not a large crocodile (that has 5 claws and likes to bask in the daytime sun), but a different creature altogether.

> Here are seen huge serpents, ten paces in length, and ten spans in the girt of the body. At the fore part, near the head, they have two short legs, having three claws like those of a tiger, with eyes larger than a fourpenny loaf (pane da quattro denari) and very glaring. The jaws are wide enough to swallow a man, the teeth are large and sharp, and their whole appearance is so formidable, that neither man, nor any kind of animal, can approach them without terror. Others are met with of a smaller size, being eight, six, or five paces long; and the following method is used for taking them. In the daytime, by reason of the great heat, they lurk in caverns, from whence, at night, they issue to seek their food, and whatever beast they meet with and can lay hold of, whether tiger, wolf, or any other, they devour; after which they drag themselves towards some lake, spring of water, or river, in order to drink. By their motion in this way along the shore, and their vast weight, they make a deep impression, as if a heavy beam had been drawn along the sands. Those whose employment it is to hunt them observe the track by which they are most frequently accustomed to go, and fix into the ground several pieces of wood, armed with sharp iron spikes, which they cover with the sand in such a manner as not to be perceptible. When therefore the animals make their way towards the places they usually haunt, they are wounded by these instruments, and speedily killed. The crows, as soon as they perceive them to be dead, set up their scream; and this serves as a signal to the hunters, who advance to the spot, and proceed to separate the skin from the flesh, taking care immediately to secure the gall, which is most highly esteemed in medicine. In cases of the bite of a mad dog, a pennyweight of it, dissolved in wine, is administered. It is also useful in accelerating parturition, when the labour pains of women have come on. A small quantity of it being applied to carbuncles, pustules, or other eruptions on the body, they are presently dispersed; and it is efficacious in many other complaints. The flesh also of the animal is sold at a dear rate, being thought to have a higher flavour than other kinds of meat, and by all persons it is esteemed a delicacy.[1]

In China, tigers are considered to be rivals of the dragon. The Chinese idiom "Dragon vs. Tiger" demonstrates this idea. It is interesting to note that Marco Polo also gave witness that through certain areas of China ("Cathay") the tigers were so numerous that the natives did not venture out of their villages at night out of fear

---

1. Ernest Rhys, *The Travels of Marco Polo the Venetian*, London: Pub. J.M. Dent and Sons Ltd., 1908, pp. 246,247. The initial serpent described being (approximately) 50 ft long by 7 ft. wide.

of being attacked by the ferocious cats.[2] In light of this, it would be reasonable to conclude that both man and tigers were mortal enemies of the dragon, or "serpent" in this case.

Differentiations

It must be stressed here that dragons were differentiated from tortoises, snakes and other reptilian animals in Asian cultures. This can be particularly seen in the zodiac. Today, many wonder why the Chinese have one single animal that is a "myth" among eleven other "real" creatures in the zodiac. Could it be that when the zodiac was arranged that the dragon was simply another creature that lived among the rest and eventually became extinct thousands, if not hundreds of years ago? In the course of time, the dragon would be delegated to the realm of myth since "no one has seen a living dragon". Though this point is often overlooked, the differentiation made between the dragon and other reptiles is an important fact to consider that the Chinese were not merely describing a large salt water crocodile or enormous python, but a kind of magnificent creature that influenced their entire culture.

Not only are dragons differentiated from other reptiles, but the Chinese differentiated dragons between themselves. Today (from a Western viewpoint) however, there seems to be essentially only one basic style of dragon portrayed in Chinese art (other than the number of toes): a long serpentine, 4-legged creature with scales, hair, and horns. This single portrayal of the dragon may lead people to believe that the long-standing Chinese culture only has one type of mythological dragon to refer to. In reality, this is not the case. There were *at the very least* nine different types of dragons described in ancient Chinese accounts. M. W. de Visser explains how the Chinese, upon observing various dragons and their behavior, would make artistic representations of the creatures to be used in their appropriate capacity. Today these accounts are only considered as legendary.

> A well-known work of the end of the sixteenth century, the *Wuh tsah tsu* (五雜俎), informs us about the nine different young of the dragon, whose shapes are used as ornaments according to their nature. The *pu'-lao* (溝牢) dragons which like to cry, are represented on the tops of bells, serving as handles. The *szĕ-niu* (四牛), which like music, are used to adorn musical instruments. The *ch'i-wen* (蚩吻) which like swallowing, are placed on both ends of the ridgepoles of roofs (to swallow all evil influences). The *chao-fung* (嘲風), lion-like beasts which like precipices, are placed on the four corners of roofs. The *ai-hwa* (睚眦), which like to kill, serve as ornaments of sword grips. The *hi-pi* (屓贔), which have the shape of the *ch'i-lung* (螭龍), are fond of literature, are represented on the sides of grave monuments. The *p'i-han* (狴犴), which like litigation, are placed over prison gates (in order to keep guard).

---
2. Rhys, pp. 264,265.

The *swan-i* (狻猊), which like to sit down, are represented upon the bases of Buddhist idols (under the Buddhas' or Bodhisattvas' feet). The *pa-hia* (霸下), finally, big tortoises which like to carry heavy objects, are placed under grave-monuments.

Further, the same author enumerates nine other kinds of dragons—there are so many, says he, because the dragon's nature is very lewd, so that he copulates with all animals, which are represented as ornaments of different objects or buildings according to their liking prisons, water, the rank smell of newly caught fish or newly killed meat, wind and rain, ornaments, smoke, shutting the mouth (used for adorning key-holes), standing on steep places (placed on roofs), and fire.[3]

The last dragon listed in the citation above, and the only creature among the nine that has a vague physical description in these passages, is the *pa-hia*, a tortoise-like dragon. If this is speaking of a real living dragon, it would be reasonable to suggest that this may possibly be what we would call today a "Talarurus" or "Shamosaurus" – both found (in fossil form) in the region of China and Mongolia. These dinosaurs were of the ankylosaur family and resemble tortoises due to their thick bony shell.

Detailed Descriptions

In addition to the *pa-hia*, the Chinese wrote many consistent descriptions of the various dragons that inhabited the land. The descriptions are quite specific and seem to indicate that they were not describing a mythical beast or some fossil in the ground, but actual living creatures. These dragons were also compared with (and in some cases related to) other scaly animals living today, like a gavial or snake. Consider the following quotes from various ancient documents collected in de Visser's extensive research[4] on Asian dragons:

Shape of the Dragons
  Wang Fu (王符) says: "The people paint the dragon's shape with a horse's head and a snake's tail. Further, there are expressions as 'three joints' and 'nine resemblances' (of the dragon), to wit: from head to shoulder, from shoulder to breast, from breast to tail. These are the joints; as to the nine-resemblances, they are the following: his horns resemble those of a stag, his head that of a camel, his eyes those of a demon, his neck that of a snake, his belly that of a clam (shen), his scales those of a carp, his claws those of an eagle, his soles those of a tiger, his ears those of a cow. Upon his head he has a thing like a broad eminence (a big lump), called ch´ih muh. If a dragon has no ch´ih muh, he cannot ascend to the sky."

---

3. M. W. de Visser, *The Dragon in China and Japan*, 1913, pp. 101, 102.
   Primary source: Sie Chao-chi's *"Wuh Tsah Tsu"* (Five Assorted Offerings), chapter 9, 1592.
4. Since M. W. de Visser's book is in the public domain, the advantage of his authoritative research which references multiple ancient texts is used estensively. The lengthy quotes taken from his book do not include the Chinese texts however, which much can be found in de Visser's work (or see source text) if a direct transcription and/or comparison of the ancient source text is needed. (Transliterated Chinese is his.).

The *P'i ya* (埤雅) states that "the dragon's 81 scales form a number consisting of nine times nine. Nine is Yang. The carp's 36 scales form a number consisting of six times six. Six is Yin."[5]

In the *Yang kuh man luh* (暘谷漫錄) we read: "The dragon has five fingers."[6]

Finally, the *Pen-ts'ao kang-muh* (本草網目, section: 鱗之一) teaches us that 'a dragon has whiskers at the sides of his mouth and a bright pearl under his chin; under his throat he has scales lying in a reversed direction; upon his head he has a broad eminence called in writing *ch'ih muh* (尺木); if a dragon has no *ch'ih muh*, he cannot ascend to the sky.

Male and female dragons

The difference between male and female dragons is described as follows: "The male dragon's horn is undulating, concave, steep; it is strong at the top, but becomes very thin below. The female dragon has a straight nose, a round mane, thin scales and a strong tail."

Different kinds of dragons

"If a dragon has scales, he is called *kiao-lung*; if wings, *ying-lung*; if a horn, *k'iu-lung*; if he has no horn, he is called *ch'i-lung*". In the Japanese Buddhist dictionary entitled *Bukkyō iroha jiten* (佛教いろは字典) we find the same enumeration with the addition of a fifth class, the *p'an-lung*, "coiled dragon", which does not yet ascend to heaven. This dragon is also mentioned in the *Fang yen* (方言), where we read: "Dragons which do not yet ascend to heaven are called *p'an-lung*". …

According to the *Wen-tszĕ tsih-lioh* (文字集略) the *ch'i-lung* is red, white and green, and the *k'iu-lung* is blue. The *k'iu* is mentioned several times in the *Pao P'oh-tszĕ* (抱朴子): "If a pond inhabited by fishes and gavials is drained off, the divine *k'iu* go away". "As to the flying to the sky of the *k'iu* of the pools, this is his union with the clouds". …

The connection between the snake and the dragon is evident from the description of the so-called *t'eng-she'* (螣蛇螣), a wingless serpent, "which can cause the clouds to rise, and, riding upon them, can fly a thousand miles. It can change into a dragon. Although there are males and females, they do not copulate. Their cry forbodes pregnancy". And Koh Hung states that "tortoises turn into tigers and snakes, into dragons". In the *Yiu-yang tsah tsu* (酉陽雜俎) we read: "Dragons and snakes are considered by the learned class to be related".

The gavial also belongs to the dragons. The *Pen-ts'ao kang-muh* describes it as follows: "There are numerous gavials in rivers and lakes. They resemble the class of the *ling-li* and their length is one or two chang. Both their backs and tails are covered with scales. By exhaling they can *make clouds and*

---

5. Korean dragons are also said to have the same number of scales.
6. According to the Houston Museum of Natural Science, many dinosaurs have five fingers but with no more than three claws on the inner three fingers. Some have three or even two fingers; which coincide with the various Chinese dragon artistic descriptions.

cause rain. It is a kind of dragon. They live in deep holes and can fly only horizontally, not vertically. Their cries are like the sound of a drum, and when they cry at night, this is called 'the gavial drum'. When the countryfolk hear it, they predict rain".

About the *shen*, a huge clam, the same work says the following: "It is a kind of *kiao*. Its shape also resembles that of a snake, but it is larger. It has a horn like a dragon, a red mane, and the scales under its loins are all lying in a reversed direction. It eats young swallows. When exhaling its breath assumes the form of towers and castles, which are seen when it is about to rain, and are called 'clam-towers', or 'sea-markets'. Of its fat, mixed with wax, candles are made, which one may smell at a distance of about a hundred steps. Also in the flames of these candles the shapes of towers and steeples are to be seen. Luh Tien [the author of the *P'i ya*, who lived during the reign of the Emperor Hwui Tsung (1101—1126)] says : 'If a kiao copulates with a tortoise, they produce a tortoise, and when with a pheasant, a clam (*shen*) is produced'".

Kiao lung

The *Shan hai king* (山海經) describes the *kiao* as follows: "(Out of the *Tao Kwo* mountains) water comes forth in waves and flows to the South, where it flows into the sea. In this water there are '*tiger-kiao*'. Their shapes consist of the body of a fish and the tail of a snake. Their voices are like those of mandarin ducks. Those who eat them, have no boils, and they (i.e. their flesh) may be used to cure piles". In three other passages of the same ancient work many kiao are said to live in special mountain rivulets.

According to the *Yang yü king* (養魚經), "Classic on the rearing of Fishes", "if there are fully 360 fishes, the *kiao lung* is made their chief, and leading the fishes flies away". …

Kwan tszĕ (管子) says: "The *kiao-lung* is the god of the water animals. If he rides on the water, his soul is in full vigour, but when he loses water (if he is deprived of it), his soul declines. Therefore I (or they) say: 'If a *kiao-lung* gets water, his soul can be in full vigour'". The same philosopher states that "when people drain marshes and catch fish, the *kiao-lung* do not dwell in those pools".

Also *Hwai nan tszĕ* (淮南子) mentions the *kiao-lung* with the following words: "The *kiao-lung* lie hidden and sleep in pools, and yet, their eggs break up (i.e. the young ones come out of them) on the hills". The commentator remarks: "The *kiao-lung* lay their eggs on hills and hide in pools.[7] Their eggs get life spontaneously". …

The *Ta tai li ki* (大戴禮記) instructs us that the *kiao-lung* is considered to be the head of the 360 scaly animals, and that "if water accumulates and becomes a river, the *kiao-lung* is born". The *Poh wuh chi* (博物志) says: "If a man has eaten swallows, he must not enter the water; (for if he does so), he will be swallowed by a *kiao-lung*'".

---

7. Compare with the Marco Polo account.

In the above texts, except in those of the *Shan hai king*, the words *kiao* and *lung* are combined to one term. The *Shan hai king*, however, speaks of the *kiao* only, and so do a large number of other works, which distinguish the *kiao* from the lung. Neither in the *Shan hai king*, nor in the *Li ki* (禮記), which says: "(In the last month of summer) the inspector of fishing is ordered to kill the *kiao*", these water animals are mentioned as divine creatures. The commentator of the former work, Kwoh P'oh (郭璞), however, states the following: "The *kiao* resembles a snake. It has four legs, and is akin to the *lung*". As we have seen above, the *Shuh i ki* (拾遺記) remarks that a water snake (水虺 "*shui-yuen*"), when five hundred years old, changes into a kiao, and a *kiao* after a thousand years becomes a *lung*. ...

Standard		Description
ch'i lung	螭龍	no horns; red, white, green.
kiu lung	虬龍	horned; blue; water diety.
kiao lung	蛟龍	scales; snake-like; 4 legs; thin neck; white ring around neck; small tiger-like head; fleshy ring on tail; brocaded flanks; some are white; some have reddish-brown breast and spotted blue on upper back; united eyebrows.
li lung	驪龍	good eyesight.
ying lung	鷹龍	winged.
p'an lung	盤龍	coiled; the status of "heavenly dragon" has not been attained.
sien lung	先龍	"first dragon"

Additional		Description
ai wha	睚眦	predatory killer.
chao fung	嘲風	lion-like; inhabits precipices.
ch'i wen	蚩吻	"swallowing".
ch'i lung	螭龍	"fond of literature".
hi pi	屓贔	"fond of literature".
"ling li"	(鲮鲤)	(a dragon class called "*ling li*", or pangolin-type) yet similar to a gavial; scaled; inhabits deep holes; cries like a drum; up to 20 feet long.
lung ma	龍馬	"dragon horse"; spotted blue, red + three other colors; covered in scales; dragon-like mane; neighs like the tone of a flute; 300 mile territory; serpent tail; frizzy hair; round eyes; horse-like head; fleshy crest; 2 white horns.
pa hia	霸下	large tortoise-like.
p'i han	狴犴	"fond of litigation".
pu' lao	蒲牢	cries (makes sound) often.
shen	蜃	snake-like; clam-like qualities (pearlescent scales?); horned; red mane; scales on underside lie in reverse direction.
szĕ-niu	四牛	likes music.

Figure 4: Non-comprehensive comparative list of various Chinese dragons.

The *P'i ya* describes this animal as follows: "The *kiao* belongs to the same kind as the *lung*. Its shape resembles that of a snake and yet it has four legs and a thin neck. Around its neck it has a white necklace. The big *kiao* are several spans thick. They are born from eggs. Their eyebrows are united, reason why they are called *kiao*".

The *Mih k'oh hwui si* (黑客琿屖) says: "The *kiao's* shape is like that of a snake, and its head is like that of a tiger. Its length reaches several chang.[8] Many of them live in rivulets and pools and under rock caves. Their voices are like the bellowing of a cow. When people walk on the shore or in the valleys of brooks, they are troubled by the *kiao*. When they see a man, they first surround him with stinking saliva, and after having made him tumble into the water they suck his blood under his armpits. When he has no blood left, they stop sucking".

In the *Pen-ts'ao kang-muh* Li Shi-chen quotes the following passage from the *P'ei yuen kwang cheu ki* (裴淵廣州記): "The *kiao* is over a chang long. It resembles a snake but has four feet and its shape is broader, resembling the beam of a railing. It has a small head and a thin neck. At its neck it has white tassels (a white necklace). The upper part of its breast is reddish brown, the upper part of its back is spotted with blue, the sides of its ribs (flanks) are like brocade. Its tail has a fleshy ring. Big kiao are several span thick, and their eggs are also larger (than those of other kiao). They can lead fishes and fly. If people catch turtles, the kiao can escape".[9] [*These descriptions will be important later!*]

Considering the description of the *kiao* in the previous paragraph, it is reasonable to conclude that just as reptiles today exhibit various colors (lizards and snakes in particular), dinosaurs no doubt did too. Paleontologists have wondered what colors the dinosaurs were, though it is impossible to tell from a fossil bone what color a dinosaur was. Even fossilized skin has offered little help in this area. Nevertheless, the Chinese in the past apparently saw the living creatures and gave us a basic description of their particular colors. For example, "According to the *Wen-tszĕ tsih-lioh* the *ch'i-lung* is red, white and green, and the *k'iu-lung* is blue."[10]

Color has deep symbolic meaning in Chinese culture (**Figure 5**). For example, it is common knowledge that red is considered good luck in modern China. Yellow traditionally represents freedom from worldly concerns (which is why it is popular in Buddhism), and so forth. As indicated, dragons were also associated with colors. The azure colored dragon was considered the highest ranking dragon and was the symbol of spring.[11] "The *Yih lin* (易林) says: "If six dragons have [an] angry fight with one another under an embankment, and the azure and yellow dragons do not conquer, the travellers will meet hardships and trouble". As we have seen above, the azure and yellow dragons especially were harbingers of felicity; so their defeat was a sign of coming trouble."[12] "King-Pang says in his *Yih chw'en* (易傳): 'When those who have virtue meet injuries (i.e. are put to death), the bad omens of this are that dragons appear in wells... In cases of execution or violent cruelty black dragons come out

---
8. A *chang* is approximately 10 ch'ih, or 3.05 meters (~10 feet).
9. M. W. de Visser, *The Dragon in China and Japan*, 1913, selections from pp. 70 - 80,
10. de Visser, p. 73.
11. de Visser, p. 30.
12. de Visser, p. 46.

of wells.'"[13]

CENTER:
Color: gold / yellow
Element: Earth
Metal: gold
Season: (Inbetween / Neutral)
Planet: Saturn
Identity: Cauldron (large metal pot or kettle)
Relationship: Husband / Wife
Virtues: Faith
Senses: Touch

NORTH
Color: black
Element: Water
Metal: Iron
Season: Winter
Planet: Mercury
Identity: Dragon
Relationship: Ruler / Minister
Virtues: Knowledge
Senses: Hearing

WEST
Color: white
Element: Metal
Metal: Silver
Season: Autumn
Planet: Venus
Identity: Tiger
Relationship: Elder / Younger
Virtues: Righteousness
Senses: Smell

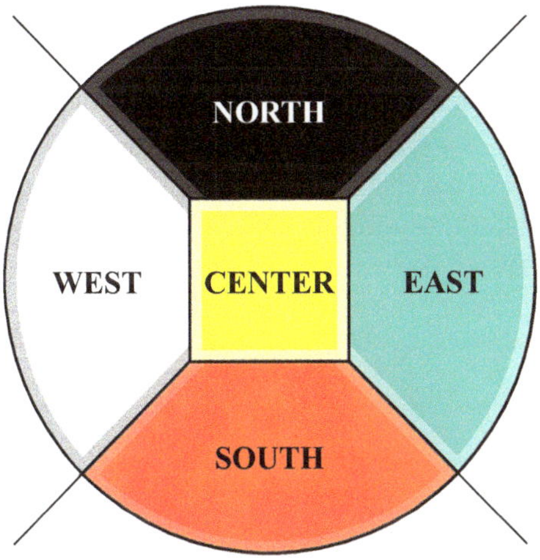

EAST
Color: azure / blue-green
Element: Wood
Metal: Lead
Season: Spring
Planet: Jupiter
Identity: Tortoise / Azure dragon
Relationship: Friends
Virtues: Benevolence
Senses: Sight

SOUTH
Color: red
Element: Fire
Metal: Copper
Season: Summer
Planet: Mars
Identity: Phoenix
Relationship: Father / Son
Virtues: Propriety
Senses: Taste

MUTUALLY PRODUCING:
wood produces fire / fire produces earth / earth produces metal / metal produces water / water produces wood

MUTUALLY OVERCOMING:
wood overcomes earth / earth overcomes water / water overcomes fire / fire overcomes metal / metal overcomes wood

4 AUSPICIOUS CREATURES: Unicorn, Phoenix, Tortoise, Dragon

Figure 5: The various relationships and extended associations of traditional Chinese colors.

    The *Shuh i ki* (4th century) tells us that the Emperor Chao of the Han dynasty (B.C. 86–74), when angling in the Wei river, "caught a white *kiao*, three chang long, which resembled a big snake, but had no scaly armour. The Emperor said: 'This is not a lucky omen', and ordered the Ta kwan to make a condiment of it. Its flesh was purple, its bones were blue, and its taste was very savoury and pleasant".

---

13. de Visser, p. 56.

The ancient Chinese apparently considered the kiao — some four-legged water animal — to be a common, dangerous creature, but afterwards it was believed to be akin to the dragon and called a dragon itself. Thus it became the principal god of rivers and brooks.[14]

In the 1700's, on the island of Japan, one particular description of a dragon may potentially be referring to a bipedal creature, like a young Lambeosaurus (albeit a rare fossil find in Japan). Though there are numerous other possibilities that could fit the following description, such as a Tsintaosaurus spinorhinus.[15]

> The *Kanden jihitsu* (閑田次筆) describes a dragon which was seen under a bridge near Unawa village, Harima province, at the foot of Mount Shiko. It was seven shaku long, had one horn, hands and feet, and its body had the colour of leaves of a tree tinged with a golden lustre. It was a beautiful animal, exactly like the red dragons on pictures. When the villagers descended from the bridge and stroked its horn, it was not afraid or angry, but apparently rejoiced. Afterwards the skin of this divine dragon was found near by, on the other side of the river. "This was not an evil dragon or a poisonous snake, but probably a lucky omen of a good reign. The fact that the crop of that very autumn was good, was brought into connection with the appearance of the dragon, which was (therefore) said to be a venerable being"[16]

Evolutionary Associations

The ancient Chinese had their version of what we would today label 'evolution' regarding dragons and how other animals came to be. As discussed, the Chinese described various dragons as being like other creatures. Thus it would be reasonable to conclude (like the ancient Chinese apparently did) that dragons begat other creatures by copulating with certain types of animals. This is mentioned here only to further demonstrate the detailed understanding of what dragons looked like and their distinct place in the animal kingdom. In one instance, "Hwai Nan Tszĕ goes as far as to declare the dragon to be the origin of all creatures, as we learn from the following passage; "All creatures, winged, hairy, scaly and mailed, find their origin in the dragon"."[17]
Like the platypus, dragons apparently had multiple physical characteristics that (to the naked eye) seemed to belong to other animals. In fact, the first specimen of a platypus was considered a hoax due to its duck-like bill and beaver-like tail, among other "mixed up" features. Ancient descriptions and artwork of dragons reflect this very concept that dragons were not simply reptilian.

---

14. de Visser, p. 79.
15. Tsintaosaurus fossils have been found in Asia and North America. They were both quad and bipedal. The function of the large protuberance on the head, that looks like an antenna, is still a matter of speculation.
16. de Visser, pp. 150, 151 (the author of *Kanden Jihitsu* is Ban, Kokei, 1733-1806 - omitted from source copy).
    A Shaku is about a foot in length.
17. de Visser, p. 64, 65.

The *yü-kia* (羽嘉) produced the flying dragon, the flying dragon gave birth to the phoenixes, and after them the *lwan-niao* (鸞鳥) and all birds, in general the winged beings, were born successively. The *mao-tuh* (毛犢 "hairy calf") produced the *ying-lung* (應龍)[18], the *ying-lung* gave birth to the *kien-ma* (建馬), and afterwards the *k'i-lin* (麒麟) and all quadrupeds, in general the hairy beings, were born successively. The *kiai-lin* (介鱗) produced the *kiao-lung* (蛟龍), the *kiao-lung* gave birth to the *kwun-keng* (鯤鯁), and afterwards the *kien-sié* (建邪) and all fishes, in general the scaly beings, were born successively. The *kiai-t'an* (介潭) produced the *sien-lung* (先龍), 'the *sien-lung* gave birth to the *yuen-yuen* (元黿 "original tortoise") and afterwards the *ling-kwei* (靈龜) "divine power manifesting tortoise") and all tortoises, in general the mailed beings were born successively".[19]

Furthermore, the ancient Chinese believed that various animals would eventually grow up/evolve to become dragons. The Koreans believed the same in that a creature called an *imugi*, or lesser dragon, that resembled a gigantic serpent, would eventually become a true dragon, or *yong*. Through the course of time, a small creature would become a larger and more majestic creature. From a practical sense, do not all animals (and plants) grow up from a small baby (or seedling) to a larger creature or organism? Consider that the Chinese call a lobster a "lóng xiá", which literally translated means "dragon shrimp" – lending some support to this concept. We know today that a shrimp will never become a clawed lobster. Though it looks quite similar, it is a different creature altogether. If modern scientific discovery had not revealed this to us, the practical misunderstanding of a shrimp being the offspring of a lobster is reasonable and understandable. Like Darwinian evolution theory, if given enough time, one thing will change into another. Therefore, the following makes sense in light of their limited understanding at the time.

The *Shuh i ki* says: "A water snake (*shui yuen*) after five hundred years changes into a *kiao*, a *kiao* after a thousand years changes into a *lung*, a *lung* after five hundred years changes into a *kioh-lung* (角龍 "horned dragon") and after a thousand years into a *ying-lung*".

Quite different, however, is, ... Liu Ngan's statement in his work entitled *Hwai nan tszĕ*, according to which the "flying dragons" are the offspring of the bird *yu-kia* ("the winged barbell"; this is the reason, says the commentary to this passage, why these dragons have wings); the *ying-lung* are the issue of a quadruped called *mao-tuh*; the *kiao-lung* are the issue of a fish called *kiai-lin*; the *sien-lung* are the issue of a mailed beast called *kiai-t'an*; and the *k'üh-lung* (屈龍) are produced by a sea plant called *hai-lü* (海閭). When the yellow dragon, born from yellow gold a thousand years old, enters a deep place, a yellow spring dashes forth, and if from this spring some particles arise, these become a yellow cloud. In the same way blue springs and blue clouds originate from blue dragons born from blue gold eight hundred

---

18. de Visser uses the Chinese character 應 ("yìng"), which means "should". The similar character 鷹 ("yíng"), which means "eagle", is more appropriate since the ying lung could fly. This is used in figure 4.
19. de Visser, p. 65.

years old; red, white and black dragons born from gold of the-same colours, a thousand years old.[20]

On the other hand, the ancient Chinese may have simply given names to particular growth stages of the dragon.

Divine Characteristics

Continuing with the observation that dragons lived long lifespans, Asian cultures, from India to Japan, considered dragons to be god-like creatures that had control over rain and water. In the philosophical work entitled *Kwan tszĕ*, it states that "a dragon in the water covers himself with five colours. Therefore he is a god (*shén*)... He whose transformations are not limited by days, and whose ascending and descending are not limited by time, is called a god (*shén*)."[21] Perhaps, like the Galapagos tortoises that can live to be hundreds of years old, dragons lived for hundreds of years too - thus giving the illusion of near immortality.

> The *Li ki* says: "What is called the four *ling* (靈)? The unicorn, the phoenix, the tortoise and the dragon, they are called the four *ling*... The effective operation of the *tsing* (精) or vital spirit of these four creatures is, indeed, enormously strong, and therefore they may be justly called "the four spiritual animals par excellence".[22]
> The Classics have taught us that the dragon belongs to the four creatures that have the most *ling*, i.e. whose *shen* manifests itself in the most powerful way. The *Rh ya yih* (爾雅翼) goes further and states that the dragon possesses the most *ling* of all creatures. According to the *Shui ying fu* (瑞應圖) "the yellow dragon is the quintessence of *shen*, and the chief of the four dragons. If a king does not drain off ponds and lakes, their water can penetrate into deep pools, and the yellow dragons, following their nature, swim in ponds and lakes".[23]

The philosopher Confucius (551 - 479 B.C.) even compared himself with horned dragons and considered them as being more noble than himself, giving credence to the idea that dragons were considered divine. Also, the importance of the comparison between dragons and fish should not be overlooked. His general comments on their living habits are based off of thoughtful observations; thus one can confidently conclude that Confucius was describing the two dragon types as real living animals. Furthermore, note that the wording is such that it assumes that the reader already knows what creature is being discussed. This would not make much sense (or lend to Confucius' fame) if Confucius, or Lü Puh-Wei for that matter, were

---
20. de Visser, p. 72.
21. de Visser, p. 63.
22. de Visser, p. 39,40. The unicorn may be the Elasmotherium and/or Rhinoceros. Both were prominent in Asia in the past. See *The Mythic Chinese Unicorn* by Jeannie Thomas Parker. www.chinese-unicorn.com
23. de Visser, p. 63, 64.

describing unrecognizable creatures.

> Lü Puh-Wei (呂不韋) relates the following: "Confucius said: 'A dragon (*lung*) eats what is pure and moves about in what is pure. A *chi* (螭)[24] eats what is pure and moves about in what is muddy. A fish eats what is muddy and moves about in what is muddy. Now I, in ascending do not reach the dragon (i.e. I am not such a high being as the dragon), and in descending do not reach the fishes (i.e. I am not such a low creature as the fishes); I am (like) the *chi*'".[25]

To press the point, Confucius also made a general comparison of three classes of animals to the dragon (His meeting with Lao-tzu / 老子 is described in the *Shih-chi*). His initial comment was from literal observations of animals; "I know how birds can fly, how fishes can swim, and how animals can run. But the runner may be snared, the swimmer may be hooked, and the flyer may be shot with the arrow. But there is the dragon. I cannot tell how he mounts on the wind through the clouds, and rises to heaven."[26] Confucius then transitioned his last sentence in a poetic comparison of the dragon to Lao-tzu. "Today I have seen Lao-tzu and can only compare him to the dragon." Thus a clear example of the majestic and mysterious dragon not only being literally compared with other animals but also is used in a figurative sense to express admiration.

Divination and Superstition

Occasionally mentioned in the Chinese Annals, the appearance of a yellow or azure colored dragon was considered to be a good omen, that is, unless they appeared in a "wrong place" or at an untimely moment. Then they were considered harbingers of misfortune and evil. These particular dragons seemed to be nocturnal since they were seen often at night. They are reported as spreading light all around them. It would seem that they had some bioluminescent qualities if this is the case. No wonder the Chinese considered these large 'glowing' creatures to be divine!

> Such a nightly apparition illuminated the palace of Kung Sun-shuh under the reign of the Emperor Kwang Wu (25–57 A.D.). The former considered it such a good omen, that in 25 A.D. he proclaimed himself Emperor of Shu (White Emperor) and changed the name of the era into Lung-Hing, "Dragon's rise". A black, horned dragon was seen one night by Lü Kwang, who lived in the fourth century A.D. Its glittering eyes illuminated the whole vicinity, so that the huge monster was visible till it was enveloped by clouds which gathered from all sides…
> Then one of Lü Kwang's attendants said to him: "A dragon is a divine animal and an omen of a man's rise to the position of a ruler. So you will attain

---
24. *chi* = a hornless dragon. See: L. P. Fung, *A Dual-Purpose Chinese Dictionary*, p. 596.
25. de Visser, p. 64.
26. *The Confucian Analects, the Great Learning & the Doctrine of the Mean*. Translated by James Legge. p. 65.

this rank". On hearing this, Lü Kwang was very much rejoiced; and actually he became a ruler after some time[27]. The dragons being such important omens, it is no wonder that Imperial proclamations often were issued on account of their appearance.[28]

Finaly [sic], we may quote a divinatory work[29] which says: "When the beginning rise of an Emperor or King is about to take place, a dragon appears in the Yellow River or in the Loh. All examine his head: if the head is black, men are correct; if white, the Earth is correct; if red, Heaven is correct".[30]

I-ching

Still in use today, the *I-Ching* (易經 "Book of Changes") is the most ancient written work of the Chinese where dragons are mentioned. For example, the bottom line of the first diagram[31] may be translated as: "A dragon hidden in the water is useless", or "Hidden dragon; do not act". In like manner, the second line reads, "A dragon out in the open; it is advantageous to see a great man". A final example would be the top line which reads, "An arrogant dragon; regret".

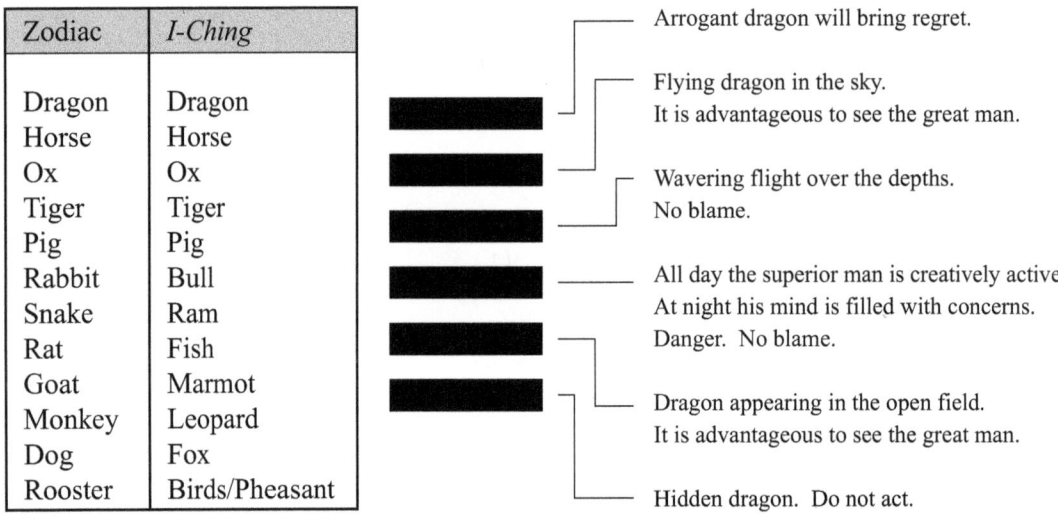

Figure 6: Comparative list (not in order) of animals used by the Chinese zodiac and the *I-Ching* (with first hexagram shown). Note that 5 animals are the same *including the dragon*. (Translation of hexagram from Richard Wilhelm and Cary F. Baynes).

A dominant view held by modern translators of the *I-Ching* is that the mythical dragon is a symbolic representation of a 'superior' man. Yet this is not the impression the oracle-book seems to present. The *I-Ching* diagrams first give an example, then the application. Dragons are not the only creatures used in this way; other animals (like

---
27. (*Pao P'oh-tszĕ*, written by Koh Hung, the fourth century; Ch. IV).
28. (The Emperor-Wen of the Han dynasty e.g. did so in B.C. 165, *Books of the Early Han Dynasty*, Ch. IV).
29. (The *Yih k'ien tsoh tu*).
30. de Visser, pp. 44, 45.
31. A diagram being made up of six lines, broken and/or unbroken. Also known as a "hexagram".

tigers and horses) are used as well (**Figure 6**). Thus one can conclude that if dragons were not mythical and were alive when the book was written, then the *I-Ching* is consistent in using dragon behavior along with other living animals as an example (or "oracle interpretation") for what an individual should be doing (to become a superior man). The ancient book simply used various animals that were common knowledge in order to convey a specific meaning. Similar to the Chinese zodiac, which also uses animals as examples of human behavior, it would be inconsistent to figure that all the animals were actual living creatures *except* the "mythical" dragon.

Dragon Bones and Medicine

In the third century, *Yü Pao* wrote about an inventor of wax-coated balls that contained a number of poisonous substances, which would expel demonic spirits from possessed persons by means of diarrhea. Of the list of ingredients, dragon bones are included; which could be attained from leading apothecaries, ground to a powder, and mixed with the other ingredients.[32] The term "dragon bones" was apparently referring to fossilized dinosaur bones, which in turn indicates that the Chinese associated fossil bones with living dragons. This assertion is supported by several ancient accounts.

Taking 27 years to complete, the *Pen-ts'ao kang-muh* (known in the West as "Chinese Medicinal Herbs") by Li Shi-chen (李時珍)(1518-1593), is considered to be an excellent source regarding dragon bones and how Chinese physicians utilized them. Referring to other authorities (one principal source being the lost book entitled *Shen Nung Pen Ts'ao King* (神農本草經), a "Classical work on Medicines of (the Emperor) Shen Nung"), Li Shi-chen mentioned that dragon bones consisted of the bones of living or dead dragons as well as their "cast-off skins". By comparing various accounts and sources, Li Shi-chen concluded and confirmed that though the dragon was considered a divine creature, it apparently died like other animals.[33]

Chinese apothecaries knew where dragon bones, teeth, and horns could be gathered and knew which types of bones were the best for medicine. Apparently, dragon bones were sometimes found fresh and were not fossilized! Various methods of medicinal preparation instruct that the bones must be soaked in hot water to soften them up before grinding to powder. This could not be done as easily using fossilized bone. Wu Pu (吳普), the author of *Wu Shi Pen-ts'ao* (吳氏本草), written in the first half of the third century, states the following;

> "At the present day all (the bones) come from Tsin land. The fresh and hard ones are not good; those bearing five colours are good. The blue, yellow, red, white and black ones also according to their colors correspond with the viscera, as the five *chi* (felicitous plants), the five crystals (*shih ying*) and the

---
32. J. J. M. De Groot, *The Religious System of China*, Vol. VI., Supplemented edition, 2007. p. 165.
33. de Visser, p. 90.

five kinds of mineral bole (*shih chi*)." The meaning of the last sentence is the following. The five colors (blue, white, red, black and yellow) correspond to the five viscera (liver, lungs, heart, kidneys and spleen) and to the so-called mansions (gall, small and great intestines, bladder and stomach), as we learn from the list given by De Groot, *Rel. Syst.* Vol. IV, p. 26. For this reason probably the use of the dragon bones as medicines was different according to their colours, with regard to the colour of the organ to be cured.[34]

It would also seem that fresh organs could also be gathered, according to the 6th century writing entitled *Shuh i ki'*; "According to tradition a dragon, when a thousand years old, casts off his bones in the mountains. Now there are dragon mounds, out of which dragon brains are taken". De Visser explains that "dragon's brains were believed to stop dysentery, and the liver of this divine animal, sometimes of a living one, was prescribed by some physicians in difficult cases. Sometimes a royal patient for this reason even ordered to kill the dragon of a pond, which used to hear the people's prayers for rain in times of drought and guarded the castle of the prince." Another instance described a Taoist doctor cutting a liver out of a living dragon to give to his patient, who recovered. Even dragon placentas and foetus were used in treating blood related diseases.[35]

The *Pen-ts'ao kang-muh* describes several specific observations made by the ancient apothecaries regarding the dragon. For instance, a dragon will definitely not eat the fruit of the Chinaberry tree, and as for the Balanophera plant, "[it] comes up in places where the wild horse and scaly dragon have dropped semen, which sinks into the ground and after a time springs up in a form like a bamboo shoot."[36]

In a number of medicines, animal skins and minerals were sometimes mixed with plants for a more powerful antidote. Some of the ingredients mentioned in the *Pen-ts'ao* sound like a strange concoction of items to mix with plants. Items like human skull bones and teeth, scaly ant eaters (pangolins), snake, rhinoceros, and elephant skins, are all in league with dragon bones. Two particular medicinal powders mentioned in Li Shih-chen's compilation are good examples in how the Chinese made these natural remedies using dragon bones.

> *Seven Candarin Powder*; Use dragon bone, borax, dragon's blood (a tree that has red sap), catechu, Cannabis indica, and Forsythia suspensa, of each equal parts; powder finely. The dose is seven candarins, and is used in the treatment of wounds as an anodyne. ...
> *Seven Precious Powder*; Use dragon bone, elephant's skin, dragon's blood, ginseng, Gynura pinnatifida, plibanum, myrrh, and laka wood, all powdered together. This is thought to promote healing in wounds, and is a military men's remedy.[37]

---
34. de Visser, pp. 91, 92.
35. de Visser, pp. 95, 96.
36. Li Shih-chen, *Chinese Medicinal Herbs*, Translated by F. P. Smith and G. A. Stuart, 1973. pp. 261, 61.
37. Li Shih-chen, *Chinese Medicinal Herbs*, pp. 352, 353.

Lips and Noses

In spite of their scaly bodies, some Asian dragons are shown with lips, large noses, ears, and other mammal-like features. These artistic representations of dragons do not fit our modern assumptions of a completely reptilian prehistoric creature. Therefore, some would say that dragons are mere depictions of man's imagination. Thus the assumption arises that since the idea of a dragon could have been artistically based loosely on fossil remains, they are not true representations of dinosaurs at all because we *know* that dinosaurs didn't have protruding ears and large noses! Needless to say, paleontologists are still playing a guessing game on what dinosaurs actually looked like when alive and if they were warm or cold blooded (the evidence weighing heavily towards warm-blooded). The job of a modern paleoartist is to reconstruct the prehistoric creature from fossil bones. In 2001, paleontologists reexamined several dinosaur skulls and found evidence for larger noses than previously thought, and lips as well. Thus artists had to go back to the drawing board.

The heads of a Diplodocus and a Brachiosaurus have typically been shown with the nostrils on top instead of the front end of the skull near the mouth (like almost all other dinosaurs). Due to the unusual position of the nasal cavities in the skulls, speculation has arisen as to whether these particular sauropods had trunks like an elephant. Several studies came to the conclusion that there was no anatomical evidence for a trunk. However, Ohio University paleontologist Lawrence Witmer indicated that though the nasal cavities were located high on the head, the actual, fleshy nostrils were located down near the snout. "The only reasonable explanation, said Witmer, is that dinosaurs had fine, long noses that extended in a fleshy tunnel from the nasal passageway near the top of the skull down to nostrils just above the mouth... This could be important to the animal because a long nose does important things."[38] Though speculation is ongoing as to some dinosaur noses, there does seem to be evidence that their noses are larger than traditionally shown by artists.

In Japan, paleoartists show dinosaurs with their mouths closed but in the West, artists show them with their mouths open, simply indicating that the dinosaur was either carnivorous or herbivorous. Could ancient artists be correct in portraying dragons with lips? Through the ages, Asian artists have consistently shown the dragon with lips and extended or bulbous noses. Reasonable speculation would conclude that if they saw living dragons they would not need to wonder what their facial features were like, as we must do today.

Another matter of artistic interpretation also regards the lips. Tyler Keillor, a paleoartist and fossil preparator at the University of Chicago, has begun showing theropod lips closed because he has found certain traits in animals that are similar to

---
38. CBS News.com, *Dino Nose Job Needed*, online article, 2009.

dinosaurs, suggesting that they did have lips.

If I can seal a dinosaur's mouth with lips like large lizards have, it allows dinosaurs to breathe in through the nose without losing air or getting dehydrated," he said. Keillor's argument, that therapods [*sic*] would have had difficulty staying hydrated with a "no lips" model because they were more terrestrial, is a valid concern.[39]

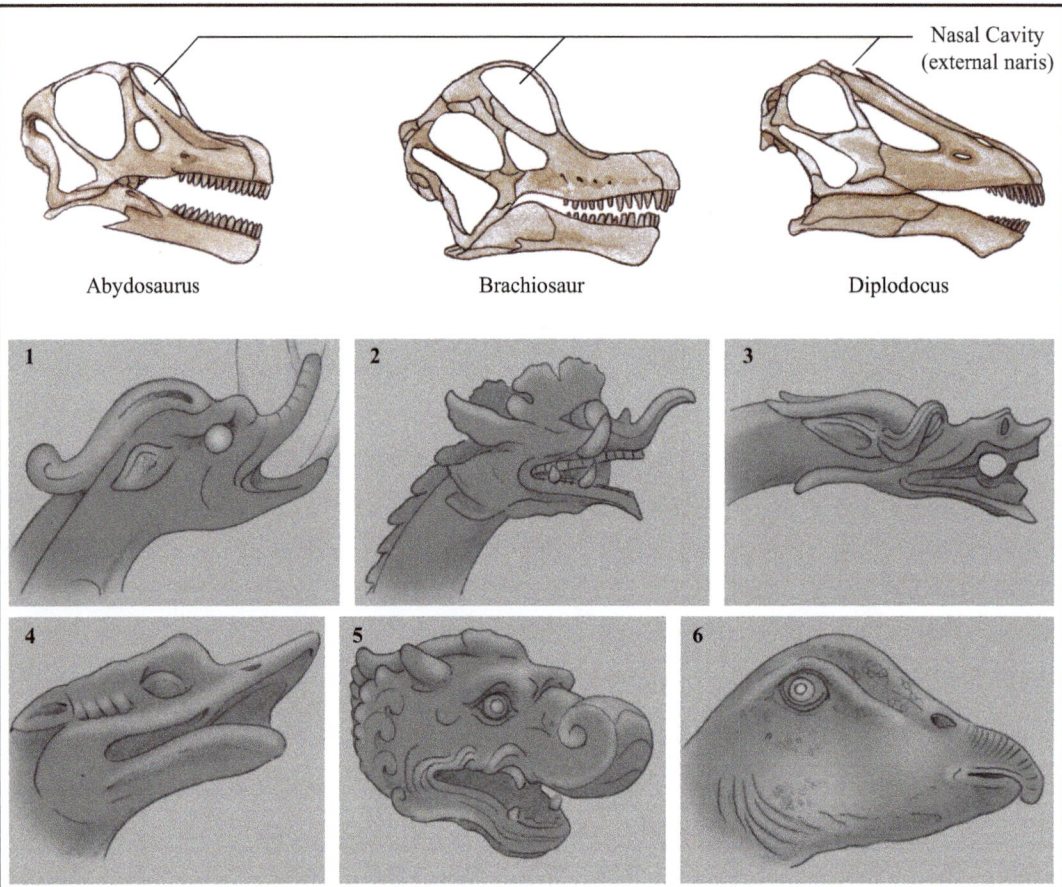

Illustrations are made from the following actual artifacts:
1: Antique porcelain, dragon handled vase, China
2: "Korean Banner Pole" of a dragon head, Unified Silla, 9th century AD, Gilt bronze, Daegu National Museum, Korea
3: Gilt bronze handle, Eastern Han Dynasty (25–220 AD). Source at the Metropolitan Museum of Art, New York.
4: Northern Wei Dynasty (386–534 AD), China
5: "Makara", Northern Qi Dynasty (550–577 AD), China
6: Martin and Neave's theoretical fleshy lipped diplodocus (modern sculpture)
Photo references used: 1,4,6; Chris Parker, *Tracking the Sauropod Dinosaur through the Art of Ancient Peoples, part 2*.
2; Unknown photographer. 3; Wikipedia. 5; Photographer - "Sailko" (Wikipedia)
Although specific Brachiosaurus and Diplodocus fossils have not been found in Asia, there are numerous sauropod types in Asia (i.e., Ultrasaurus), some belonging to the brachiosaur family (i.e., Abydosaurus mcintoshi - shown above), that have similar nasal features. The point here is that there *is* archeological evidence for fleshy lips and typical nasal placement (particularly for reptiles), which are coincidentally reflected in ancient dragon art throughout the world.

Figure 7: Atypical sauropod skulls compared with dragon sculptures depicting fleshy lips and nostril placement. Note the ears are all similar.

---

39. Hallie D. Martin, *Paleoartists See Bones and Make Dinosaurs*, online article, 2008.

Robert T. Bakker, Ph.D. (a paleontologist and advocate for warm-blooded dinosaurs) analyzed many dinosaur skulls and compared them with modern creatures. He found in some dinosaur skulls deep lip holes along the dentary and mandibular that indicate large muscular lips. Thus the possibility of an extended proboscis-like upper lip (like a rhino, giraffe, or even a Baird's tapir) as indicated in Asian art (**Figure 7**). "Lips require blood for nutrition and nerve fibers to carry sensory information to the brain... Through these holes passed the requisite blood vessels and nerve tracts. An identical pattern of holes can be found in the jawbones of living lizard species."[40] Bakker further indicates that some dinosaur skulls were different from others in this respect.

> But the Diplodocus's lips were definitely different from those of lizards – the gum lines along its jawbones were not bevelled, and the holes for blood vessels and nerves did not make an evenly spaced row like the one in lizards. Diplodocus's lips were different from those of crocs too... Diplodocus's jawbones were quite smooth compared to crocs.[41]

There is more to be said regarding noses and lips on dinosaurs (and the evidence for them being warm blooded), but that is beyond the scope of this book. The point here is that it would seem that modern science is beginning to uncover evidence supporting the ancient artistic descriptions of the dragon. The more details they discover in fossil remains, the gap between ancient descriptions and modern interpretation decreases.

A brief note on another feature in Asian dragon art that seems to elude credibility; the horns on the back of the head. Many assume that Asian dragon art is portraying only sauropod type dinosaurs, *if* they are portraying a literal creature to begin with! However, that may not be the case. There are a couple possibilities as to why horns are not found on the sauropod fossils yet shown on Asian dragon art: 1. The assumption does not include other dinosaurs that have horns and comparatively long necks. (There are many dinosaur species with long necks found in Asia that do have horns). 2. Asian dragon art may be a conglomeration of several dragon types to make one representative creature out of many. 3. Sauropods may indeed have horns, but that feature has not yet been discovered in the fossil record – like dorsal spines which have only been discovered in the late 20th century (this is perhaps the least likely). Despite these possibilities, there are written eyewitness accounts (expressed in several descriptions earlier in this chapter) describing certain dragon types as having horns on the head which coincide with artistic representations. As to which specific dinosaur(s) having such horns described remains to be seen.

---

40. Robert T. Bakker, *The Dinosaur Heresies*, p. 143.
41. Bakker, pp. 143, 144.

Territorial Fights, Wells, and Omens

The following accounts not only describe dragons fighting, but also reveal how people revered dragons, being superstitious of how the impressive creatures were somehow influential over the weather or political events.

The *Tso chuen* (左傳) tells of a large flood that was attributed to some dragons that were fighting in a pool. This happened during the 19th year of the reign of the duke of Chao (523 B.C.). "There were great floods in Ch'ing; and [some] dragons fought in the pool of Wei, outside the She gate. The people asked leave to sacrifice to them; but Tsze-ch'an refused it, saying, "If we are fighting, the dragons do not look at us; when dragons are fighting, why should we look at them? We may offer a deprecatory sacrifice, but that is their abode. If we do not seek anything of the dragons, they will not seek anything from us." On this, [the people] desisted [from their request]."[42]

..."In the sixth month of the fifth year of the P'u t'ung era (524 A.D.) dragons fought in the pond of the King of K'üh o (?). They went westward as far as Kien ling ch'ing. In the places they passed all the trees were broken. The divination was the same as in the second year of the T'ien kien era (503 A.D.)[43], namely that their passing Kien ling and the trees being broken indicated that there would be calamity of war for the dynasty, and that it was a sign that the Imperial tombs would be destroyed. At that time the Emperor considered the holding of discussions to be his only task, and did not think of ploughing. His fighting generals were careless, his soldiers idle, and the Tao of the Ruler was injured. Therefore there was the corresponding fact of the dragons' evil. The Emperor did not at all become conscious (of the danger). In the first year of the T'ai Ts'ing era (547 A.D.) there was again a dragon fight in the waters of Li cheu. The waves seethed and bubbled up, and clouds and fog assembled from all sides. White dragons were seen running to the South, followed by black dragons. That year Heu King came with troops to submit, and the Emperor accepted his submission without taking precautions. The people of the realm were all frightened, and suddenly rebellion arose. The Emperor in consequence thereof had a sad death". He died in 549, and eight years later the Liang dynasty came to an end.

In A.D. 579 a black dragon was killed by a red one. Moreover, in the same year there was a fight of a white dragon with a black one, the result of which was that the white one ascended to the sky and the black one fell on the earth and died. As black was the colour of the Later (i.e. Northern) Cheu dynasty, these dragon fights were forebodings of its approaching fall, which actually took place two years later.

As to inundations announced beforehand by dragon fights, we may refer to the *History of the Sung dynasty* where we read that in the fifth year of the K'ien Tao era (A.D. 1169) such a battle in the air was seen amidst a heavy thunderstorm. "Two dragons fled and pearls like carriage wheels fell down

---

42. James Legge, *The Chinese Classics, Vol V, Part II*, (book X, year XIX), Chinese: p. 674; English translation: p. 675.
43. T'ien-chien (天監), of the Liang Dynasty. (502 - 557 AD.).

on the ground, where they were found by herdsboys. In the following years inundations afflicted the country". ...

When dragons, wounded in a battle, tumbled down and died, this was believed to be a very bad omen. The *Books of the Han dynasty* relate the following: "On the day jen-tszĕ of the sixth month of the seventh year of the Yen-hi era (A.D. 164), under the Emperor Hwan, there was a dragon which died on Mount Yé Wang in Ho néi (one of the districts of that time). Its length was about some tens of chang. Siang K'iai was of the following opinion: 'Taking into consideration that the dragon is a felicitous symbol of an Emperor or King, and that the *Yih lun ta jen* says: "In the T'ien-feng era (A.D. 14—19) there was a dead dragon in the Hwang-shan palace. The Han troops killed Mang (i.e. the Emperor Wang Mang, killed in A.D. 22), and Shi Tsu (i.e. Kwang Wu, the first Emperor of the Eastern Han dynasty) rose again (ascended the throne, in A.D. 25)", this omen must be a sign of change (of the dynasty)'. In the 25th year of the Kien-ngan era (A.D. 220) the Emperor Wen of the Wéi dynasty replaced the House of Han".

In the fifth year of the Kien-teh era (A.D. 576), under the Later Cheu dynasty, a black dragon fell from the sky and died. The dragon is the symbol of the Ruler, black was the colour of the dynasty, and falling and dying is a most unlucky omen'. So it was a foreboding of the Emperor's death, which happened two years later (A.D. 578), and of the dynasty's fall (A.D. 581), which was announced also by the dragon fights mentioned above.[44]

In De Visser's work *The Dragon in China and Japan*, we are reminded that in China dragons were symbols of imperial power. He indicates that if a dragon was born in the house of a common family, or emerged from their well, that was considered a very bad omen, particularly for the Emperor personally, or one of his feudal lords. The event meant that those in authority would be degraded from their state of power to a common level. It could also mean the death of the ruler or one of his representatives.

For instance, "*The Books of the Tsin Dynasty* contain the following passage: "Under the reign of Sun Hao of the Wu dynasty (the fourth and last Emperor of that dynasty, A.D. 242—283), in the T'ien-ts'eh era (A.D. 275—276), a dragon was hatched in (the house of) a family in Ch'ang-sha, and ate the chickens. King Fang says in his *Yih yao*: 'If a dragon is hatched in a man's house, a king will become a commoner'. Afterwards Hao submitted to Chin (the Chin dynasty)."[45] In addition, *The Books of the Tsin Dynasty give* the following account from the same section.

"Under the Emperor Ming of the Wei dynasty (A.D. 227—239), in the first year of the Ts'ing-lung era (233), on the day kiah-shen of the first month, a blue dragon appeared in a well at Mo-p'o (a place) in the suburbs. If only a lucky omen rises at a wrong time, it becomes an evil. How much more is this the case, when it (the dragon) is in straits in a well! This is not a felicitous

---
44. de Visser, pp. 47 - 50 (selections).
45. de Visser, pp. 54, 55.

omen! It was wrong that Wei on account of it changed the name of the era. Yu Pao says: 'From the end of the reign of the Emperor Ming under the Wei dynasty the appearances of blue and yellow dragons were signs corresponding with the fall and rise of its rulers. As to the fate of the land of Wei, blue is the colour of wood and yet it does not conquer metal; it was a sign of yellow getting the throne and blue losing it. The frequent appearance of blue dragons means that the virtue of the sovereign and the fate of the dynasty are in inner conflict with each other. Therefore Kao Kwei Hiang Kung (Ts'ao Mao, A.D. 241—260, who in 254 became the fourth Emperor of the Wei dynasty) was utterly defeated in war.'"

"According to Liu Hiang's explanation the dragon, the symbol of dignity, when being imprisoned in a well means calamity consisting in a feudal lord being about to be secretly seized. In the Wei dynasty there was no dragon which was not in a well. It was an omen of the oppressive measures of those men who occupied the highest ranks. The poem on the 'Dragon lying in the deep', written by Kao Kwei Hiang Kung, has this meaning".[46]

Hibernation of the Water Gods in China and Japan

As mentioned earlier, some dragons were considered gods of the water animals, since they lived in and were associated with large bodies of water, or the god of rain, since they came out of hibernation at the beginning of the rainy season.

> Even when the dragons were only leaping in their pools, no calamity was to be feared… Winter, when they hibernate and sleep in pools, is the dry season in China. But in spring, in the third of the twenty four seasons into which the year was divided even in olden times, the "Resurrection of the hibernating animals" takes place, and it begins to rain a little. In the "beginning of summer", however, i.e. in the first of the six summer seasons, "the winds arrive and the dragons ascend to the sky" for this is the time when the abundant rains come down, a blessing to mankind.[47]

In the ancient Chinese work entitled *Cheu li* (周禮), it describes the use of official metal tablets of the envoys of the Empire. Tablets that had tigers engraved or painted on them were used as a form of passport and symbols of authority in mountainous regions. Tablets with human figures on them were used in plain (flat land) regions, while tablets with dragons on them were used in regions with lots of water (rivers, lakes, and ponds). Ching K'ang-ch'ing commented on why the metal tablets were divided in such a manner. "In the mountains are many tigers. In the plains are many men, and in the waters are many dragons." This is why the Chinese believe the dragon symbolized water.

Furthermore, the *Cheu li* explains that in painting and embroidery "water is represented by means of dragons." Cha'o P'uh (趙溥) commented that "the dragon is a

---
46. ibid.
47. de Visser, pp. 38, 39.

divine being in the water. If one represents water without representing dragons, there is nothing to show the divinity of its phenomena." Ching K'ang-ch'ing added, "The dragon is a water creature; it is (depicted or embroidered) on clothes."[48]

"Li Tao-yuen (麗道元), in his commentary on the *Shui king*, states that the expression 'fishes and dragons consider the autumn days as night' means that "at the autumnal equinoctium the dragons descend and then hibernate and sleep in pools."[49]

Dragons were also associated with water in Japan, both in historical accounts as well as myths and legends. The *Fusō ryakki* (扶桑略記 "Concise Chronicles of Japan") gives an account of the history of Shitenno-ji (四天王寺), the Buddhist monastery built by Shotoku Taishi at Namba (Osaka). A deep pond near one of the monastery buildings was the dwelling place of a blue dragon.[50] Another account of a Japanese dragon is the following:

> Among the eighty five Shintō shrines to which messengers were despatched by the Court to pray for rain, the *Engishiki* (延喜式) mentions several river and water-deities, e.g. the gods of Kibune and Nibu no kawakami but also the Wind-gods of Tatsuta, the Thunder-god of Kamo and many others. The *Nihongi* repeatedly uses the same words in regard to these prayers, namely: "The Emperor sent *daibu* (大夫 officials of a high rank) as envoys to the different Shintō temples in order to pray for rain; he also despatched messengers to pray to the god Ō-imi of Hirose and to the Wind-gods of Tatsuta, (龍田 'Dragonfield')". … They identified these *tatsu* with the *lung*, and… wrote the name of their "water-fathers", *mizuchi*, with the character 虬, k'iu (the horned dragon), while the word *okami* was written by means of a character, partly consisting of rain and dragon.
>
> Their dragons were *kami*, gods, who lived in rivers and seas, valleys and mountains (in rivulets, lakes and ponds), bestowing rain on their worshippers… So the three kinds of dragons, to be found in Japan, original Japanese, Chinese and Indian, all have one feature in common, i.e. the faculty of causing rain; while the winds belong to the dominion of the former two.[51]

A different type of hibernation that may seem incredible when read at first can also be explained by natural means. In Africa, the amazing lungfish buries itself in the drying mud during a drought. It can last up to four years without water by surrounding itself with mucous. Upon the next rain however, the lungfish 'rehydrates' and "comes back to life". Those who build their houses with bricks made of the same mud where the lungfish have hidden themselves are surprised to find the creatures coming out of their walls during a storm![52]

In like manner, the *Fei süeh luh* (霏雪錄 approximately 12th century) describes the following account. "… a little snake, which crept out of a small crack of the

---
48. de Visser, p. 41.
49. de Visser, p. 66.
50. Fusō ryakki, Ch. III, p. 495 (Cited by de Visser, p. 181).
51. de Visser, pp. 153, 154.
52. See: Animal Planet video *Fooled by Nature: Lungfish*.

unplastered wall of a house, became bigger and bigger, changed into a dragon and flew away amidst storm and rain."[53] Perhaps this particular flying dragon had a similar ability to hibernate like the lungfish and appeared to grow in size due to being rehydrated. Even if hibernation was not involved, the tale is not far-fetched in light of contemporary animal capabilities, and lend to the dragon's magical mystique. (For example, consider the Australian Thorny Devil lizard that "drinks" water from its skin and swells in size by doing so).

Domestication

According to ancient documents, the Chinese were able to domesticate (with a degree of success) some dragons! Chinese historians gave a number of accounts where dragons were kept and raised for various purposes. The philosopher Han Fei[54] wrote about his familiarization with dragons and stated, "Ah, a dragon, as being an animal, is so mild, that one may approach him (be familiar with him, i.e. tame him) and ride on him. But under his throat he has scales, lying in a reverse direction, one *ch'ih* (foot) in diameter. If a man touches them, the dragon is sure to kill him".[55] Notice the specific descriptive details of the physical creature and consequent behavioral warning! Anyone during Han Fei's time could have written the contrary if this description were not true. Han Fei's reputation was on the line in other words, and was written in a matter-of-fact manner.

Another description that matches Han Fei's is found in the *Pen-ts'ao kang-muh*.[56] It describes a dragon as having whiskers at the sides of its mouth, a bright "pearl" under his chin and has scales lying in a reverse direction under the dragon's throat. The detail of the scales lying in reverse direction is unusual for an animal. It is worthy to note here that no contrary accounts have been found to counter these two consistent descriptions.

Wang Ki, a popular physician of the 16th century who wrote the *Pen-ts'ao hui-pien* (本草會編), says "From the saliva spit out by dragons perfume is made." Li Shi-chen (author of the *Pen-ts'ao kang-muh)* confirmed this by saying, "Dragon's saliva is seldom used as a medicine; it is only mixed into perfumes. It is said that it can bind camphor and musk for several tens of years without evaporating. Further, it is said that, when it is burned, a blue smoke floats through the air."[57]

> According to the *Lang hüen ki* the Emperor Shun used the saliva of a purple dragon as ink in writing the names of holy ministers on tablets of jade, those of sages, on tablets of gold and those of talentful ministers on tablets

---
53. de Visser, p. 113.
54. Han Fei Tszĕ, 韓非子 (4th century B.C).
55. de Visser, p. 63, 64.
56. de Visser, p. 71.
57. de Visser, p. 96, 97.

of quartz-crystal; those of ordinary ministers were written with ordinary ink on tablets of wood. In order to obtain the saliva he ordered Yu Hu to rear a purple dragon. The latter daily made the animal drop saliva by holding a swallow, which he had cooked (the favourite food of the dragons...) before it without immediately giving it to eat. This made the dragon's mouth water, and a large quantity of saliva dripped down. Then Yu Hu filled a vessel with it, whereupon he gave the swallow to the dragon. In this way he daily got one *koh* (a gill) of saliva, which was mixed with *hwui shih* (the "Herb of the Sien") In the time of Yao this herb grew before the audience hall. It wore flowers in all four seasons. If one rubbed its fruit and mixed it with a purple dragon's saliva, a liquid of a genuine red colour was produced, which penetrated into gold and jade and thus could be used in writing names on the tablets mentioned above.[58]

Before doubt is ascribed to this tale, consider that Marco Polo confirms that various tablets of gold and silver were used in East Asia by government officials for proving their authority.[59] Furthermore, a depiction from the *Nan-Pu-Sin-Shu* indicates that a dragon's disposition is ferocious, and the *King-Ts'ing* (a type of dragon) loves to eat cooked sparrows.[60] Furthermore, the *Pen-ts'ao kang-muh states,* "The dragon's nature is rough and fierce, and yet he likes beautiful gems and *k'ung-ts'ing*, and is found [*sic*, fond] of (roasted) swallows...Those who have eaten swallows avoid [crossing] the water, and those who pray for rain use swallows.[61] Thus, the use of tablets and the fact that a particular type of dragon liked to eat birds is confirmed by separate reports.

The Li Ki states that the dragon is considered to be a domestic animal, so much so that "fishes and sturgeons do not flee away."[62] It is also documented that in ancient times during the feast of the fifth moon, Chinese dumplings, called *zòng*, made from glutenous rice and filled with meat, were thrown into appropriate rivers to feed scaly dragons.[63] Thus particular types of dragon were not only brought under human control but were also considered peaceful animals that could be admired in the wild, like fish in a pond. The dragon described here may be a type of *lung*, but most likely was not the *ai-hwa*, which (as previously mentioned), likes to kill, indicating that it was most likely too dangerous or precarious to domesticate. The point is that though the Chinese accounts make general statements that the dragon is a domesticated animal, that does not mean that they are necessarily referring to *all* types of dragons since some are considered dangerous and some peaceful.

Another account of dragon domestication, told by Szĕ-ma Ts'ien in the *Historical Records*, is about the Chinese emperor K'ung Kiah who had two dragons (a male and female). Though the dragons were held captive by him, the emperor did not

---

58. de Visser, p. 97, 98. *Lang hüen ki* (瑯嬛記)
59. Rhys, *The Travels of Marco Polo the Venetian*, p. 161, 162.
60. Charles Gould, *Mythical Monsters*, p. 403 (appendix).
61. de Visser, p. 68, 69.
62. de Visser, p. 39.
63. Li Shih-chen, *Chinese Medicinal Herbs*, pp. 469 [Pinyin Mandarin - *zòng*; Cantonese - *júng*].

know how to feed or care for them and therefore searched for one who could raise the dragons correctly. A man by the name Liu Léi was found who was from the Dragon-rearer family. He knew how to tame dragons and therefore entered into the service of K'ung Kiah, who bestowed upon Liu Léi the family name of Yü-lung (Dragon-ruler). Eventually, the female dragon died and Liu Léi craftily fed the dragon meat to the emperor without telling him the situation. Shortly thereafter, the emperor found out that the female dragon was missing and ordered a search for it. Fearing for his life, Liu Léi fled. The emperor, K'ung Kiah died afterwards and his son ascended the throne. An almost identical account of the same story is found in chapter four of the *Tso chw'en*.[64]

Chariots of the Gods and Dragon Horses

It is noted that the emperor Shun instituted the Dragon-rearer family.[65] It was their duty to raise dragons for the emperor; one purpose was for pulling chariots. "Among the ancients there were the Dragon-rearer and the Dragon-ruler families, who ruled the dragons only by means of their knowledge of what they desired and disliked."[66] Sun Ch'oh Tszĕ says, "Kao Tsu (probably the Emperor of the Han dynasty, who reigned B.C. 206—159) drove in a dragon carriage, Kwang Wu (who reigned A.D. 685—717) drove in a tiger carriage".[67] "Yü, the celebrated founder of the Hia dynasty, drove in a carriage drawn by two dragons, which had descended in his court-yard..."[68] (Note that none of these are references from Marco Polo's account. This is being pointed out here because many have continued the unsupported claim that he is the one who indicated that the Chinese emperor's chariot was pulled by dragons, yet this is never mentioned in Marco Polo's records. *See appendix D*)

> The *Tso chw'en*: "In autumn (of the 29th year of Chao kung, i.e. Chao, duke of Lu, who reigned B.C. 541—509) a dragon appeared in the suburbs of Kiang. Wéi Hien tszĕ asked Ts'ai Mih saying: "I have heard that none of the animals is the dragon's equal in knowledge, and that for this reason the dragon cannot be caught alive. Can we believe that it is right to ascribe this (his not being caught alive) to his knowledge?" Mih replied: "Men really do not know; it is not that the dragon is really knowing. The ancients kept dragons; therefore the State had a Dragon-rearer family (豢龍氏 *Hwan-lung shi*) and a Dragon-ruler family (*Yü-lung shi*)". Hien tszĕ said: "I too have heard about those two families, but I do not know their origin; what is it said to be?" The answer was: "In olden times there was Shuh Ngan of Liu, who had a distant descendant called Tung Fu, very fond of dragons and able to find out their tastes and likings, so as to supply them with drink and meat. Many dragons

---
64. de Visser, p. 50, 51. Emperor K'ung Kiah was from the Hia dynasty, approximately 2000 B.C.
65. de Visser, p. 123.
66. de Visser, p. 68.
67. de Visser, p. 67.
68. de Visser, p. 123. See: *Poh wuh chi*, Ch. II, p. 2a.

sought refuge with him and he reared the dragons according to their nature in order to serve the Emperor Shun, who gave him the surname of Tung, and the family name of *Hwan-lung* (Dragon-rearer). He was [also] invested with [the principality of] Tsung-chw'en, and the family of Tsung I is of his posterity. Thus in the time of the Emperor Shun, and for generations after, dragons were reared.[69]

A different type of dragon that had characteristics of a horse was mentioned by a commentator on the *Yih king (I-Ching)*, who explained where such a creature (as well as a large tortoise) was found and what it looked like. "The water of the Ho sent forth a dragon horse; on its back there was curly hair, like a *map of starry dots*. The water of the Lo sent forth a divine tortoise; on its back there were riven veins, *like writing of character pictures*".[70] The *T'ung kien ts'ien pien wai ki* confirms this by saying, "At the time of T'ai Hao (i.e. Fuh-Hi) there was a lucky omen consisting of a dragon horse which carried a map on its back and came out of the Ho river. Therefore in giving titles to the officials he began to arrange them by means of the dragon, and called them 'Dragon-officers'." The *Annals of the Three sovereigns* further explains these titles: "He (Fuh-Hi) had the lucky omen of a dragon; by means of the dragon he arranged the officials and called them 'Dragon-officers'.[71] Also a passage in the *Shih i ki* describes how the Emperor Muh (Cheu dynasty, in the thirty second year of his reign) drove around to various places in a carriage pulled by eight dragon horses.[72] These descriptions do not have the appearance of myths since they are tied to actual rulers and dates. They could have been debunked by contemporary scholars, but none have been found to counter their claims.

Another description was given in the *Shui ying t'u* (瑞應圖). "It is a benevolent horse, the vital spirit of river water. Its height is eight ch'ih five ts'un[73]; its neck is long, and its body is covered with scales. It has wings at its shanks, and its hair hangs down its sides. Its cry consists of nine tones, and it walks on the water without sinking. It appears at the time of famous sovereigns". K'ung Ngan-kwoh, in his commentary on the *Shu king* gives a similar description, "A dragon horse is the vital spirit of Heaven and Earth. As a being its shape consists of a horse's body, yet it has dragon scales. Therefore it is called 'dragon horse'. Its height is eight ch'ih five ts'un (~6.5 feet). A true dragon horse has wings at its sides and walks upon the water without sinking..."[74]

As late as 741 A.D., a dragon horse was seen and was considered to be a good omen for the Emperor at the time. The *T'ai-p'ing yü-lan* (太平御覽) described it as being covered in scales with blue and red spots. The dragon horse had a hairy mane

---

69. de Visser, p. 82.
70. Taoist tradition claims these accounts are how the concepts of the I Ching were derived. Emphasis in italics mine.
71. de Visser, p. 57, 58. (通鑑前編外紀 "T'ung kien ts'ien pien wai ki")
72. de Visser, p. 59.
73. Measurements of ch'ih varied slightly with each dynasty. One ch'ih is approximately 22.5 to 23 cm. One ts'un is approximately 3.7 cm. See: *Man and land in Chinese history: an economic analysis*, by Gang Zhao, p. 65, 66.
74. de Visser, p. 58.

that resembled those of a dragon and its neighing was like a flute. Apparently it had a territorial range of about 300 miles. About a hundred years earlier, in 622 A.D., a dragon horse also appeared. It was described in a similar manner as having a dragon-like body that was covered in scales, spotted with five colors, and a horse-like head that sported two white horns. This particular dragon horse carried an object about three or four ch'ih long in its mouth. It was seen on a river, travelling about a hundred steps on the surface of the water. After looking around, it quickly left never to be seen again. "The *Shui ying t'u* added that the dragon horse was the vital spirit of the river. The dragon horse is also described in *Yuen kien lei han* (淵鑑類函), written in 1710 by Chang Ying: "A horse with dragon scales, the tail of a huge serpent, frizzy hair, round eyes and a fleshy crest".[75] The description of the fleshy crest and long serpent-like tail are intriguing details that make one wonder if the author had seen the actual creature, or heard consistent reports as to what it looked like. Considering that there are several crested dinosaur fossil types found in East Asia, perhaps these descriptions are referring to them, or maybe a type of plesiosaur, where the flippers were identified as wings?

Just because the Chinese called this creature a dragon horse does not mean that it was simply a very large horse. Nor should the dragon horse be confused from actual horses that were considered magnificent and powerful. This should be obvious from the consistent descriptions of it having scales. According to the *Yih king*, the dragon is considered to be "a heavenly kind of being, the horse an earthly one".[76] In addition to the differentiations made between dragons and horses, consistent descriptions of this particular animal show that the dragon horse was indeed a dragon that had horse-like resemblances and was revered as a spiritual water creature. Culturally speaking, this naming convention is not unique to Asia. Europeans, for example, technically call the hippopotamus a "river horse" (*Hippos* (Greek) a horse; *potamos* (Greek) a river).

Some propose that the dragon horse was simply a clever depiction of a star constellation or cloud formation that foretold omens. This does not appear to be the case due to the following accounts differentiating the dragon horse from such an idea. For one example, the Japanese work *Nihon Sandai jitsuroku* (日本三代実録)[77] compared a cloud vapor that hung under the sun on a specific day (the 27th day of the 7th month of 883 A.D.) with a dragon-horse. It also stated that in 885 A.D. the "dragon-star" appeared twice in the night sky, which consequently was the reason why the name of the era was changed.[78] This dragon star must not be confused with a dragon horse, since stars do not have scales and swim about in the river.

To drive home the fact that the dragon horse was not a mere mythological representation of an omen, consider the following account which placed a limitation

---

75. de Visser, p. 59.
76. de Visser, p. 66.
77. Written in 901 A.D.
78. de Visser, p. 148.

on the creature in reference to a historical flood event in Japan. The Japanese historical epic, *Masu kagami* (増鏡), indicated that in 1221 A.D., when Hojo Yoshitoki marched from Kamakura to Kyoto against the Emperor Juntoku, the rivers Fujigawa and Tenryugawa were flooded by rains to such an extent, that "even a dragon horse would not be able to cross them".[79] This raises the question as to why would one make that kind of statement if he were merely referring to a star or cloudy portent? It doesn't make sense since stars would be able to figuratively "cross" a flooded river. Therefore one can reasonably conclude that the dragon horse was a real documented creature.

To wrap up this section, the following is another matter-of-fact historical account that demonstrates that the dragon horse was described and discussed as though it were a real creature. As mentioned, dragons were believed to be some sort of divine creature by the ancient people of East Asia. This can be seen in the superstitious manner in which the dragon horse is said to be a "metamorphosis of the Fang constellation"; meaning that it is not the actual constellation but believed to be a *physical representative* of it.

> An interesting passage with regard to the dragon horse is found in the *Taiheiki* (太平記), where such an excellent horse is said to have been presented by Enya Takasada to the Emperor Godaigo (1318—1339). His Majesty praised it highly, and said that it was certainly a "Heavenly horse". At his question whether the fact that such a horse had appeared during his reign, was a good or a bad omen, the answer of the courtiers was, that it was an extremely lucky sign, due to His Majesty's own virtues. As phoenixes appeared at the Chinese Emperor Shun's time (supposed to have reigned B.C. 2255—2205), and a *kilin* in the age of Confucius, so this heavenly horse was an excellent omen for the period, foreboding at the same time the Emperor's long reign and life... They further related how at the time of a Chinese Emperor, Muh Wang of the Cheu dynasty, eight heavenly horses had appeared, all having different names, and how the Emperor, drawn by them all, had visited every place of the world. So all those present congratulated Godaigo with his horse, except Fujiwara no Fujifusa. When his opinion was asked, he declared to be convinced that it was not a good omen, and he too referred to Chinese examples to confirm his statement. The houses of two Emperors of the Han dynasty, Wen and Kwang Wu, who had refused such presents, had had a long and lucky reign, he said, while that of Muh, who had used the eight heavenly horses, had soon declined. Those horses were only a metamorphosis of the Fang constellation (the eleventh of the zodiacal constellations), and an omen of the fall of the Cheu dynasty. Godaigo, on hearing these words, was angry and put a stop to the festivities of the day. Not believing Fujifusa's pessimistic prediction he accepted the horse, and a few years later (1336) the great schism of the Southern and Northern Courts seemed to prove the truth, of Fujifusa's words.
>
> The same work relates how the Emperor Godaigo gave the aforesaid dragon-horse to Nitta Toshisada, when he despatched him to Owari province (1335). It was expected to cover the distance, which would have required four

---

79. de Visser, p. 148. The *Masu Kagami* was written in 1340—1350; Ch. II, K.T.K. Vol. XVII, p. 1012.

or five days with an ordinary horse, in half a day, so that he could be back in Kyoto that very evening. In a few hours he arrived in Omi province, but there the animal suddenly died, which was, of course, a very evil foreboding.[80]

The popular adage, "Lung ma jihng shén" (龍馬精神 the spirit or energy of a horse and/or dragon; i.e. great vitality) may not be referring to two separate animals as might be thought of today, but may be referring to the actual dragon horse described in antiquity.

Fire!

In many cultures, dragons are described as being able to "breathe" fire. East Asia is no different. The following descriptions are particularly interesting since they specifically describe a dragon's fire as behaving more like a chemical fire instead of a typical wood-burning fire. A chemical fire makes more sense naturally when it comes to an animal's ability to create it. Consider the bombardier beetle, which can instantaneously mix a few chemicals together to create an explosive charge that can be fatal to other insects. In like manner, but to a larger degree, perhaps a dragon's jaw had separate sacs filled with appropriate chemicals that when combined, would cause a fire to break out on the intended (and unfortunate) target.

> The *Rh ya yih* quotes the following passage from a work of Wang Fu; When rain is to be expected, the dragons scream and their voices are like the sound made by striking copper basins. Their saliva can produce all kinds of perfume ...
> Dragon fire and human fire are opposite. If dragon fire comes into contact with wetness it flames, and if it meets water it burns. If one drives it away by means of fire, it stops burning and its flames are extinguished".
> The *P'i ya* states the same fact with regard to the dragon fire ...[81]

Eagle Vision

Apparently, dragons could see very well. The Chinese were one of the few, along with the Greeks, to indicate this specific characteristic. Other accounts only describe a dragon's eyes as being large or glaring.

> ... according to popular belief the dragon's vital spirit lies in his eyes, for this is the case because he is deaf. The "Discussions on the spontaneous phenomena of Yin and Yang" say: 'The *li-lung's* pupils see a mustard plant or a straw at a distance of a hundred miles'.[82]

Though other Chinese accounts concur that some dragons were deaf, it is

---
80. de Visser, pp. 148, 149.
81. de Visser, pp. 66, 67. Note: *saliva can produce perfume* is confirmed in other accounts. (See *Domestication* section).
82. de Visser, pp. 67.

interesting that they concluded that these particular dragons were deaf due to their excellent vision and not by other natural means.

Babylonian Dragons

The eighth gate to the city of ancient Babylon was devoted to the goddess Ishtar and was constructed in approximately 575 B.C. under King Nebuchadnezzar II. This inner gate, made of blue lapis lazuli, had two types of creatures in bas relief carved on it, an auroch[83] and a dragon ("*mušḫuššu*"). Like the Chinese zodiac, this is another example of a dragon being presented along with a known (albeit now extinct) animal. An interesting detail of the long-necked dragon is that it has horns on the head and is shown with a forked tongue; similar in description to the Chinese water dragon *kiu lung*. Another interesting similarity to the Chinese *kiu* is that the city of Babylon was situated on both sides of the Euphrates river (the river ran through it). Perhaps the dragon shown on the gate lived in the Euphrates? The dragon image is claimed to be a mythological animal due to it having eagle-like hind legs and the forelegs of a lion. Though the dragon portrayed on the gate *may be* a potential myth, do not some dinosaurs have these very features—having bird-like hind feet with clawed forearms? To reiterate a previous point, paleontologists can only make educated guesses as to what nearly all dinosaurs actually looked like in the flesh. Also, would not the beastly auroch be considered mythical if it were not confirmed by other sources?

Perhaps confirmation can be found for the Babylonian dragon in the extended (apocryphal) book of Daniel. In this additional chapter, a dragon is described as being worshipped as a god by the Babylonians. Daniel wisely dispatched the dragon by utilizing ingredients he knew would cause intestinal failure/blockage. This tale took place in approximately 550 B.C., shortly *after* the Ishtar gate was constructed.

> There was also a great dragon, which the Babylonians revered. And the king said to Daniel, "You cannot deny that this is a living god; so worship him." Daniel said, "I will worship the Lord my God, for he is the living God. But if you, O king, will give me permission, I will slay the dragon without sword or club." The king said, "I give you permission." Then Daniel took pitch, fat, and hair, and boiled them together and made cakes, which he fed to the dragon. The dragon ate them, and burst open. And Daniel said, "See what you have been worshiping!"[84]

The Druk, Makara, and Näga

Similar to China, the people of Bhutan use the dragon as a national symbol,

---
83. Aurochs are presented in prehistoric cave paintings and were described by Julius Caesar for their brute strength and "elephantine" size. These bull-like creatures became extinct approximately 400 years ago.
84. Apocrypha, *Bel and the Dragon*, 1:23–27.

called in the Dzongkha language a *druk* (འབྲུག "thunder dragon"), . The country itself is referred to as the "Land of the Druk", and the leaders are called dragon kings (*druk gyalpo*). The *druk* is depicted on their national flag and is quite similar to those described in China.

The *makara* (मकर in Sanskrit)[85] is a sea dragon that is commonly described in Hindu mythology. The Vedic sea-god Varuna is described as riding on a *makara* and is the king of the *makaras* (and *nāgas*), which is also associated with the Ganges river. It is artistically portrayed in entryways as a guardian to Hindu and Buddhist temples. In Tibet, the *makara* is called the "chu-srin", and is considered a hybrid creature. The modern view is that this creature is simply a developed mythical form of the mugger crocodile, which is quite common in India. Though the Hindi actually call crocodiles makara (or makar) this does not explain the described physical differences between the so-called mythical *makara* and the crocodile.

Ancient stories that involve the *nāgas* continue to be a part of cultural traditions in the Hindu and Buddhist regions of East Asia. The *nāga* is considered to be the same type of creature as the *lung* in China. These creatures inhabit springs, wells, and rivers, and are also bringers of rain and are harbingers of natural disasters, like flooding. Traditionally, the *nāgas* were docile unless provoked and were regarded as guardians of treasure. Similar to the Chinese, the *nāga* is venerated and even worshipped in India where they are considered to bring fertility and prosperity. An interesting note is that one particular people group in India, the Nagavanshi, consider themselves (like the Chinese kings) to be descendants of the *nāga*.

Persian Legends

The *Shahnameh* ("The Book of Kings") is an Iranian epic poem that was written by the Persian poet Ferdowsi between 977 and 1010 A.D. Being considered part legendary and part historical, it describes a number of accounts with elephants, rhinos, and (of course) dragons. One of these stories will be given to demonstrate some apparent similarities with other unrelated accounts.

The Persian king, Sekandar, was encamped with his army by a mountainous region in a foreign country. Wanting to pass through the mountains, the local people were asked to show them the way, but the king found that they feared a great dragon that lived near the only path through the mountains. The local people explained that to appease the dragon, they brought five cows near its lair each night and ran away before he arrived to devour them. They proceeded to describe the dragon in this manner:

> His poison sickens birds that venture there,
> The noxious vapors reach the moon, there's no

---
85. See Figure 7 for an example; particularly illustration 5.

Safe route by which your warriors could go.
His massive maw breathes fire, and he could snare
An elephant with his two locks of hair...
 (Sekandar later described the dragon as):
... like a huge dark cloud: his tongue purple, his eyes blood red, and fire issuing continuously from his maw. [86]

Drawing the dragon out in the open, Sekandar's army shot at the dragon with arrows, which seemed to have little effect. In reply, the dragon breathed fire and killed some of the attackers. The dragon fled only after hearing the beating of the ominous military drums. Eventually, the dragon was killed by means of filling dead cows with poison and oil, which were then presented to the dragon to eat. The poison burst open the intestines and spread to the rest of the dragon's body. While the dragon was thrashing about in misery, the army showered the beast again with arrows, which finally died.

Turkish Dragons

In the region of Turkey, Bulgaria and Western Russia, a well known though repulsive serpent-dragon is called (in English) a *zilant*. The Tatars call it a *yilan* (juʻlan), and sometimes refer to this dreaded creature with the Persian word *ajdaha-yilan*, which means dragon-snake. A *zilant* not only possessed the ability of flight, but its blood was also believed to have medicinal properties. It could be used as a remedy or as a deadly poison, depending on how it was concocted for use.

It was believed that a *zilant* would eventually grow to become a large white serpent, called an *aq yilan*, after living one hundred years. Similar to ancient Chinese beliefs, the Idel-Ural people in particular believed that any snake that lived over one hundred years would become a *ajdaha* (dragon). The century old *aq yilan* was then considered to have benevolent qualities, unlike the *zilant* "stage" of the creature's life. Kazan Russians held negative feelings for the *zilant* and some consider it to be a *wyvern* as described in the West.

There are several legends involving the *zilant*. One tells of a dragon-snake that lived in a pagan temple at Alabuğa. This serpent lived for quite some time, despite Islamic domination beginning in the 10th century[87], until the invasion of Tamerlane[88]. Ibn Fadlan[89], while in Volga Bulgaria during the 10th century, told of numerous snakes that inhabited trees. He also wrote about a huge fallen tree where he saw a large serpent that was almost as large as the tree itself! Despite its intimidating size,

---
86. *Shahnameh: The Persian Book of Kings*, Firdawsi, Translated by Dick Davis, 2006. (See 506 - 508).
87. Islam adherents would destroy such serpents, most likely to symbolize the victory of Islam over pagan religions.
88. Derived from the Persian *Timur-i lang.* His armies invaded central Asia from 1370 until his death in 1405 A.D.
89. Ahmad ibn Fadlān ibn al-Abbās ibn Rāšid ibn Hammād (Arabic: أحمد بن فضلان بن العباس بن راشد بن حماد) was a 10th century Arab traveler. He is famous for his accounts as a member of an embassy of the Arab Abba-sid Caliph of Baghdad to the king of the Volga Bulgars. See MS 5229, a 13th century (7th century Hijra) manuscript.

the Bulgars assured Ibn Fadlan that the serpent was not dangerous.

> These flying snakes were also known in Bolghar, Suar, Bilär and the other cities of Volga Bulgaria. For the most part, these snakes were benevolent. However, in the boundary fortresses of Kazan, Alabuğa and Cükätaw, legends about flying monsters flourished. One particular fortress on the Shishma River was known as Yılantaw [Zilantaw Hill (originally Tatar Yılantaw/Елантау/Жылантау, Snake Mount), associated with Zilant legends, was formerly situated on the bank of Kazanka River.], later russified as Yelantovo.[90]

Camouflage?

In this section, a divergence from the more accepted historical accounts will be taken in order to offer a hypothetical proposal regarding those accounts that are considered legendary. To begin with, there are four types of camouflage known in the modern animal kingdom:

> *Concealing Coloration*: Using coloration to hide against a similar background color.
>
> *Disruptive Coloration*: Using patterns to "break up" a creature's outline so it does not stand out against the background.
>
> *Disguise*: Blending in with the surrounding area by shape and/or coloration.
>
> *Mimicry*: Taking on the characteristics of, or mimicking other creatures or objects.

Most creatures utilize only one or two of these types of camouflage and can not willfully alter it in any way. A zebra cannot change its stripes in other words. However, cephalopods (i.e. octopi and cuttlefish) are exceptional in this regard since they can utilize three or all four types of camouflage at the same time and alter it at will instantaneously. Not only the color, but also the shape of the creature can practically morph into whatever background is available. Some octopi can even mimic plants to the point of being visually indistinguishable from it. Even the popular color-changing chameleon pales in comparison to the stealth abilities of the cephalopods. A "higher form" of camouflage (disguise) is not only limited to ocean dwelling invertebrates. A recent discovery found an Ecuadorian frog (Pristimantis mutabilis) that can rapidly change its camouflaged skin texture (disruptive coloration) from smooth to spiny.

Consider again that many ancient descriptions of dragons indicate that they were unusual creatures that had a grab-bag of physical features like scales, hair, and some even having mammal-like ears; similar to a platypus' odd assemblage of

---

90. See: http://the-book-of-dragons.deviantart.com/journal/Legendary-Zilant-241125073. Brackets inserted for clarity.

features. Perhaps this extraordinary ability of visual disguise is another feature? If so, it would explain many ancient accounts that are currently considered as legendary where dragons could change into another creature or "disappear".

Instead of quickly writing off a particular ancient account simply because it seems too far-fetched for the modern mind to believe, a reexamination is called for. Perhaps these types of ancient observations of dragons were the basis for *exaggerated* accounts and legends—that dragons were spiritual or magical creatures that could change into anything they wanted? Knowing human behavior, this concept is not absurd. There are too many accounts that seem to indicate the same profound capability, that some dragons may have had mimicry camouflage![91]

Much non-poetic ancient literature seems more historical in nature than heroic fantasy, particularly the closer we come to modern times. In these later works, it would be unlikely as well as inconsistent with other verifiable historical accounts for the writers to spontaneously insert a mythical creature into a work that is understood by their contemporaries as being non-fiction. For instance, some ancient Asian chronicles describe lengthy and mundane historical accounts except for one or two specific events that entail dragons performing amazing feats. These stories pop up almost unexpectedly but are described in the same manner and style as the rest of the historical work.

Proposal: If some dragons did indeed possess the ability to camouflage themselves in a similar manner of cephalopods, then it is reasonable to consider that people in ancient times thought that dragons were magical creatures, let alone considered them as gods that could "appear" and "disappear" or change their shape at will. Without the scientific knowledge of the animal kingdom that we have today, such capabilities of physical alteration would cause us to think these creatures were in some ways supernatural, as the ancients apparently did. (This is not to say that *all* ancient accounts that are considered semi-legendary, allegorical, or mythological are to be believed in part or at all!) Some tales of dragons would naturally be over-exaggerations if not deliberate fables of the imagination due to the belief that the creatures were indeed magical. (i.e., Shinto and Buddhist allegorical tales describing dragons becoming humans (or vice-versa), or large multi-headed dragons becoming small snakes (physical impossibilities), waterspouts or fierce weather ascribed to being dragons, etc.) *Careful discernment is in order here!*

The problem is how does one determine if an account is reasonably true or not? Though it is beyond the scope of this book to go into a full explanation of determining literary style and genre, there are certain criteria that can be applied to a particular work that help in making such a determination.

---

91. This proposal was written approximately four years before the blockbuster movie *Jurassic World* (2015) was released which had a scene where a genetically modified dinosaur had mimicry camouflage capability.

Here are a few basics to consider:

a) *Specific actual location.* In some instances, the location is still known and can be visited.

b) *Specific historical individuals.* When the account was written, contemporaries would know if the person described did or did not exist and could refute the claim.

c) *Specific time.* In some instances, rulers were mentioned to verify the date.

d) *Normal setting.* The hero is not superhuman. The shape-changing ability is attributed to the dragon as being a normal or expected behavior.

e) *Literary consistency.* The account is included with other historical events and is described in the same literary style.

f) *Genre and implication.* Was the text written as an allegory, or does it give concise eyewitness reports of events that happened in space and historical time?

g) *Physically possible.* The shape and size of the dragon is similar to the shape and size it appears to change into.

In ancient Japan, for example, during the semi-legendary period of the Emperor Nintoku (313—399 A.D.), horned 4-legged water dragons were called *mizuchi* (蛟 or みずち *midzu-chi*), also known as "water fathers". Coincidentally, these specific creatures were considered (like the Chinese) to be rain-controlling snake deities. The collection of Japanese chronicles entitled *Nihongi* (日本紀), describe two separate events where men supposedly tricked the *mizuchi* with calabashes (a type of gourd) for their own personal ends. The second account (paraphrased below) that took place in 379 A.D. is what will be focused on here since it pertains to the killing of a water dragon that apparently had the (potential) capability of mimicry camouflage.

The *Nihongi* states that at a fork of the river Kahashima, in the central division of the province of Kibi, there was a large *mizuchi* that went about harassing the local people. When travelers passed by the area, they were poisoned by the dragon and many died. Wanting to rid the land of the menacing beast, a man of great strength and hot temper named Agata-mori, ancestor of the Omi of Kasa, stood over the waters of the river-fork and threw into the water three calabashes as a challenge. Agata-mori said, "You are continually belching up poison and plaguing the people. I will kill you, water dragon! If you can sink these calabashes, then I will leave you alone. But if you cannot sink them, then I will cut your body to pieces!" The dragon changed itself into a deer in an attempt to draw down the calabashes, but it could not do so. Upon seeing the dragon's failed attempt, Agata-mori entered the water with his sword drawn and he slew the dragon. He then went on and sought to kill the remaining *mizuchi* that lived in a cave at the bottom of the river pool. Agata-mori was so successful in killing the remaining water dragons that the river water was said to have turned to blood; thus the reason for the pool in the river to be named the "pool of Agata-mori".[92]

It should be highlighted that the only unusual event described in this first example is that the dragon turned itself into a deer (a creature that is coincidentally similar in shape to the 4-legged dragon according to other descriptions of water dragons). Note that the speed or method of metamorphosis is not explained in any manner but is mentioned as though it was a matter-of-fact event. If this ancient water-creature did have camouflage capabilities, perhaps it *appeared* to change into a semblance of a deer, or alternatively perhaps an actual deer entered the river unseen until it came within view of the hero (who subsequently thought it to be the dragon in disguise). The dragon was also not necessarily responding to the man's challenge (insinuating the ability to understand human speech), but was most likely responding naturally to the calabashes floating in the water, like koi fish do with floating objects or food pellets. Another factor of the "deer" description may be similar to the *lung ma* in that the name applied is merely describing a resemblance, but not necessarily what the creature transforms into. Unfortunately one will never know for sure since the account is briefly described.

Another example is described in deVisser's work (below). Note how the dragon's form is not described except that it could change into a black dog. Apparently, the creature was more than just a common black dog since a temple was built on the spot in honor of the dragon (and common dogs don't live in ponds).

> The *Kiang-si t'ung-chi* speaks about a very deep "Dragon-rearing pond" near the castle of Kwang ch'ang district in Kien ch'ang fu, inhabited by a dragon. Over the pond there was a stone tray, in which remains of food were always laid for the animal, which used to change into a black dog and eat the food. This pond was still there in the author's time, and a "Dragon-well temple" had been built on the spot.[93]

Admittedly, this hypothetical proposal is not a strong argument for substantiating the reality of dragons living with humans, but the theory that some dragons may have had the potential for mimicry camouflage is reasonable (or at least entertaining) to consider. Chapter 7 presents another example of this profound ability (Leelanau lake monsters). Since camouflage is demonstrated in a variety of ways in our modern animal kingdom, why not for extinct creatures in the past? Whether or not dragons had the ability to camouflage themselves may never be known and is debateable. In any event, there are even more Asian historical accounts not presented in this chapter

---

92. William G. Aston, 1896. *Nihongi: Chronicles of Japan from the Earliest Times to A.D. 697*, Vol. 1, p. 298,299.
93. de Visser, p. 129. (江西通志 "Kiang-si t'ung-chi").

that describe these amazing creatures in a consistent realistic manner (regardless of them using camouflage or not), further lending to historical eligibility. Is it any wonder why these amazing serpents of the past greatly influenced the cultures of the Far East?

Speech?

To address another conjectural side-issue; in some accounts and stories, dragons are described as being able to talk and reason! Now if they did possess such an ability, then it would coincide with African grey parrots and mynah birds, both of which have a high clarity of voice with some understanding of what they are saying (ability to reason). Parakeets can also talk but do not have a high clarity of voice nor are they as adept at reasoning. Consider also Koko the gorilla, who had a greater than 1000-word sign-language vocabulary, and how the Superb Lyre bird can mimic any sound. Dogs, elephants, and young beluga whales can mimic human speech sounds to some questionable degree but do not appear to understand what they are mimicking.

The point here is that though it may be unbelievable that some dragons were able to speak and reason, this is not an exception in the animal kingdom! The conjectural point here, like the previous section, is that the possibility of such capabilities are substantiated by other existing examples and should not be quickly dismissed. If one or two types of dragons had this capability, even to some degree, then it would certainly support why early Asian observers considered dragons to be a divine creature.

Here be Dragons

It is often believed that most ancient maps had the Latin phrase *hic sunt dracones* ("here be dragons") written on them when pointing out unexplored regions. This is not so. Early cartographers did, however, often incorporate images of dragons and sea serpents in blank regions of their maps. The only time the Latin phrase *hic sunt dracones* was used was on the Hunt-Lenox Globe,[94] where, coincidentally, the words were placed in East Asia. Thus the crossover from East to West will be made here.

---

94. The Hunt-Lenox Globe is one of the first known Western globes ever made of the earth. 1507 A.D. (approximately)

4: Western Historic Dragons

Depicted in ancient artwork and literature, horns are a particular physical feature that dragons sport, which causes our current society to separate the modern view of dinosaurs (with relatively hornless heads) with the mythical dragon. In other words, to say that the dragon and dinosaur were one and the same would be preposterous! Yet this is not a foregone conclusion. Take for instance the recently discovered fossil named "Dracorex hogwartsia" found in the Hell Creek Formation of central South Dakota. This fossil skull looks very similar to what one would think a classic fantasy dragon skull would look like due to its atypical horned head. Many other dinosaurs had horns too. This particular chapter will focus on various documented dragons in Europe, Africa and the Americas, occasionally reflecting back on similar Asian descriptions.

Iaculus (Latin: jaculus)

Known best for his prolific artwork, Leonardo da Vinci (1452 - 1519 A.D.) was also considered a scientific genius who epitomized the ideals of the Renaissance. Leonardo wrote several notebooks[1] on human character attributes and frequently associated such behavior with animals (i.e., vain glory with the peacock). In a similar fashion to the Chinese *I-Ching*, his notebooks describing such behaviors utilize many "real" animals yet also include a few animals that modern society would consider humorous fables, or mythical animals. Yet when compared with other accounts of similar so-called mythical creatures throughout the world (despite them having different names by different cultures), they may be reporting the same type of creature. Similar to the *zilant* that was described in the previous chapter, Leonardo described the *iaculus* as being a winged serpent that liked to hide in trees while

---

1. See: *The Literary Works of Leonardo da Vinci, Volume 2*, edited by Jean Paul Richter. p. 322.

waiting to fall (or throw itself down like a dart) on its prey. He was not alone in this particular description.

Lucan depicted the *iaculus* in his *Pharsalia* (book 9:848): "Swift *jaculus* there..." (962-966): "Upon branchless trunk a serpent, named by Libyans *jaculus*, rose in coils to dart his venom from afar. Through Paullus' brain it rushed, nor stayed; for in the wound itself was death."[2]

> The *iaculus* is a snake which flies. Lucan says of it: 'The *iaculus* that can fly' (*Pharsalia*, 9:720). For they spring into trees and when anything comes their way, throw themselves on it and kill it. As a result, they are called *iaculi*, 'javelin-snakes'.
> Of *sirens*
> In Arabia there are white snakes, with wings, called *sirens*, which cover the ground faster than horses, but are also said to fly. Their is [sic] poison is so strong that if you are bitten by it you die before you feel the pain.[3]

Pliny the Elder also tells of the *iaculus* in his *Natural History* (book 8:35): The *iaculus* hurls itself from the branches of a tree, so that it is not only dangerous to the feet, but flies through the air like a missile from a catapult.[4]

In addition, Isidore of Seville explained in his *Etymologies* (book 12, 4:29) that the *iaculus* was a flying snake that jumped from trees and darted onto passing animals, from which they get their name, darter (*iaculi*).[5]

The *iaculus* cannot be one of the known flying snake species as is typically conjectured. The differences are considerable between the two types of creatures. First, the *iaculus* inhabits the North African region and Eastern Mediterranean whereas flying snakes only inhabit Southeast Asia and to a lesser degree Southern India and Sri Lanka. Their bite is mildly venomous to small animals and are harmless to humans due to their small fixed fangs being in the back of their mouths. *Iaculi*, on the other hand, have a fast-acting deadly venom and are described as being aggressive in attacking any animal (or human) that comes their way, in a dart-like fashion. In comparison, the term "flying snake" is actually a misnomer since they glide (a better term would be parachute) through the air by means of belly concavity and twisting undulations; nor do they sport wings (among other described differences).

The creature now referred to as the *amphiptere* (a legless winged serpent found in European heraldry) may simply be the *iaculus* or a related species. In addition, it is known from fossil records that there are many species of pterosaurs that come in a wide range of sizes. Though admittedly none seem to portray the exact physical attributes

---

2. A first century Roman poet. The *Pharsalia* is an epic poem that tells of the civil war between Julius Caesar and the forces led by Pompey. The *iaculus* is described as living in Libya.
3. See: *Aberdeen Bestiary*, a 12th century English illuminated manuscript. Folio 69v.
4. A first century Roman author, naturalist, and natural philosopher. The encyclopedic work, *Naturalis Historia*, became a model for subsequent similar works.
5. Considered to be the last scholar of the ancient world. (560 – 636 A.D.) His work, *Etymologiae*, incorporated a major part of his summation of universal knowledge at the time.

of the *iaculus* as described by the aforementioned sources. Perhaps the *kuehneosaur*[6] would be a candidate. Nevertheless, the similarities to various extinct animals are striking. The archaic European drawings of the *iaculus* may be oversimplifications of what the creature actually looked like. These oversimplifications may be due to the creature living hundreds of miles away (from European eyes), with art direction from the descriptive memory of an eyewitness being relayed to the artist. Despite this possibility, in his travels, the Greek historian Herodotus gives a first-hand description of a strikingly similar creature living in the same reported region. His description seems to fit the smaller pterosaur species more exactly and they are also referred to as flying snakes. This will be discussed in more detail in the following chapter.

Lumerpa

As the root of its name implies, this flying creature apparently had some sort of bioluminescent quality. According to Leonardo da Vinci, the *lumerpa* was found in Asia Major, and shined so bright that it did not cast a shadow. Nor did that light fade after death or its feathers fall out. However, if a feather was plucked from the creature, the luminous qualities of the feather ceased. Today, scientists scoff at such nonsense; and reasonably so since there are no creatures known that are remotely like it living today. However, when one realizes that some pterodactyls or "prehistoric" birds did have feathers, or "proto-feathers", the creature described may have indeed existed. Especially when one considers modern reports of bioluminescent[7] flying creatures mentioned in other regions of the world (see next chapter).

The Macli

Another one of Leonardo's "mythical" creatures with an unfamiliar name is the *macli*. (Apparently, Leonardo was quoting Pliny).[8] According to the description, it may have been a type of sauropod. Leonardo stated that the creature was born in Scandinavia. This is reasonable since sauropod fossils have been found on every continent, including Antarctica. Specifically to Scandinavia, various sauropod tracks have recently been found in the Bagå formation that is situated in the Baltic Sea in Southern Sweden.[9] Continuing, Leonardo described the *macli* as having the shape of a huge horse, except that it had an exceptionally long neck and its ears were different from a horse as well. The *macli* went backwards while eating grass due to its long upper lip. (Leonardo explained that if it went forward, the *macli* would cover up the

---
6. An extinct flying reptile, approximately 2 feet long.
7. See Appendix B for a list of bioluminescent creatures existing today.
8. Plinius Secundus *The Historie of the World.* Book VIII. Chapter XV. (Also spelled "Machli")
9. See: Jesper Milàn's article entitled, *New theropod, thyreophoran, and small sauropod tracks from the Middle Jurassic Bagå Formation, Bornholm, Denmark.*

grass with its upper lip!) This specific detail about a long necked creature sounds humorous at first until one considers the evidence for a fleshy lipped "prehistoric" animal, as discussed in the previous chapter. Risking his reputation on such an unusual creature, Leonardo da Vinci also described the *macli's* behavior.

> Its legs are all in one piece; for this reason when it wants to sleep it leans against a tree, and the hunters, spying out the place where it is wont to sleep, saw the tree almost through, and then, when it leans against it to sleep, in its sleep it falls, and thus the hunters take it. And every other mode of taking it is in vain, because it is incredibly swift in running.[10]

Thus, if Leonardo's (Pliny's) account of the *macli* is true, and the creature was indeed a living animal (considering that many long-necked dinosaurs or macrauchenia-like[11] animals have existed, lending to its credibility), then we can surmise that man is the main reason for this particular creature's extinction.

Dragons, Serpents, and the Roman Army

Among all the other living animals accounted for in his notebooks, Leonardo da Vinci also wrote about dragons and serpents as though they were actual living creatures. Like the Asian chroniclers of old, Leonardo described specific behaviors and historic events. As previously mentioned, his reputation was on the line and his accounts could have been debunked, yet none of Leonardo's contemporaries did so. Consider the following accounts and the details described.

> These [dragons] go in companies together, and they twine themselves after the manner of roots, and with their heads raised they cross lakes, and swim to where they find better pasture; and if they did not thus combine they would be drowned, therefore they combine.

> The serpent is a very large animal. When it sees a bird in the air it draws in its breath so strongly that it draws the birds into its mouth too. Marcus Regulus, the consul of the Roman army was attacked, with his army, by such an animal and almost defeated. And this animal, being killed by a catapult, measured 123 feet, that is 64 1/2 braccia and its head was high above all the trees in a wood.[12]

Note that Leonardo da Vinci specified the serpent from the family of dragons. Though the serpent sounds like it could be a long-necked dinosaur from the description. Perhaps all long-necked dinosaurs were considered serpents while other dinosaurs were called dragons? Just because modern science grouped the land

---
10. *The Literary Works of Leonardo da Vinci, Volume 2.* pp. 328
11. Macrauchenia: an extinct camel-like animal that had a long neck and snout. Found only in South America however.
12. *The Literary Works of Leonardo da Vinci, Volume 2.* pp. 327

dwelling dinosaurs into one classification does not mean the Medieval Europeans classified them in the same manner.

The event that Leonardo was referring to was initially described by the highly respected Roman historian Livy (Titus Livius Patavinus) who stated, "[Y.R. 496. B.C. 256.] Attilius Regulus, consul, having overcome the Carthaginians in a sea-fight, passes over into Africa: *kills a serpent of prodigious magnitude, with great loss of his own men.*"[13] If this serpent was a common reticulated python (long though it may have been) as many claim today, then that does not account for the heavy toll of soldier deaths since a python will only attack one creature at a time, or at best two. Even a python that was over 120 feet in length would not be able to nearly defeat an entire Roman army. If the serpent is a different creature altogether, then that is another matter! Yet Livy comments on another physical detail about serpents in the following passage that clearly indicates that it was not simply a large snake or python.

> Before the consuls cast lots for their provinces, several prodigies were reported: that in the Crustumine territory, a stone fell from the sky into the grove of Mars; that in the Roman territory, a boy was born defective in his limbs; *that a serpent with four feet had been seen*; that at Capua, many buildings in the forum were struck by lightning; and, that at Puteoli, two ships were burned by lightning."[14]

Elephants vs. Dragons vs. Panthers

The *Aberdeen Bestiary*, a 12th century English illuminated manuscript that depicts various animals, describes a dragon in a similar manner as many other accounts throughout the Eurasian continent. Due to the spread of Christianity in Europe, many Medieval manuscripts incorporated religious allegorical comparisons. Because of this, it could be reasonably argued that real physical creatures were used as an allegory for spiritual concepts (similar to the *I-Ching* which allegorizes a person's character with an animal, as discussed earlier). More specifically, dangerous dragons became associated with Satan (aka: the Devil). This makes sense, especially in light of how the dragon is analogous to various deities in Eastern philosophies. A good example is given in the Aberdeen Bestiary itself, which describes a particular kind of dragon in detail.

> "The dragon is bigger than all other snakes or all other living things on earth. For this reason, the Greeks call it dracon, from this is derived its Latin name draco. The dragon, it is said, is often drawn forth from caves into the open air, causing the air to become turbulent. The dragon has a crest, a small mouth, and narrow blow-holes through which it breathes and puts forth

---

13. Titus Livius, *The History of Rome*, Vol. 1. Books I.- XX. Translated by D. Spillan. (Book XVIII) p. 745. (Italics added for emphasis). See: Appendix D.
14. Titus Livius, The History of Rome, Book XLI, Chapter 9. McDevitte. (See: www.perseus.tufts.edu). "prodigies" being extraordinary events in this case.

its tongue. Its strength lies not in its teeth but in its tail, and it kills with a blow rather than a bite. It is free from poison. They say that it does not need poison to kill things, because it kills anything around which it wraps its tail. From the dragon not even the elephant, with its huge size, is safe. For lurking on paths along which elephants are accustomed to pass, the dragon knots its tail around their legs and kills them by suffocation. Dragons are born in Ethiopia and India, where it is hot all year round. The Devil is like the dragon; he is the most monstrous serpent of all; he is often aroused from his cave and causes the air to shine because, emerging from the depths, he transforms himself into the angel of light and deceives the foolish with hopes of vainglory and worldly pleasure. The dragon is said to be crested, as the Devil wears the crown of the king of pride. The dragon's strength lies not in its teeth but its tail, as the Devil, deprived of his strength, deceives with lies those whom he draws to him. The dragon lurks around paths along which elephants pass, as the Devil entangles with the knots of sin the way of those bound for heaven and, like the dragon, kills them by suffocation; because anyone who dies fettered in the chains of his offences is condemned without doubt to hell."[15]

A similar description with additional details (and allegory) is given in another bestiary.

The dragon's strength is found in its tail, not in its teeth. Its lashing tail does great harm, and the dragon kills anything it catches in its coils. The dragon is the enemy of the elephant, and hides near paths where elephants walk so that it can catch them with its tail and kill them by suffocation. It is because of the threat of the dragon that elephants give birth in the water. The dragon's venom is harmless. The dragon has a crest and a small mouth. *When the dragon is drawn from its hole into the air, it stirs up the air and makes it shine*. Dragons are found in India and Ethiopia. Dragons are afraid of the peridexion tree and stay out of its shadow, which will harm them. Doves roost in the tree to be safe from the dragon.[16] Dragons cannot stand the sweet smell breathed out by the panther *and hide in a hole when the panther roars.*
The Devil is likened to a dragon because he is the worst of all serpents. *As the dragon makes the air shine*, so the Devil makes himself appear as the angel of light to deceive the foolish. The crest of the dragon represents the Devil crowned with pride. As the dragon's strength is not in its teeth but in its tail, the Devil, deprived of his strength, deceives with lies. The way in which the dragon attacks elephants represents the way the Devil attacks people, lying in wait along their path to heaven, wrapping them in his coils, and suffocating them with sin.[17]

Note that the description of the dragon effecting the surrounding atmosphere as it emerges from its lair is strikingly similar to Asian accounts, not to mention its dread of the panther! As a side note, the Aberdeen Bestiary concurs that the dragon's enemy is the panther - which is identical (i.e., tigers) to accounts in the East.

---
15. *Aberdeen Bestiary*. See "of the Dragon", Folio 65v - 66r.
16. See the Perindens tree, discussed in the *Aberdeen Bestiary*, f64.
17. *Harley* MS 3244, f59r British Library. (italics mine - for emphasis)

> There is an animal called the panther, multi-coloured, very beautiful and extremely gentle. Physiologus says of it, that it has only the dragon as an enemy. When it has fed and is full, it hides in its den and sleeps... Only the dragon, hearing its voice, is seized by fear and flees into the caves beneath the earth. There, unable to bear the scent, it grows numbed within itself and remains motionless, as if dead.

These bestiaries (and other authors such as Claudius Aelianus) were in agreement with Pliny the Elder's earlier encyclopedic work on *Natural History*, where the contention between elephants and dragons are explained. Though his understanding of elephants (and dragons) may be lacking or naive exaggerations compared with modern scientific understanding, Pliny was indeed comparing two *concurrent* animals in a matter of fact way and not as an allegorical tale.

> Africa produces elephants... But it is India that produces the largest, as well as the dragon, which is perpetually at war with the elephant, and is itself of so enormous a size, as easily to envelope the elephants with its folds, and encircle them in its coils. The contest is equally fatal to both; the elephant, vanquished, falls to the earth, and by its weight, crushes the dragon which is entwined around it.
>
> The sagacity which every animal exhibits in its own behalf is wonderful, but in these it is remarkably so. The dragon has much difficulty in climbing up to so great a height, and therefore, watching the road, which bears marks of their footsteps when going to feed, it darts down upon them from a lofty tree. The elephant knows that it is quite unable to struggle against the folds of the serpent, and so seeks for trees or rocks against which to rub itself. The dragon is on its guard against this, and tries to prevent it, by first of all confining the legs of the elephant with the folds of its tail; while the elephant, on the other hand, endeavours to disengage itself with its trunk. The dragon, however, thrusts its head into its nostrils, and thus, at the same moment, stops the breath and wounds the most tender parts. When it is met unexpectedly, the dragon raises itself up, faces its opponent, and flies more especially at the eyes; this is the reason why elephants are so often found blind, and worn to a skeleton with hunger and misery. What other cause can one assign for such mighty strifes as these, except that Nature is desirous, as it were, to make an exhibition for herself, in pitting such opponents against each other? There is another story, too, told in relation to these combats —the blood of the elephant, it is said, is remarkably cold;[18] for which reason, in the parching heats of summer, it is sought by the dragon with remarkable avidity. It lies, therefore, coiled up and concealed in the rivers, in wait for the elephants, when they come to drink; upon which it darts out, fastens itself around the trunk, and then fixes its teeth behind the ear, that being the only place which the elephant cannot protect with the trunk. The dragons, it is said, are of such vast size, that they can swallow the whole of the blood; consequently, the elephant,

---

18. There is no basis for this idea and is therefore not the actual reason why dragons preyed upon elephants.

being thus drained of its blood, falls to the earth exhausted; while the dragon, intoxicated with the draught, is crushed beneath it, and so shares its fate.

Æthiopia produces dragons, not so large as those of India, but still, twenty cubits in length. The only thing that surprises me is, how Juba came to believe that they have crests. The Æthiopians are known as the Asachæi, among whom they most abound; and we are told, that on those coasts four or five of them are found twisted and interlaced together like so many osiers in a hurdle, and thus setting sail, with their heads erect, they are borne along upon the waves, to find better sources of nourishment in Arabia.[19]

Dragontites

The scholar Isidore of Seville relayed similar descriptions of the dragon in his *Etymologies*. Note that he also indicated how dragons disturbed the air around them. He also gave fascinating details as to the reason why dragons were hunted down!

The dragon is the largest serpent, and in fact the largest animal on earth. Its name in Latin is draco, derived from the Greek name drakon. When it comes out of its cave, it disturbs the air. It has a crest, a small mouth, and a narrow throat. Its strength is in its tail rather than its teeth; it does harm by beating, not by biting. It has no poison and needs none to kill, because it kills by entangling. Not even the elephant is safe from the dragon; hiding where elephants travel, the dragon tangles their feet with its tail and kills the elephant by suffocating it. Dragons live in the burning heat of India and Ethiopia.

Dracontites is a stone that is forcibly taken from the brain of a dragon, and unless it is torn from the living creature it has not the quality of a gem; whence magi cut it out of dragons while they are sleeping. For bold men explore the cave of the dragons, and scatter there medicated grains to hasten their sleep, and thus cut off their heads while they are sunk in sleep, and take out the gems.[20]

Perhaps dragontites were the basis for the mythological tales of the *wyverns* of France,[21] that were said to possess a gem-like "eye" (or carbuncle) *in the forehead* that was considered to be of great value, particularly to magicians.

Many of these stones are mentioned by Pliny as being widely known among the Romans in his day, or as being mentioned in the writings of the older Greek writers whose works have long since disappeared.[22]

Despite the gem-like quality, dragontites (aka dragonites) were listed among

---
19. John Bostock, *The Natural History. Pliny the Elder.* Book 8, chapters 11 - 13.
20. Isidore of Seville, *Etymologies*, Book 12 (Animals), 4:4-5 and Book 16 (Stones and Metals), 14:7.
21. *Wyvern*, (or *Vouivre*) in French, is equivalent to the old French word "Wurm"; a type of dragon species.
22. Frank Dawson Adams, Development of the Geological Sciences. p. 104.

at least a dozen other animal "stones" that were thought to cure certain diseases by those in the past. One such person, Camillus Leonardus, in his *Speculum Lapidum* (1505), described many of these "stones" and each were given a specific name.[23] Included among these were dracontites (dragontites), which were taken from the head of a dragon. Dragonites are also mentioned in the *De Hortus Sanitatis*[24] and were considered useful for curing some maladies.

The Ch'ih Muh Revisited

In the *Detailed Descriptions* section of the previous chapter, it was indicated through observation that particular types of dragons could not fly if they did not have a *ch'ih muh*. This description sounds absurd if taken alone, however, it may bear some significance in light of the following unrelated Western descriptions. Hugo de Folieto explained that a dragon was "lifted by the strength of its venom into the air as if it were flying, and the air is set in motion by it. It lies in wait for the elephant, the most chaste of animals, and encircling its feet with its tail it tries to suffocate it with its breath, but is crushed by the elephant as it falls dead."[25] Perhaps the Asian observers noted that dragons with the cranial lumps could mysteriously fly, but did not correlate their breath specifically as helping them levitate. Nevertheless, Bartholomaeus Anglicus concurs more specifically with the Asian account. "The Dragon is most greatest of all serpents, and oft he is drawn out of his den, and riseth up into the air, and the air is moved by him, and also the sea swelleth against his venom, *and he hath a crest...*"[26]

Here we have an account that specifies that particular dragons with a crest (i.e. *ch'ih muh*) have the ability to levitate using their vaporous breath as a means. In addition, some Asian accounts also describe dragons as affecting or moving the air around them. Such "venom" may have been kept in the so-called *crown*, or *ch'ih muh*; similar to a viper's poison glands that puff out their cheeks, giving them the distinctive triangular-shaped head. Bartholomaeus explained further, like other European accounts, that the venom of these crested dragons was not effective enough to kill their prey yet indicated it was used for the purposes of flight.

Since the air was described as being noticeably affected around the dragons as they flew, there may be a scientific explanation to this phenomenon. Perhaps these dragons performed a type of acoustic levitation, ultimately using sound that travels through a fluid (usually a gas) to balance the force of gravity. On earth, this can cause objects and materials to hover unsupported in the air. In other words, they may have breathed a certain type of gas that enveloped their bodies and then produced a high or low frequency sound (i.e. a growl) which allowed the dragon to rise into the air. Of

---

23. Frank Dawson Adams, Development of the Geological Sciences. See pp. 104-105.
24. *De Hortus Sanitatis*. Printed by Jacob Meyderbach. (1491 - 1497?)
25. Hugo de Folieto, *Elephants, dragon, and mandrake*, Sloane 278, folio 48v. British Library MS, Druce translation.
26. Bartholomaeus Anglicus, *De Proprietatibus Rerum*, book 18, 13th century CE. (italics mine)

course any magi seeing this capability would indeed risk hunting down a dragon to gain that ability! Whether the crests and dragontites were one and the same, or were separate features altogether remains to be seen. Consider that there are many types of dinosaur fossils found all over the world that have odd shaped crests and cranial protrusions.

Pins and Needles

Similar to Daniel's account of slaying the dragon,[27] there is a European tale of a dragon that was killed by feeding it bread filled with pins. Folklore known as the *Straw Dragon*, or *Cuélebre*,[28] originated in the Asturias, located in Northern Spain. Though tales of the *Cuélebre* border on the unbelievable; dealing with far off legendary lands, beautiful nymphs and so forth, the tales rooted in superstition also bear some similarities to other unrelated descriptions. This large flying dragon lived in caves and, like a rat, hoarded shiny valuables or treasure. (Compare with the serpentine *nāgas,* mentioned in the previous chapter, that also guarded treasure). As it grew older, its scales became increasingly thick and impenetrable. It would usually slumber in its cave, but on occasion would go out and hunt down cattle and unsuspecting people. One account described the *Cuélebre* being killed by offering it bread with pins inside, and another was killed by means of a red-hot stone. The spit of this serpent would eventually harden to a rock-like consistency and was considered as a magic stone with healing powers. The idea of the *Cuélebre's* spit hardening into a magic stone is similar to that of the magical carbuncle on the basilisk's head. It also is reminiscent of how the Chinese used dragon spit (saliva) for more utilitarian purposes.

A similar tale occurs in Southern Poland, which also depicts the founding of the city of Kraków. Note that Kraków is situated along the Vistula river and is one of the oldest cities in Poland; dating back to the seventh century. This tale is also pre-Christian, ruling out the claim that it is an allegorical tale of spiritual virtue, nor was it copied from Old Testament manuscripts. Thus the "Legend of the Wawel Dragon":

A fire-belching dragon lived in a cave at the bottom of Wawel Hill. It would occasionally roam about, eating farm animals and scaring the farmers. The dragon was so deadly that the farmers did not leave their homes from fear nor let their livestock graze near the fields along the river. Consequently the region became increasingly poor. The king wanted the dragon killed and offered his daughter in marriage, with the promise of becoming king when he died. Many brave knights attempted to kill the dragon but only met their doom. During this time, a shoemaker's apprentice, named Krak, asked the king if he could attempt to kill the dragon. The king gave his

---
27. See *Babylonian Dragons* section, previous chapter.
28. References and tales of the *Cuélebre*, or *Culebre*, can be found in various places online.

permission but saw that the apprentice had no weapons or armor. Krak confidently explained that he had a clever plan and went forth to put it into action. He bought a dead lamb and some powdered sulphur. With his shoemaker's knife he cut open the lamb's body and put the sulphur within; then proceeded to sew up the lamb with his thread. He placed the lamb's body near the dragon's cave and then hid himself, waiting for the dragon to appear. The dragon eventually came out of the cave and quickly devoured the lamb. The sulphur caught fire and injured the dragon's stomach. The dragon ran to the river and drank a great amount in an attempt to ease the "fire within" but this only made him sluggish and sickly. Krak came forth and attacked the dragon by throwing rocks at it. The dragon was unable to produce fire nor could it run about due to the internal damage done by the sulphur and water-swelled stomach. After a while, the dragon burst asunder and Krak was victorious. He married the princess and, as promised, became king after his father-in-law died. Krak built a castle on top of Wawel Hill and a city grew from it which the people called Kraków.[29]

These old tales of killing dragons through unconventional means (as opposed to slaying with swords and javelins) are few and far between, which is what one would expect if these were historical accounts. In other words, if dragons were complete fabrications of man's imagination, then the expected amount of stories that tell of dragons being killed by such means would be far more prevalent since they would proudly demonstrate man's applied wisdom over brute force.

Slavic Snakes / Naming Conventions

Though the generic term *dragon* is used today to refer to all sorts of dragons, European cultures (like Asia) had specific names for specific dragons. For instance, in Slavic culture, *zmaj* (and variants thereof) are used to describe dragons. *Zmaj* is the masculine form for "snake", despite the feminine form that is normally used. This would indicate that these dragons were not only reptilian but were larger than actual snakes. Other names for particular dragons and dragon-like creatures in Slavic folklore are *smok* (смок, цмок), *lamya* (ламйа, ламја), and the purely evil and hostile *aždaja*.

In Southern Slavic cultures in particular, dragons are considered to be magical creatures that are quite intelligent, having great strength. They are capable of belching fire too. Like other wild predators, dragons (other than the *aždaja*) were considered as being "neutral" in that they were neither entirely evil nor entirely good. They simply behaved according to their nature.

---

[29]. *The Legend of the Wawel Dragon.* (various versions found online). Kraków is an archaic possessive form (Polish) of Krak and essentially means "Krak's town".

Dragon Kings?

Mentioned briefly in the previous chapter, dragons were known to be lewd creatures that copulated with other animals.[30] There are even Asian mythical accounts of women bearing the offspring of dragons; several of which became known as dragon kings. Some European rulers and heroes, both mythical and historical, also claimed to be descended from dragons.[31] Now if these tales are based on historical events, then perhaps that would lend to the horrific reason why maidens in both (Eastern and Western) cultures were sacrificed to dragons for appeasement. Nevertheless, due to the lack of genetic evidence, to argue that dragons actually copulated with women is an argument in futility and will not be further entertained here.

What can be gathered from these tales is that human aggressive behavior was in some ways compared with a dragon's behavior. However, if *some* dragons were considered to have a "neutral behavior", as indicated in both the East and the West, then why are these violent men associated with dragons specifically? Perhaps it is also due to a dragon's "kingly" status among the animal kingdom. It is common knowledge that kings were associated with lions and other predatory animals too. It is therefore reasonable to conclude that cultures in the past compared human behavior to living *observable* creatures. The parallels between both cultures are intriguing and indicate that this particular association of dragon behavior with kings or heroic men and women is not an isolated cultural idea.

Two Heads are Deadlier than One

The evil *aždaja* (pronounced "azhdaya"), also known as the *hydra*, that lived in dark and adverse places, is often described as being multi-headed, having up to as many as nine heads! This creature is also reported to produce fire. This well known mythical multi-headed creature is also described in similar fashion in ancient Middle Eastern, Egyptian, and Asian accounts (i.e., the *näga*).

The first mention of a dragon in ancient Greece can be found in the Iliad. It describes Agamemnon as having an image of a three-headed dragon on his breastplate, not to mention another dragon motif on his belt. It is interesting to note at this point that the English word "dragon" is derived from the Greek δράκων (drákōn). The meaning is descriptive of a serpent of huge size or a very large water-snake. In addition, the word is associated with the Greek verb δρακεῖν (drakeîn), which means "to see clearly". Did not the Chinese indicate that some dragons could see very well?[32]

Like the hydra, Russian dragons had heads that grew back if every individual head was not cut off. One particular legendary Ukranian dragon-like creature, the

---
30. See Chapter 3, *Differentiations* section (Sie Chao-chi's "*Wuh Tsah Tsu*").
31. Some examples: Celtic PenDragons; Tuatha de Danaans; Vlad III Dracula; the dragon queens of Egypt.
32. Chapter 3, *Eagle Vision* section.

Zmey Gorynych, was green and had three heads. It could "breathe" fire and walked upright on two back legs, and had two smaller front arms. Other than the amount of heads, the physical description sounds strikingly similar to a theropod dinosaur (i.e. *Tyrannosaurus Rex or Allosaurus*). Multi-headed animals are rare in nature today, nevertheless, some creatures sport several heads (*bicephaly*) and live to maturity. Though the mythical tales of multi-headed dragons are often beyond belief, the fact remains that multi-headed creatures do indeed exist and should therefore at least give some credit to such a notion. Due to the fact that not all dragons are described as having multiple heads, and that such consistent descriptions are found throughout the world, perhaps there were several dragon types that existed that were prone to having bicephaly. Consider also the following quote from Aristotle, which perhaps gives an alternate view on how the multi-headed dragon came to be perceived.

> Long animals devoid of feet, like serpents and muraenae, intertwine in coition, belly to belly. And, in fact, serpents coil round one another so tightly as to *present the appearance of a single serpent with a pair of heads.* The same mode is followed by the saurians; that is to say, they coil round one another in the act of coition.[33]

Coat of Arms and Other Insignias

Demonstrated in DeVisser's book, *The Dragon in China and Japan,* Asian countries placed dragons on their military flags, clothing, and other regalia to represent the ruling authority and military power. The same is true for European nations. The main difference is that the graphic portrayals of dragons between the two regions are varied. To some extent, Asians seemed to focus on snake-like dragons while Europeans seemed to focus on flying dragons. The different kinds of represented dragon types is what one would expect from one geographic region to another since animals of all kinds have variances between them from one locale to another.

Take birds for instance. There are thousands of bird types and each is given a specific name. Though they vary significantly from one region to another (i.e. compare an ostrich to a hummingbird), we may refer to them all generically as birds. In like manner, a nation may take a certain animal as a form of symbolic emblem. For example, the bald eagle was chosen as the emblem of the United States due to its great strength and majestic appeal, as did ancient Rome. It is therefore reasonable for a multitude of nations, both in Asia and Europe, to choose particular dragons for their national emblems and coat of arms.

One example is the well-known story of St. George who (according to legend) killed a dragon. The *Golden Legend*[34] tells of a dragon that made its home near the

---
33. Aristotle, *Historia Animalium*, Book 5, section 4. (italics mine).
34. Jacobus de Voragine, *The Golden Legend* (Latin: *Legenda aurea*). A collection of hagiographies. 1260 A.D.

spring that provided water for the city of "Silene" (i.e., modern Cyrene in Libya?). In order to collect water, the people needed to subdue the dragon by means of offering it sheep. When they eventually ran out of sheep, they turned to offering maidens who were chosen by drawing lots. The story comes to a climax when Saint George fights and slays the dragon. This event has been represented on the coat of arms of Moscow since the 16th century.

Also, though not so well known, is the dragon of the city of Ljubljana (the capitol of Slovenia). The legendary account of *Jason and the Argonauts* tells of the this very dragon, that lived in the marshes around the city and of its ultimate demise by Jason. Due to the legendary battle, this particular dragon has been incorporated into the city's coat of arms.

Note that the city is a real place and the description of the surrounding landscape, along with the dragon, are described accordingly from the tale of the Argonauts. In addition, lending additional historical validity to this tale, "Some have hypothesized that the legend of the Golden Fleece was based on a practice of the Black Sea tribes; they would place a lamb's fleece at the bottom of a stream to entrap gold dust being washed down from upstream. This practice is still in use, particularly in the Svaneti region of Georgia."[35]

Another example would be the Welsh red dragon, *Y Ddraig Goch,* which is the symbol of their Government and is prominently displayed on the nation's flag. The initial (mythical) history behind it lies in a collection of eleven medieval Welsh (Cymry) manuscripts called the *Mabinogion*[36]; in particular, the story of Lludd and Llevelys. In the same manner as ancient Asian beliefs (that by seeing certain types of dragons and their behavior would be a prophetic sign, omen, or allegory regarding the nation or government), King Vortigern gained insight through the interpretation of two fighting dragons (red vs. white) observed in the immediate vicinity. Vortigern was told that the white dragon symbolized the Saxons and the red dragon symbolized Vortigern's people. Fortunately for the king, the red dragon defeated the invading white dragon, as were the invading Saxons defeated by Vortigern's army.

> The same story is repeated in Geoffrey of Monmouth's History of the Kings of Britain, where the red dragon is also a prophecy of the coming of King Arthur. It is notable that Arthur's father was Uther Pendragon ("chief dragon", erroneously translated by Geoffrey as "dragon's head").
>
> The Welsh Dragon appears on the national flag of Wales (the flag itself is also called "Y Ddraig Goch"). During the reigns of the Tudor monarchs, the red dragon was used as a supporter in the English crown's coat of arms (one of two supporters, along with the traditional English lion)...
>
> The Tudors' livery was white and green. As he marched his troops

---

35. *Greek Mythology - Heroes and Creatures.* (e-book) p. 145.
36. *Mabinogion,* translated by Lady Charlotte Guest in 1877.

through Wales to Bosworth, Henry Tudor – shortly to be Henry VII – flew the red dragon of Cadwallader, from whom he claimed ancestry, on the white and green Tudor colours. After the battle the flag was carried in state to St. Paul's Cathedral to be blessed. It was the beginning of the flag as we know it today.[37]

The Welsh flag is considered to be one of the oldest national flags in Europe.[38]

Anglo-Saxon Chronicles

Speaking of omens, consider the following historical records. Particularly note how the Anglo-Saxons, like the Asians, considered the appearance of dragons and impressive serpents as noteworthy or as omens of foreboding events.

> A.D. 774. This year the Northumbrians banished their king, Alred, from York at Easter-tide; and chose Ethelred, the son of Mull, for their lord, who reigned four winters. This year also appeared in the heavens a red crucifix, after sunset; the Mercians and the men of Kent fought at Otford; and wonderful serpents were seen in the land of the South-Saxons. ...
> A.D. 793. This year came dreadful fore-warnings over the land of the Northumbrians, terrifying the people most woefully: these were immense sheets of light rushing through the air, and whirlwinds, and fiery dragons flying across the firmament. These tremendous tokens were soon followed by a great famine: and not long after, on the sixth day before the ides of January in the same year, the harrowing inroads of heathen men made lamentable havoc in the church of God in Holy-island, by rapine and slaughter. Siga died on the eighth day before the calends of March.[39]

Dragon Slayers

In similar fashion to *Saint George and the Dragon*, there are many other historical people who were considered to be (mythical) dragon slayers throughout Europe. Though a few of these tales may be mere allegories based on Christian influences, some of the descriptions of dragons are consistent with other (cultural) descriptions. Besides, even allegories generally stem from actual things and events. To assign sainthood to someone who defeated a living dragon (an allegory to Jesus defeating Satan), would also be appropriate at that time.

The following are a few notable examples out of many:

---

37. Found online at: http://theresagreen.wordpress.com/tag/welsh-flag
38. Image compliments of welshflag.org.
39. *The Anglo Saxon Chronicle Part 2: A.D. 750 - 919. Online Medieval and Classical Library.*

Ragnar ("hairy-breeches") Lodbrok: A legendary Norse ruler known as the scourge of France and England during the ninth century. He rescued a princess by killing a large two-legged poisonous lindworm[40] (a theropod?) with a spear.

Saint Martha (first century):
> There was that time upon the river of Rhone, in a certain wood between Arles and Avignon [Southern France], a great dragon, half beast and half fish, greater than an ox, longer than an horse, having teeth sharp as a sword, and horned on either side, head like a lion, tail like a serpent, and defended him with two wings on either side, and could not be beaten with cast of stones ne with other armour, and was as strong as twelve lions or bears; which dragon lay hiding and lurking in the river, and perished them that passed by and drowned ships. He came thither by sea from Galicia, and was engendered of Leviathan, which is a serpent of the water and is much wood, and of a beast called Bonacho, that is engendered in Galicia. And when he is pursued he casts out of his belly behind, his ordure, the space of an acre of land on them that follow him, and it is bright as glass, and what it toucheth it burneth as fire. To whom Martha, at the prayer of the people, came into the wood, and found him eating a man. And she cast on him holy water, and showed to him the cross, which anon was overcome, and standing still as a sheep, she bound him with her own girdle, and then was slain with spears and glaives of the people. The dragon was called of them that dwelled in the country Tarasconus, whereof, in remembrance of him that place is called Tarasconus, which tofore was called Nerluc, and the Black Lake, because there be woods shadowous and black.[41]

The cross that Martha bore, if golden or shiny, may have indeed had a mesmerizing effect on the dragon, enough for Martha to accomplish her feat. The reasoning here is that since some dragons are reported (cross-culturally) to hoard and protect treasure (similar to rats), then they may have had some affinity to shiny objects, or at least easily distracted by such. Unfortunately, since this tale does not adequately describe the cross that Martha used, it is impossible to gain support in this case for such a conjectural possibility. In spite of this, as a side note, there is another account that supports the widespread (cross-cultural) notion that dragons were enticed by golden-colored things. Consider the following quote from a pamphlet entitled (briefly) *True and Wonderfull*; "... Elian reports, that there was (a man who kept oxen, and) a dragon fell in love with, for his yellow hair, which seemed in its amiable color to resemble gold; and often came creeping unto him like an amorous lover, licking his hair and face so gently, as the man professed he never felt the like."[42]

Note that the dragon Tarasconus, other than the physical description that is similar to Asian depictions, did not "breathe fire", but produced a shiny substance that burned upon touch. This indicates that it may have been acidic in composition or a

---
40. aka: *Lindorm*, or "lindon tree serpent", so called for its habit of laying eggs at the base of a lindon tree.
41. See *The Golden Legend - The Life of Saint Martha*. Compiled by Jacobus de Voragine. Text in brackets mine.
42. *True and Wonderfull...*, by A.R. 1614. Parenthesis mine - for brevity.

substance that caused a chemical burn, possibly emitted from glands like a pangolin or skunk.[43]

Saint Beatus of Lungern (aka: Beatus of Beatenberg) (2nd century): The coat of arms of Beatenberg, depicts him fighting a dragon that he encountered in a cave.

Saint Crescentinus (died 303 AD): He is considered to have been a Roman soldier who converted to Christianity. After killing a dragon in the Umbria region of Italy, he had successfully evangelized the region along with his companions.

Saint Donatus of Arezzo (mid 300 AD): He reportedly fought and killed a dragon that poisoned a well in the vicinity of Arezzo, Italy.

Saint Clement of Metz (late 3rd century): He vanquished a dragon (called "Graoully") from the local Roman amphitheater. The inhabitants of the town felt trapped due to the poisonous breath of the beast, along with the many snakes with it. The local inhabitants agreed to convert to Christianity if Saint Clement would rid them of the dragon. After doing so however, King Orius did not keep his promise to convert to Christianity. Though later, when the king's daughter died, Saint Clement brought her back from the dead, which compelled the king to convert.

Saint Mercurialis (died 406 AD): As the first bishop of the city of Forli (Italy), he saved the city by slaying a dragon.

Saint Veran (6th century): A village in the French Alps is named after him. Saint Veran was a Bishop who, according to legend, drove out a dragon, and by doing so caused the superstitious pagans to accept Christianity.

Saint Leonard of Noblac (or of Limousin) (485-559 AD): During his fight with a dragon, St. Leonard became injured and his blood spilled on the ground in a forested area where Lilies of the Valley still grow today (the flowers are often linked with this tale). Though at that time it was considered to be the last dragon in England, dragons were still being seen and reported around the country. For instance, *Ethelward's*[44] *Chronicle*[45] (770 AD) states that "Monstrous serpents were seen in the country of the Southern Angles that is called Sussex".

---

43. See Appendix B.
44. Ethelward (aka Æthelweard), (died 998 AD) An Anglo-Saxon historian, who was descended from King Æthelred I (brother of Alfred the Great), and was the earl of the western provinces.
45. J. A. Giles, *Old English Chronicles.* George Bell & Sons. London. 1906. p. 18.

The Serpents of Sussex and the Chinese Connection

Apparently dragons lived (at least) in Sussex, England, for quite some time. Not only were they documented in *Ethelward's Chronicle*, but centuries later, in August 1614, a pamphlet was published with the following lengthy title; *"True and Wonderfull: A Discourse relating a strange and monstrous Serpent (or Dragon) lately discovered, and yet living, to the great annoyance and divers slaughters both of men and cattell, by his strong and violent Poyson: in Sussex, two miles from Horsam, in a woode called St. Leonards Forrest, and thirtie miles from London, this present month of August, 1614."*[46] The description of the "monstrous serpent" is strikingly similar to Asian sightings of the *kiao*[47]; particularly the white neck-ring and the shape of the scaly body. Here is the main portion of the pamphlet:

To THE READER.
  The just reward of him that is accustomed to lie, is not, to be believed when he speaketh the truth: so just an occasion may sometimes be imposed upon the pamphleting pressers; and therefore, if we receive the same reward, we cannot much blame our accusers, which often falls out either by our forward credulity to but-seeming true reports, or by false copies translated from other languages, which (though we beget not) we foster, and our shame is little the less. But, passing by what's past, let not our present truth blush for any former falsehood sake: the country is near us, Sussex; the time present, August; the subject, a Serpent; strange, yet now a neighbour to us; and it were more than impudence to forge a lie so near home, that every man might turn in our throats; believe it, or read it not, or read it (doubting) for I believe ere thou hast read this little all, thou wilt not doubt of one, but believe there are many serpents in England. Farewell.
By A. R.
He that would send better news, if he had it.

A DISCOURSE
A STRANGE AND MONSTROUS SERPENT OR DRAGON.

  In Sussex, there is a pretty market-town called Horsham, near unto it a forest, called St. Leonards forest, and there, in a vast and unfrequented place, heathy, vaulty, full of unwholesome shades, and overgrown hollows, where this serpent is thought to be bred ; but, wheresoever bred, certain and too true it is that there it yet lives.
  Within three or four miles compass are its usual haunts, oftentimes at a place called Faygate, and it hath been seen within half a mile of Horsham, a wonder, no doubt, most terrible and noisome to the inhabitants thereabouts. There is always in his track or path left a glutinous and slimy matter (as by a small similitude we may perceive in a snail's) which is very corrupt and offensive to the scent, insomuch that they perceive the air to be putrified

---
46. *True and Wonderfull...*, by A.R. 1614. Text modernized in areas for clarity.
47. See: *Detailed Descriptions* section in chapter 3.

withal, which must needs be very dangerous.

For though the corruption of it cannot strike the outward part of a man, unless heated into his blood, yet by receiving it in at any of our breathing organs (the mouth or nose) it is by authority of all authors, writing in that kind, mortal and deadly, as one thus saith:

Noxia serpentum est admixto sanguine pestis. -Lucan

The serpent, or dragon, as some call it, is reputed to be nine feet, or rather more, in length, and shaped almost in the form of an axletree of a cart, a quantity of thickness in the midst, and somewhat smaller at both ends. The former part, which he shoots forth as a neck, is supposed to be an ell long, with a white ring, as it were, of scales about it.

The scales along his back seem to be blackish, and so much as is discovered under his belly appeareth to be red; for I speak of no nearer description than of a reasonable occular distance.

For coming too near it hath already been too dearly paid for, as you shall hear hereafter. It is likewise discovered to have large feet, but the eye may be there deceived; for some suppose that serpents have no feet, but glide upon certain ribs and scales, which both defend them from the upper part of their throat unto the lower part of their belly, and also cause them to move much the faster.

For so this doth, and rids way, as we call it as fast as a man can run. He is of countenance very proud, and, at the sight or hearing of men or cattle, will raise his neck upright, and seem to listen and look about, with arrogancy. There are likewise on either side of him discovered two great bunches so big as a large foot-ball, and, as some think, will in time grow to wings ; but God, I hope, will defend the poor people in the neighbourhood, that he shall be destroyed before he grow so fledged.

He will cast his venom about four rod from him, as by woeful experience it was proved on the bodies of a man and woman coming that way, who afterwards were found dead, being poisoned and very much swelled, but not preyed upon.

Likewise a man going to chase it and, as he imagined, to destroy it, with two mastiff dogs, as yet not knowing the great danger of it, his dogs were both killed, and he himself glad to return with haste to preserve his own life. Yet this is to be noted, that the dogs were not preyed upon, but slain and left whole; for his food is thought to be, for the most part, in a cony-warren, (rabbit warren) which he much frequents, and it is found much scanted and impaired in the increase it had wont to afford.

These persons, whose names are hereunder printed, have seen this serpent, beside divers others, as the carrier of Horsham, who lieth at the White Horse, in South wark, and who can certify the truth of all that has been here related.

John Steele.
Christopher Holder.
And a Widow Woman dwelling near Faygate.

To press the point of reporting consistency; the Western *"True and Wonderfull"* pamphlet described a creature that had features specific to the Chinese dragon called the *kiao* 蛟, as described by several ancient documents; the *P'i ya* 埤雅, the *P'ei yuen kwang cheu ki* 裴淵廣州記, and the *Mih k'oh hwui si* 黑客揮犀. Thus, there are two separate yet consistent cultural descriptions of a particular extinct creature that:

a) had 4 legs
b) was reptilian / scaly
c) was larger than a man
d) had a long thin neck and tail with thicker body
e) had a white ring around its neck – like a necklace
f) had a dark colored ("blackish" or blue) back
g) had a red colored breast
h) used a type of venom to subdue its victim
i) both cultures classified it as a dragon (Chinese = "*lung*" 龍)

Bearded Dragons

Due to modern media and entrenched contemporary ideas, Western people today only view dragons as completely reptilian, having no hair. Yet as has already been pointed out, dragons were described repeatedly in eyewitness accounts as being chimera-like, having not only armored scales but could have flesh-like skin and hair as well. Though Asian dragon art reflects this almost universally (a hairy head), Western dragon art does not. Despite this, there are indeed Western accounts that describe dragons as having hair.

> Beyond the Oasis of Egypt there is a great desert which extends for seven days' journey, succeeded by a region inhabited by the Cynoprosopi, on the way to Aethiopia. These live by the chase of goats and antelopes. They are black, with the head and teeth of a dog, of which animal, in this connection, the mention is not to be looked upon as absurd, for they lack the power of speech, and utter a shrill hissing sound, and have a beard above and below the mouth *like a dragon*; their hands are armed with strong and sharp nails, and the body is equally hairy with that of dogs. (Book X, chapter 25)
>
> The masculine sex also seems to be privileged by nature among brutes, inasmuch as the male dragon is distinguished by a crest and hairs, with a beard. (Book XII, chapter 26)[48]

The Piasa (aka: Piasa Bird) was a North American dragon that was depicted in a mural painted by Native Americans on a limestone cliff in Illinois above the Mississippi river. While exploring in 1673, Father Jacques Marquette was perhaps the first European to see the paintings of the Piasa. He wrote down the following

---

48. Aelian, Claudii. *De Natura Animalium.* English translation via: Charles Gould. *Mythical Monsters.* Appendix II, pp. 379, 382. (See Appendix D for reference discrepancies). Italics added for emphasis.

description which not only included a beard, but had other physical similarities to other dragons throughout the Eurasian continent.

> While Skirting some rocks, which by their height and length inspired awe, we saw upon one of them two painted monsters which at first made us afraid, and upon which the boldest savages dare not long rest their eyes. They are as large as a calf; they have horns on their heads like those of a deer, a horrible look, red eyes, *a beard like a tiger's*, a face somewhat like a man's, a body covered with scales, and so long a tail that it winds all around the body, passing above the head and going back between the legs, ending in a fish's tail. Green, red, and black are the three colors composing the picture. Moreover, these two monsters are so well painted that we cannot believe that any savage is their author; for good painters in France would find it difficult to reach that place conveniently to paint them. Here is approximately the shape of these monsters, as we have faithfully copied it.[49]

The original Piasa graphic that was described no longer exists. Several versions have been made over the centuries however, and the current image is several hundred yards away from the original site. As demonstrated above, the initial report of the Piasa did not include wings. The idea that the creature was some type of bird seems to have been a creative (and "somewhat illustrated") addition by John Russell,[50] which gave rise to the common belief that the Piasa was a type of bird instead of a flightless dragon.

Divination and Superstition

Again, like the Asians, dragons were sometimes associated with divination practices, albeit through a culturally different method.

> There is a peculiar divination of the dragon, for in Lavinium, a town of the Latins but in Lavinium, there is a large and dense sacred grove, and near it the shrine of the Argolic Juno. Within the grove is a cave and deep den, the lair of a dragon.
> Sacred virgins enter this grove on stated days, who carry a barley cake in their hands, with bandaged eyes. A certain divine afflatus leads them accurately to the den, and gently, and step by step, they proceed without hindrance, and as if their eyes were uncovered. If they are virgins, the dragon admits the food as pure and fit for a deity.
>
> If otherwise, it does not touch it, perceiving and divining them to be impure.[51]

---

49. *The Journal of Père Jacques Marquette*. Section 7.
50. William McAdams. *Records of Ancient Races in the Mississippi Valley*. See chapter 2.
51. Aelian, Claudii. *De Natura Animalium*. Book XII, chapter 16. Cited by Gould. pp.381,382. (See Appendix D).

Eating Habits

In his work *Historia Animalium* (The History of Animals), Aristotle wrote down two separate accounts of what dragons eat. "The sheatfish (a very large catfish) is destroyed in great quantities in shallow waters by the serpent called the dragon."[52] And, "The dragon, when it eats fruit, swallows endive-juice; it has been seen in the act."[53]

Also, in Claudius Aelian's work, *De Natura Animalium*, two accounts were given as to a dragon's eating habits. Notice how these African dragons ate birds like those in Asia.

> Aethiopia generates dragons reaching thirty paces long; they have no proper name, but they merely call them slayers of elephants, and they attain a great age. So far do the Aethiopian accounts narrate. The Phrygian history also states that dragons are born which reach ten paces in length[54]; which daily in midsummer, at the hour when the forum is full of men in assembly, are wont to proceed from their caverns, and [near the river Rhyndacus], with part of the body on the ground, and the rest erect, with the neck gently stretched out, and gaping mouth, attract birds, either by their inspiration, or by some fascination, and that those which are drawn down by the inhalation of their breath glide down into their stomach--[and that they continue this until sunset,] but that after that, concealing themselves, they lay in ambush for the herds returning from the pasture to the stable, and inflict much injury, often killing the herdsmen and gorging themselves with food. (BOOK II, chapter 21)
>
> When dragons are about to eat fruit they suck the juice of the wild chicory, because this affords them a sovereign remedy against inflation. When they purpose lying in wait for a man or a beast, they eat deadly roots and herbs; a thing not unknown to Homer, for he makes mention of the dragon, who, lingering and twisting himself in front of his den, devoured noxious herbs. (BOOK VI, chapter 4)

Dragon Scales and Dragon Tales

Many claim the following account to be nothing more than a description of a crocodile (or alligator), despite the fact that crocodiles can be easily killed by arrows which can pierce their armored spines. Though the noted crest is the same as other eyewitness descriptions of male dragons (previously mentioned), a crested crocodile has yet to be discovered. Besides, if a crocodile was being described, then why not use that word (*Latin: crocodīlus*, already in use at that time) instead of "dragon"? Also consider the Biblical passages describing dragons (leviathan) as having impenetrable scales (See Appendix C).

---

52. Aristotle, *Historia Animalium*, Book 8, section 20.
53. Aristotle, *Historia Animalium*, Book 9, section 6.
54. 10 paces is about 25 to 50 feet, depending on variant measurement equivalents (i.e. 30 inches or 5 feet).

In these times (1405 AD), close to the town of Bures, near Sudbury, has appeared a disaster for the country, a dragon, with a huge body, a crested head, serrated teeth and a very long tail. After having killed a shepherd the dragon killed many sheep. The men of the lord, Richard Waldegrave, the knight of the domain in which the dragon had appeared, then came out to shoot at the dragon with arrows. The dragon's body was unhurt, however, despite being hit by arrows that bounced off his back as if it were iron or hard rock. The arrows that hit the spine of his back gave a ringing or chiming sound as they hit, as if they had hit a burning plate, and then fell down; the hide of this enormous beast being impenetrable. Then, in order to destroy the dragon, all the country was summoned. And when the dragon saw that he was to be attacked by arrows again, he fled into a marsh and hid himself among the long reeds and was never seen again.[55]

A completely different account, occurring centuries earlier, describes the same scaly feature. Either the Roman army had blunt arrows for warfare (which was not the case), or the scales were stronger than a common python or "adder". True, the creature described in the following tale apparently had no legs, so it was either an unusually enormous snake or it was a true serpent. Note that the largest snake ever discovered in the fossil record is the *Gigantophis garstini*, found coincidentally in North Africa. This snake reached about 33 feet, and was related to the (smaller) modern pythons. If the largest snake ever discovered in history was only 33 feet, then the serpent described in this tale was a different creature due to its size and impenetrable armor.

... Regulus undertook the war against Carthage, and whilst he was encamped near a river, called Bagrada, an immense adder came out of the water, and all those who approached the river where killed by this adder. On this Regulus collected all the archers of his army, that they might destroy the serpent; but when they shot at him, the arrows glanced over his scales, as if they were made of smooth iron. Then Regulus ordered that they should try to transfix the monster with a balista (which they demolish walls with during a siege) and this struck the serpent on one of its ribs, so as to break it, after which the monster could make no defense, but was easily killed; because it is the nature of the adder-kind, that their strength and confidence is in their ribs, as it is in the feet of other creeping worms. When the monster was thus slain, Regulus directed it to be stuffed, and sent the skin to Rome, where being extended to its full length, on account of its singularity, it was found to measure 88 feet.[56]

The following 15th Century chronicle (the manuscript is currently located at Canterbury Cathedral's library) took place near a marsh region and the river Stour (near the village of Little Cornard). Today, many claim that this is merely an allegorical tale that actually relates two opposing armies that waged a battle. However, the account

---

55. *Chronica et Annales*, by John de Trokelowe and Henry de Blaneford. Translated and reproduced in the *Rolls Series*. 1866. ed. H.T. Riley. p. 402. Quoted text modified (for clarity) from various public sources.
56. *The Anglo-Saxon Version of the Historian Orosius.* Alfred (King of England). 1773. pp. 142, 143.

appears to be more of a practical description instead of allegory and is written as a short memorandum (of an unusual, albeit noteworthy event) amongst other historical events. Besides, it was witnessed (among other town folk) by two of the most respected Englishmen of the time: John Steel and Christopher Holder.

> Memorandum that on Friday the 26th of September in the year of our Lord 1449, about the hour of Vespers, two terrible dragons were seen fighting for about the space of one hour, on two hills, of which one, in Suffolk, is called Kydyndon Hyl (Kedington Hill) and the other in Essex Blacdon Hyl (Ballingdon Hill). One was black in colour and the other reddish and spotted. After a long conflict the reddish one obtained the victory over the black, which done, both returned into the hills above whence they had come, that is to say, each to his own place to the admiration of many beholding them.[57]

Ulysses Aldrovandus, a famous naturalist of his time, described an eyewitness encounter between an Italian farmer and a small dragon. He obtained the small carcass, documented and illustrated it in his book, and (allegedly) had the dragon mounted and placed in a museum in 1592. The following is a translation of the described encounter.

> On May 13, 1572, a dragon was encountered that made a kind of whistling or hissing sound. It had been hiding on the estate of Master Petronius which was near Dosius in a place named Maonolta. Later, at about 5:00 pm. the dragon was encountered again by a man named Baptist of Camaldulo on a public highway about a mile away. Baptist was following his ox cart when his oxen suddenly came to a halt. Though he kicked and shouted at them, the oxen got down on their knees out of fear and refused to advance. He then heard the great hissing sound of the dragon and was startled by the sight. In a panic, Baptist immediately struck the dragon on the head with his rod and killed it.[58]

Many suggest that the dragon could have been a *tanystropheus*. However, the illustration of the bipedal creature (shown in Aldrovandus' work) does not entirely match the proposed long-necked quadruped in the fossil record, though it could have been a type of cousin.

A similar creature (cousin candidate?) that resembles the *tanystropheus* more closely was presented near the end of Ulysses' work. It was a long necked quadruped with wing-like appendages. (**Figure 8, C**) This same creature (and variants) was also shown in Athanasius Kircher's book *Mundus Subterraneus* (1678). Similar dragons were shown in Edward Topsell's *The History of Four-footed Beasts and Serpents* (1658), and Pierre Belon's serpent illustration (not shown).[59]

---

57. Roger Frith: *Dragons in Essex*, in *The East Anglian Magazine*, Vol.21 (Nov.1961-Oct.1962), pp.523-4. Text in parenthesis added for clarity. Cited also in: *Folklore, Myths and Legends of Britain*, Contributors: Geoffrey Ashe, et al., Reader's Digest, 1973, p. 241.
58. Ulysses Aldrovandus, *Serpentum, et Draconum Historiae libri duo*. 1640. p. 402, 403, with drawing on p. 404. (Translation mine). Also see Appendix D, #3 *Clarification*.
59. Pierre Belon, *Portraits d'oyseaux, animaux, serpens, herbes, arbres, hommes et femmes d'Arabie et d'Egypte*. p. 109. His serpent is similar to "B" in fig. 8, but is claimed to be found near Mt. Sinai (Egypt / Arabia).

An interesting theory about these wing-like appendages was presented by James Edward Gilmer, Ph.D. in his book entitled *100 Year Cover-Up Revealed*. He suggested that the undersized wing-like appendages shown on the dragon illustrations were not wings at all but were used in a similar fashion as a frilled dragon lizard does today (aggression, mating, etc.). The frills of the frilled dragon seem to be similar in structure and appearance as those in Ulysses' illustrations. Many ancient flightless dragons sporting these wing-like frills were perhaps confused with dragons that could fly since they had similar looking bat-like wings.

Figure 8: Comparison of dragons reported by Ulysses Aldrovandus and Athanasius Kircher.
A) Bipedal dragon [like two legged lizards today]. B) Draco Aethiopicus; "Ethiopian dragon". C) Dragon.

In his work mentioned above, Athanasius Kircher devoted a whole chapter (*De Draconibus Subterraneis*) to dragons. Some of his descriptions were of dragons that lived in caves, like the dragon of Rhodes island.

... The dragon "had a head shaped like that of a large horse, but was wide like a cow's head. The head was scaled like a snake's, and was situated at the end of a long neck... It's *[sic]* horrific gaping mouth was outfitted with massive teeth; it had oversized eyes, breath which burned like fire, and four feet with claws like those of a bear. Its tail and other hind parts were similar to those of a crocodile. The entire body was well-protected by an extremely tough hide of overlapping scale; it had two membranous wings..." When alarmed and running, the creature "seemed partly to fly, and partly to go about on its feet..."

... It had "membranous wings" (bat-like) that it apparently used for speed when alarmed and running on the ground, which suggests another possible function of the bat-like undersized wings... Furthermore, ... the dragon had breath that "burned like fire." Here the reporter does not embellish and make the metaphoric leap to say the dragon breathed fire. Instead, he uses a more credible simile, comparing the heat of its breath to that of fire.[60]

Polo's Serpent Resurfaces

The Nordic saga, *The Story of the Völsungs*, describes how Sigurd killed a dragon named Fafnir in a similar manner as the Chinese, though much more courageously! Note the similarity from Marco Polo's account in relation to how Fafnir dragged his body to the water making an impression in the ground, also how Regin tries to downplay the size of the dragon in order to encourage Sigurd to go slay it.

> Regin answered, "Fafnir is his name, and but a little way hence he lies, on the waste of Gnita-heath; and when thou comest there thou mayst well say that thou hast never seen more gold heaped together in one place, and that none might desire more treasure, though he were the most ancient and famed of all kings."
> "Young am I," says Sigurd, "yet know I the fashion of this worm, and how that none durst go against him, so huge and evil is he."
> Regin said, "Nay it is not so, the fashion and the growth of him is even as of other lingworms, and an over great tale men make of it; ... (chapter XIII)
>
> ... But when Sigurd had been at home but a little, came Regin to talk with him, and said--
> "Belike thou wilt now have good will to bow down Fafnir's crest according to thy word plighted, since thou hast thus revenged thy father and the others of thy kin." ... (chapter XVII)
>
> Now Sigurd and Regin ride up the heath along that same way wherein Fafnir was wont to creep when he fared to the water; and folk say that thirty fathoms was the height of that cliff along which he lay when he drank of the water below. Then Sigurd spake: "How sayedst thou, Regin, that this drake was

---

60. James Edward Gilmer, Ph.D. *100 Year Cover-Up Revealed – We Lived With Dinosaurs!* p. 50.

no greater than other lingworms; methinks the track of him is marvellous great?"

Then said Regin, "Make thee a hole, and sit down therein, and whenas the worm comes to the water, smite him into the heart, and so do him to death, and win thee great fame thereby."

Now crept the worm down to his place of watering, and the earth shook all about him, and he snorted forth venom on all the way before him as he went; but Sigurd neither trembled nor was adrad at the roaring of him. So whenas the worm crept over the pits, Sigurd thrust his sword under his left shoulder, so that it sank in up to the hilts; then up leapt Sigurd from the pit and drew the sword back again unto him, and therewith was his arm all bloody, up to the very shoulder.

Now when that mighty worm was ware that he had his death-wound, then he lashed out head and tail, so that all things so ever that were before him were broken to pieces. (chapter XVIII)[61]

A particular Danish account also describes a large and powerful serpent creature that dragged its body along the ground. In like manner, this creature was killed by means of piercing the underbelly due to its impenetrable scaly hide.

Fridleif... set forth on his voyage; and his fleet being becalmed, he invaded some villages to look for food... but, while going back to his own country, he had a bad voyage, and was driven on the shores of an unknown island. A certain man appeared to him in a vision, and instructed him to dig up a treasure that was buried in the ground, and also to attack the dragon that guarded it... Therefore, to test the vision, he attacked the snake as it rose out of the waves, and for a long time cast spears against its scaly side; in vain, for its hard and shelly body foiled the darts flung at it. But the snake, shaking its mass of coils, uprooted the trees which it brushed past by winding its tail about them. Moreover, by constantly dragging its body, it hollowed the ground down to the solid rock, and had made a sheer bank on either hand, just as in some places we see hills parted by an intervening valley. So Fridleif, seeing that the upper part of the creature was proof against attack, assailed the lower side with his sword, and piercing the groin, drew blood from the quivering beast. When it was dead, he unearthed the money from the underground chamber and had it taken off in his ships.[62]

Beowulf

Many today believe that the ancient epic poem *Beowulf* is nothing more than an allegorical work of fiction influenced by Christianity. This common belief does not coincide with the facts however. The poem was written before the Christianization of the Saxons and Danes. The mention of God, creation, and Cain are also found in other pre-Christian works and Saxon genealogies. The historical validity of this purely

---
61. *The Story of the Volsungs, (Volsunga Saga) - With Excerpts from the Poetic Edda.* Project Gutenberg. Anonymous. 2009. Text based from William Morris and Eirikr Magnusson's translation. 1888.
62. Saxo Grammaticus, *The Danish History, Books I-IX.* Late 12th–Early 13th Century A.D., Book six.

pagan account has been established by many scholars, not to mention the accuracy of personal names and genealogy. None of the features poetically expressed in Beowulf (i.e., burial of king Scyld, descriptions of armor, etc.) are without archeological parallel either. The *Sutton Hoo*[63] discovery is one prime example. In other words, *Beowulf* is a reasonably reliable historical account. (To establish these claims in further detail is beyond the scope of this book and can be found in other scholarly works.[64] It is also assumed here that the reader is familiar with the tale.)

Beowulf provides (arguably more than any other single ancient manuscript) a great amount of information regarding an extensive variety of large reptilian creatures inhabiting Denmark. Also keep in mind that the Anglo-Saxon language at that time had a simplistic method of word construction. For example, a body was called a bone-house (*banhus*), and the sun was called a world-candle (*woruldcandel*). Likewise, the word for serpent was worm-kind (*wyrmcynnes*, or more generic as *wyrmas*), and sea dragons were called sea-drakes (*saedracan*). Other creatures that are mentioned were known as a *nicor*, which later developed into knucker, a Middle English word for a water dwelling dragon, and where we get knucker hole (a dragon cave). A surface-swimming creature was called a *ythgewinnes*, which meant wave-thrasher. "...[this] would explain the ease with which the creature was harpooned from the shore of the mere [by Beowulf and his men]. It is also probably the *ythgewinnes* whose likeness was portrayed so often on the prow of Viking ships... [having] the very practical purpose of deterring other wave-thrashers from attacking the vessel."[65]

Many readers of *Beowulf* would agree that the most memorable monster described was (the) Grendel. In light of the naming conventions above, Grendel was the name given to a specific species of animal, not a personal name (i.e. how we give our pets names).

> This is evidenced by the fact that in the year AD 931, King Athelstan of Wessex issued a charter in which a certain lake in Wiltshire (England) is called (as in Denmark) a *grendles mere*. The Grendel in Beowulf, we note with interest, also lived in a mere. Other place-names mentioned in old charters, *Grindles bec* and *Grendeles pyt*, for example, were likewise places that were (or had been) the habitats of this particular species of animal. Grindelwald, lit. Grendelwood, in Switzerland is another such place. But where does the name Grendel itself come from?
>
> There are several Anglo-Saxon words that share the same root as Grendel. The Old English word *grindan*, for example, and from which we derive our word *grind*, used to denote a destroyer. But the most likely origin of the name is simply the fact that Grendel is an onomatopoeic term derived from the Old Norse *grindill*, meaning a storm or *grenja*, meaning to bellow. The

---

63. *Sutton Hoo* (in Suffolk county, England): a site of two 6th- and early 7th-century cemeteries. One is an undisturbed ship burial containing many Anglo-Saxon archaeological significant artefacts.
64. Suggested reading: *After the Flood*, by Bill Cooper. See Chapter 11, and Appendix 9 "The Historical Characters of Beowulf".
65. Bill Cooper, *After the Flood*. p. 161.

word Grendel is strongly reminiscent of the deepthroated growl that would be emitted by a very large animal and it came into Middle English usage as *grindel*, meaning angry.

To the hapless Danes who were the victims of his predatory raids, however, Grendel was not just an animal. To them he was demon-like, one who was *synnum beswenced* (afflicted with sins). He was *godes ansaca* (God's adversary), the *synscatha* (evil-doer) who was *wonsaeli* (damned), a very *feond on helle* (devil in hell)! He was one of the *grund-wyrgen*, accursed and murderous monsters who were said by the Danes to be descended from Cain himself. And it is descriptions such as these of Grendel's nature that convey something of the horror with which the men of those times anticipated his raids on their homesteads.[66]

The narrative hints that the "otherworldly" Grendel was bipedal since the two creatures described [female ("mother") and male ("son")], were said to have a human-like shape, but twisted, and far larger than a man. Grendel also had an impenetrable hide (a type of scale armor in other words), which was the main reason why the Danes were not able to kill Grendel with common weapons. Grendel was also a very stealthy night stalker that quickly devoured its prey with its jaws. The speed at which Grendel was able to eat its victims indicated that the mouth was of considerable size! When Beowulf fought Grendel, he managed to tear off Grendel's entire arm, which was fatal to the young beast.

If Grendel was larger than a man and more powerful, yet Beowulf was able to break off its arm, then this would indicate that Grendel's arm was the monster's weak point. It should be obvious for those familiar with dinosaur kinds that Grendel could easily fit the description of a theropod (a bipedal dinosaur with small arms). One only needs to look at a *tyrannosaur* skeleton in particular (bipedal, oversized head and jaws, with undersized arms) to see the similarities with Grendel and realize that the description is of a plausible creature.

The poetic saga indicated that the last creature to be killed by Beowulf "was a flying reptile which lived on a promontory overlooking the sea at Hronesness on the southern coast of Sweden."[67] The Saxons called this flying creature a *widfloga* (a far-ranging flyer) and also referred to it as a *ligdraca* (fire-dragon). This fire-drake was described as having a poisonous bite (which killed Beowulf), along with the ability of "breathing" fire (ruining a warrior's shield). It was thought to be hundreds of years old and about 50 feet long (wing span?). Consider the following selected passages describing this particular creature.

> The dragon came raging wildly, seeking his enemies with hot-gleaming fire. With blazing breath he burned the wooden shield to its edges: The armor failed then to furnish any protection to the youthful spear-wielding

---
66. Bill Cooper, *After the Flood.* pp. 153-154.
67. Bill Cooper, *After the Flood.* p. 152.

> hero; but the young man quickly advanced beneath his kinsman's shield, since his own had been ground in the grip of the fire...
>
> The fierce-raging fire-drake charged on the strong one, and when chance was afforded, seized on his neck with teeth that were bitter...
>
> The wound then began to burn and to swell from the dragon's bite. Beowulf quickly realized that he had been poisoned...
>
> They saw the dragon in front of them lying in the field like a worm. Their great foe was dead before them; that fire-spewing dragon. Ghost-like and grisly were his terrors. As he lay there he measured fifty feet.[68]

Like other accounts, this flying dragon also hoarded treasure taken from its victims and kept it in its cavernous lair.

> Sparkling golden treasure was spread on the bottom of the worm-creature's cavern. The ancient dawn-flyer had gathered vessels and cups of the ancients; he robbed them of their ornaments. There were helmets in numbers, old and rust-eaten, and many arm-bracelets that were artfully woven...
> Within his den the dragon died. He would enjoy no other earth-hollowed caverns. There stood round about him beakers and vessels; dishes were lying alongside valuable weapons, the iron implements rusting away, as in earth's mighty bosom a thousand winters there they had rested.[69]

Modern scholars claim that this description of the *lyftfloga* is nothing more than a poetic means to describe a comet. The details given in the epic, however, do not afford such an inconsistent notion. Why would a comet *live in a cavern*, or why would several men need to put forth *physical effort* to push the dragon's dead carcass over a cliff wall to discard it via the sea? ("the dragon eke (with great effort) pushed they, the worm o'er the wall, let the wave-currents take him") On the other hand, paleontologists surmise that the pteranodon/pterodactyl species (that are similar i size described in Beowulf) lived along coastline cliffs in nooks and caves.

The West Describes Dragons in the East

In approximately 217 AD, Flavius Philostratus described the various dragons[70] found throughout India. These descriptions are strikingly consistent with many others. Note the mention of 'dragontites' and how dragons were considered to have mystical powers, among other *familiar* physical features (i.e., beards and protruding

---
68. Reference: *Beowulf - an Anglo-Saxon Epic Poem*, by Lesslie Hall, Ph.D., Translated from the Heyne-Socin text. D.C. Heath & Co., 1892. (text updated for clarity - i.e., translation mine)
69. *Ibid.*
70. Dragon = δράκων, [drákōn]. Flavius Philostratus = Greek: Φλάβιος Φιλόστρατος.

eyebrows, like Asian dragons). In addition, Philostratus noted that the age of a dragon was not easily determined, alluding to (as did the Chinese) the potential of great age, as well as the benefits of killing such dangerous creatures.

> And the statements by Nearchus and Pythagoras, about the river Acesines, to the effect that it debauches into the Indus, and that snakes breed in it seventy cubits long, were, they say, fully verified by them (Apollonios of Tyana, a 1st century pagan prophet, and Damis); but I will defer what I have to say till I come to speak about dragons, on whose capture Damis gives an account.[71]

> Now as they descended the mountain (Caucasus), they say they (Apollonios and Damis) came in for a dragon hunt, which I must needs describe. For it is utterly absurd for those who are amateurs of hare-hunting to spin yarns about the hare as to how it is caught or ought to be caught, and yet that we should omit to describe a chase as bold as it is wonderful, and in which the sage was careful to assist; so I have written the following account of it:
> The whole of India is girt with dragons of enormous size; for not only the marshes are full of them, but the mountains as well, and there is not a single ridge without one. Now the marsh kind are sluggish in their habits and are thirty cubits long, and they have no crest standing up on their heads, but in this respect resemble the she-dragons. Their backs however are very black, with fewer scales on them than the other kinds; and Homer has described them with deeper insight than have most poets, for he says that the dragon that lived hard by the spring in *Aulis* had a tawny back (*Iliad* 2.308); but other poets declare that the congener of this one in the grove of Nemea also had a crest, a feature which we could not verify in regard to the marsh dragons.
> And the dragons along the foothills and the mountain crests make their way into the plains after their quarry, and get the better all round of those in the marshes; for indeed they reach a greater length, and move faster than the swiftest rivers, so that nothing escapes them. These actually have a crest, of moderate extent and height when they are young; but as they reach their full size, it grows with them and extends to a considerable height, at which time also they turn red and get serrated backs. This kind also have beards, and lift their necks on high, while their scales glitter like silver; and the pupils of their eyes consist of a fiery stone, and they say that this has an uncanny power for many secret purposes. The plain specimen falls the prize of the hunters whenever it draws into its folds an elephant; for the destruction of both creatures is the result, and those who capture the dragons are rewarded by getting the eyes and skin and teeth. In most respects the tusks resemble the largest swine's, but they are slighter in build and twisted (flexible), and have a point as unabraded as sharks' teeth.
> Now the dragons of the mountains have scales of a golden color, and in length excel those of the plain, and they have bushy beards, which also are of a golden hue; and their eyebrows are more prominent than those of the plain, and their eye is sunk deep under the eyebrow, and emits a terrible and ruthless glance. And they give off a noise like the clashing of brass whenever

---
71. Flavius Philostratus, *Life of Apollonius of Tyana*, book 2:17.

they are burrowing under the earth, and from their crests, which are all fiery red, there flashes a fire brighter than a torch.

They also can catch the elephants, though they are themselves caught by the Indians in the following manner. They embroider golden runes on a scarlet cloak, which they lay in front of the animal's burrow after charming them the runes to cause sleep; for this is the only way to overcome the eyes of the dragon, which are otherwise inflexible, and much mysterious lore is sung by them to overcome him. These runes induce the dragon to stretch his neck out of his burrow and fall asleep over them: then the Indians fall upon him as he lies there, and dispatch him with blows of their axes, and having cut off the head they despoil it of its gems.

And they say that in the heads of the mountain dragons there are stored away stones of flowery color, which flash out all kinds of hues, and possess a mystical power as resided in the ring, which they say belonged to Gyges.[72] But often the Indian, in spite of his axe and his cunning, is caught by the dragon, who carries him off into his burrow, and almost shakes the mountains as he disappears. These are also said to inhabit the mountains in the neighborhood of the Red Sea, and they say that they heard them hissing terribly and that they saw them go down to the shore and swim far out into the sea. It was impossible however to ascertain the number of years that this creature lives, nor would my statements be believed. This is all I know about dragons.

They tell us that the city under the mountain is of great size and is called Paraca, and that in the center of it are enshrined a great many heads of dragons, for the Indians who inhabit it are trained from their boyhood in this form of sport. And they are also said to acquire an understanding of the language and ideas of animals by feeding either on the heart or the liver of the dragon.[73]

Claudius Aelianus (aka: Aelian) was born in (approximately) 165 AD in Italy. Though only fragments of his work survive today, he devoted a considerable amount of his writing on dragons, particularly those found in India.

Onesicritus Astypalæus writes that there were two dragons in India [nurtured by an Indian dancer], one of forty-six and the other of eighty cubits, and that Alexander (Philip's son) earnestly endeavoured to see them. It is affirmed in Egyptian books that, during the reign of Philadelphus, two dragons were brought from Ethiopia into Philadelphia alive, one forty, the other thirty cubits in magnitude.

Three were also brought in the time of King Evergetis, one nine and another seven cubits. The Egyptians say that the third was preserved with great care in the temple of Aesculapius.

It is also said that there are asps of four cubits in length. Those who write the history of the affairs of Chios say that a dragon of extreme magnitude was produced in a valley, densely crowded and gloomy with tall trees, of the Mount Pelienaeus in that island, whose hissing struck the Chians with horror.

As none either of the husbandmen or shepherds dare, by approaching

---

72. Told by Plato; Gyges was able to make himself invisible and thus became king of Lydia.
73. Philostratus, *Life of Apollonius of Tyana*, book 3:6-9.

near, estimate its magnitude, but from its hissing judged it to be a large and formidable beast, at length its size became known by a remarkable accident. For the trees of the valley being struck by a very strong wind, and the branches ignited by the friction, a great fire thence arising, embraced the whole spot, and surrounded the beast, which, being unable to escape, was consumed by the ardour of the flame. By these means all things were rendered visible in the denuded place, and the Chians freed, from their alarms, came to investigate, and lighted on bones of unusual magnitude, and an immense head, from which they were enabled to conjecture its dimensions when living.[74]

Onesikritos (Onesicritus) of Astypalaia says that at the time of the expedition of Alexandros [Alexander the Great], the son of Phillipos, there were in India two Drakones (Serpent-Dragons) kept by Abisares the Indian, and that one of them measured a hundred and forty cubits, the other eighty. He says also that Alexandros had a great desire to see them.[75]

Alexander (while he attacked or devastated some portions of India, and also seized others), lighted on, among other numerous animals, a dragon, which the Indians, because they considered it to be sacred, and worshipped it with great reverence, in a certain cave, besought him with many entreaties to let alone, which he agreed to. However, when the dragon heard the noise made by the passing army (for it is an animal endowed with a very acute sense of hearing as well as of vision), it frightened and alarmed them all with a great hissing and blowing. It was said to be seventy cubits long.

It did not, however, show the whole of itself, but only exposed its head from the cave. Its eyes were said to have been of the size (and rotundity) of a Macedonian shield.[76]

This concludes the main literary evidence for (mostly) land-dwelling dinosaurs as being dragons living on the Eurasian and African continents. The following two chapters will focus on air and sea dwelling creatures. Though such creatures are technically not considered to be dinosaurs *per se* by paleontologists today, many still consider air and sea dwelling prehistoric creatures as 'dinosaurs'; as did those in the past who considered (air and water dwelling) serpentine creatures as being dragons.

---

74. Aelian, Claudii. *De Natura Animalium*. Book XVI, chapter 39. Cited by Gould. p.382.
75. Aelian, *On Animals*, book 16:39 - Greek Natural History, 2nd - 3rd Century AD.
 [Alexander the Great lived between 356 to 323 BC].
76. Aelian, *De Natura Animalium*. Book XV, chapter 21. Cited by Gould. p.383.

5: Flying Fiery Serpents and Thunderbirds

Enemy of the Ibis

There are many kinds of lizards commonly called "flying dragons" that live in southeast Asia. These small reptiles simply glide and eat insects. Other creatures (that are not typically associated with flying) can glide as well, like the flying squirrel, some tree frogs, and geckos. None of these are dangerous to mankind, especially when compared with the flying serpents described by Herodotus,[1] the Bible[2], and other historians.

> There is a region moreover in Arabia, situated nearly over against the city of Buto, to which place I came to inquire about the winged serpents: and when I came thither I saw bones of serpents and spines in quantity so great that it is impossible to make report of the number, and there were heaps of spines, some heaps large and others less large and others smaller still than these, and these heaps were many in number. This region in which the spines are scattered upon the ground is of the nature of an entrance from a narrow mountain pass to a great plain, which plain adjoins the plain of Egypt; and the story goes that at the beginning of spring winged serpents from Arabia fly towards Egypt, and the birds called ibises[3] meet them at the entrance to this country and do not suffer the serpents to go by but kill them. On account of this deed it is (say the Arabians) that the ibis has come to be greatly honoured by the Egyptians, and the Egyptians also agree that it is for this reason that they honour these birds.
>
> ... As for the serpent its form is like that of the watersnake; and it has

---

1. Herodotus was a Greek historian. 484 – 425 BC. Known as the "Father of History"; known for systematically collecting materials and info, testing their accuracy and arranging them in a well-constructed narrative.
2. See Appendix C.
3. *Ibis aethiopica* (aka: black ibis). Virtually nonexistent in Egypt since the 1800's; now found in Sudan.

wings not feathered but most nearly resembling the wings of the bat. Let so much suffice as has been said now concerning sacred animals.[4]

Herodotus continues discussing flying serpents and further distinguishes them from vipers and ordinary snakes. Like the viper, these flying serpents were most likely poisonous (to some degree) since they were not only associated with vipers but were considered "noxious", troublesome, and aggressive. Herodotus also indicated through comparison that "other" serpents were not hurtful to man. In addition, if these serpents posed no threat to mankind and were beneficial by eating only insects and vermin, then why would the Egyptians honor the ibis for killing such a small migratory reptile? It would seem that these flying creatures are similar in description to the deadly *iaculus*.

> Then again Arabia is the furthest of inhabited lands in the direction of the midday, and in it alone of all lands grow frankincense and myrrh and cassia and cinnamon and gum-mastich. All these except myrrh are got with difficulty by the Arabians. Frankincense they collect by burning the storax[5], which is brought thence to the Hellenes by the Phenicians, by burning this, I say, so as to produce smoke they take it; for these trees which produce frankincense are guarded by winged serpents, small in size and of various colours, which watch in great numbers about each tree, of the same kind as those which attempt to invade Egypt: and they cannot be driven away from the trees by any other thing but only the smoke of storax.
>
> The Arabians say also that all the world would have been by this time filled with these serpents, if that did not happen with regard to them which I knew happened with regard to vipers: and it seems that the Divine Providence, as indeed was to be expected, seeing that it is wise, has made all those animals prolific which are of cowardly spirit and good for food, in order that they may not be all eaten up and their race fail, whereas it has made those which are bold and noxious to have small progeny...
>
> Just so also, if vipers and the winged serpents of the Arabians were produced in the ordinary course of their nature, man would not be able to live upon the earth; but as it is, when they couple with one another and the male is in the act of generation, as he lets go from him the seed, the female seizes hold of his neck, and fastening on to it does not relax her hold till she has eaten it through. The male then dies in the manner which I have said, but the female pays the penalty of retribution for the male in this manner:—the young while they are still in the womb take vengeance for their father by eating through their mother, and having eaten through her belly they thus make their way out for themselves. Other serpents however, which are not hurtful to man, produce eggs and hatch from them a very large number of offspring. Now vipers are distributed over all the earth; but the others, which are winged, are found in great numbers together in Arabia and in no other land: therefore it is that they appear to be numerous.[6]

---
4. Herodotus, *The History of Herodotus, Vol. 1*. By G. C. Macaulay. Chapter II, Lines 75, 76. p. 128.
5. "Storax" - A brownish aromatic resin used in perfume and medicine and obtained from particular trees.
6. *The History of Herodotus, Vol. 1*. By G. C. Macaulay. Chapter III, Lines 107-109. p. 224.

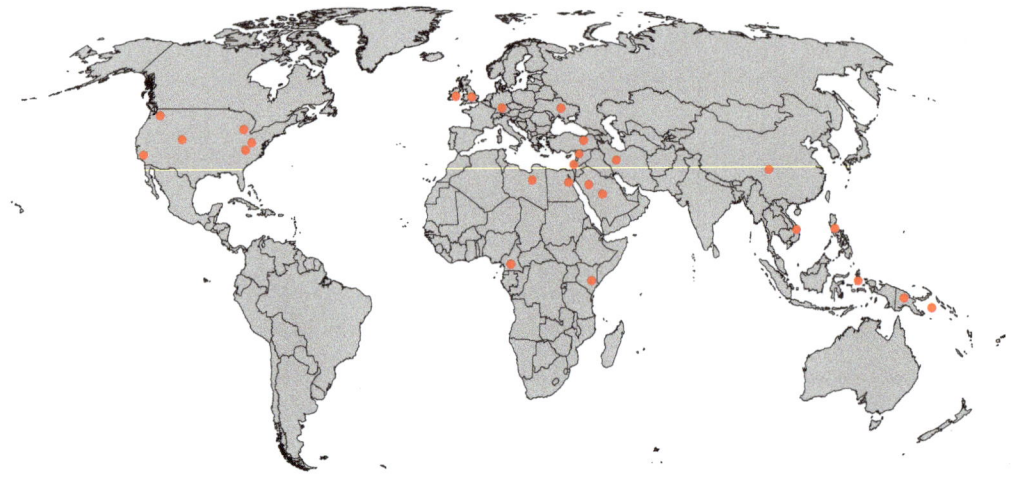

Figure 9: General overview map of documented pterodactyloid sightings through history.

The killing of the male while mating and consequent matriphagy ("mother eating") does occur in the animal kingdom, as some arachnids and insects occasionally demonstrate. Nevertheless, the behavior and perhaps the explanation for the extinction of these colorful creatures has been documented by more than one historian! Pliny the Elder mentions the ibis as being used by the Egyptians against "the coming of serpents".[7] Josephus also gives witness to these flying serpents in his book *Antiquities*.

> But Moses... took and led his army before those enemies were apprized of his attacking them; for he did not march by the river, but by land, where he gave a wonderful demonstration of his sagacity; for when the ground was difficult to be passed over, because of the multitude of serpents (which it produces in vast numbers, and, indeed, is singular in some of those productions, which other countries do not breed, and yet such as are worse than others in power and mischief, and an unusual fierceness of sight, some of which ascend out of the ground unseen, and also fly in the air, and so come upon men at unawares, and do them a mischief), Moses invented a wonderful stratagem to preserve the army safe, and without hurt; for he made baskets, like unto arks, of sedge, and filled them with ibes[8], and carried them along with them; which animal is the greatest enemy to serpents imaginable, for they fly from them when they come near them; and as they fly they are caught and devoured by them, as if it were done by the harts; but the ibes are tame creatures, and only enemies to the serpentine kind: but about these ibes I say no more at present, since the Greeks themselves are not unacquainted with this sort of bird. As soon, therefore, as Moses was come to the land which was the breeder of these serpents, he let loose the ibes, and by their means repelled the serpentine kind, and used them for his assistants before the army came upon that ground.[9]

---
7. Plinius Secundus. *Pliny's Natural History.* Book 10, chapter 28.
8. Alternate spelling: ibis.
9. Flavius Josephus. *The Works of Flavius Josephus.* Book 2, Chapter 10: 2.

Foul Weather

In Scotland, 1793, an unusual report was given as an "off topic" footnote to the subject of quarrying stones around Aberdeen. At first glance, the writer of the report seems to distance himself from the eyewitness' odd claim by calling the observation as "uncommon phenomena". However, the account indirectly indicates that the eyewitnesses were adamant in their claim of what they actually saw. Specifically indicating that the 'phenomena' was a "red fiery colour", the people seemed to have experienced this event before since they knew how to predict the weather due to such a sighting. A "meteor shower" (as some authorities have claimed what the sighting was) would not help an agrarian people with such a consistent prediction, in other words. Furthermore, if they were indeed meteors, more people than those from the Aberdeen area would have seen them and would have reported such. Consistent with the Chinese, the following official record indicated that the people could predict the weather from observations of what they claimed to be flying dragons:

> In the end of November and beginning of December last, many of the country people observed very uncommon phenomena in the air, (which they call dragons), of a red fiery colour, appearing in the N. and flying rapidly towards the E. from which they concluded, and their conjectures were right, a course of loud winds, and boisterous weather would follow.[10]

One thousand years earlier, the *Anglo-Saxon Chronicle* presented a similar account from the natural observations of the people and how dragons were considered as omens of misfortune.

> A.D. 793. This year came dreadful fore-warnings over the land of the Northumbrians, terrifying the people most woefully: these were immense sheets of light rushing through the air, and whirlwinds, and fiery dragons flying across the firmament. These tremendous tokens were soon followed by a great famine: and not long after, on the sixth day before the ides of January in the same year, the harrowing inroads of heathen men made lamentable havoc in the church of God in Holy-island, by rapine and slaughter. Siga died on the eighth day before the calends of March.[11]

Multiple Eyewitnesses

Though the following accounts had nothing to do with foul weather, they indicated that flying dragons were seen by multiple eyewitnesses simultaneously. According to a leaflet (i.e., canard) distributed at the time; on February 18, 1579, in Paris, France, a "great and wondrous flying serpent or dragon" appeared. The dragon

---

10. Sir John Sinclair, Bart., *A Statistical Account of Scotland*, Volume VI, 1793. p. 467. (N. = North / E. = East).
11. *The Anglo-Saxon Chronicle*. Part II. 750–919 AD. The "heathen men" were the first Viking raiders in England.

was seen in the sky by many Parisians from about two o'clock in the afternoon until the evening.[12] Two centuries later, another account, that occurred on February 5, 1780, in Bussieres, France, stated that *"About 6 p.m. a flaming "dragon" was seen in the sky for 15 minutes, illuminating everyone below."*[13]

Many researchers believe that these accounts are nothing more than a poetic means to describing a meteor or other natural atmospheric phenomenon. Note however that meteors or falling stars do not last more than but a few seconds at best, nor do they illumine people and things on the ground - that is, unless they are very close! If a meteor was that close, then why do these reports not mention them hitting the ground? Surely a meteor that was bright enough to illumine bystanders would be big enough to not burn up entirely in the atmosphere and would hit with some significance. Nevertheless, no meteor would last several hours as it made its way through earth's atmosphere. As would be expected, celestial events and meteors are more commonly mentioned than reports of dragons. More so as time passed and dragons were becoming less prolific.

Reputable Eyewitnesses

Ordinary people from the countryside were not the only eyewitnesses claiming to see flying dragons. People of high status saw them too, risking their reputations by relating what they saw with conviction. Note that the eyewitness was able to distinguish the dragon from a meteor.

> Herr Christophorus Schere, prefect of Uri County, saw a bright, long object, fiery in color, near Flüelen, flying along Lake Uri: "As I was contemplating the serene sky by night, I saw a very bright dragon flying across from a cave in a great rock in the mount called Pilatus toward another cave, known as Flue, on the opposite side of the lake.
>
> "Its wings were agitated with much celerity; its body was long as well as its tail and neck. Its head was that of a serpent with teeth, and when it was flying, sparkles were coming out of it like the ones thrown by an incandescent iron when struck by smiths on an anvil. At first, I thought it was a meteor, but after observing more closely, (I saw) it was truly a dragon from the recognizable motion of the members. This I write to you with respect, that the existence of dragons in nature is not to be doubted any more."
>
> Source: Athanasius Kircher, *Mundus Subterraneus*, (Amsterdam, 1665), Lib. VIII, 93-94.[14]

---

12. Source title: *Du serpent ou dragon volant, grand et merveilleux, apparu et veu par un chacun, sur la ville de Paris, le mercredi XVIII. Febvrier 1579, depuis deux heures apres midijusques au soir.* Cited by: Jacques Vallee and Chris Aubeck. *Wonders In The Sky - Unexplained Aerial Objects from Antiquity to Modern Times and their Impact on Human Culture, History, and Belief.* See item #207.
13. Source: *Lumieres dans la Nuit* 338. A French magazine. Cited by: Vallee and Aubeck. *Wonders In The Sky.* See item #359.
14. Jacques Vallee, Chris Aubeck, *Wonders in the Sky: Unexplained Aerial Objects from Antiquity to Modern Times.* 2009. Part 1, #224.

Conrad Gessner (1516–1565) was a respected Swiss botanist, zoologist, and bibliographer. His five-volume *Historiae Animalium* is considered the beginning of modern zoology. In his fifth volume entitled *De Serpentibus*, under the section of Dragons (*De Dracone*) he wrote, "In the year 1543, I heard in the recesses of Germany near Styria, many flying four-legged serpents, resembling lizards appeared, winged, and with an incurable bite."[15] The consistency of this report with others should be obvious.

Flying Fiery Serpents

The etymology of the word "dragonfly" (1620's) is unknown. Some conjecture that it may have been derived from the idea that these insects were a type of dragon, or that they had similar characteristics to dragons, having an iridescent body and wings. Like the dragonfly, some dragons are described as being multicolored ("sparkling with all the colors of the rainbow"). In Wales, reliable sightings of flying serpents were seen as late as 1649 AD.

> The woods around Penllin Castle, Glamorgan, had the reputation of being frequented by winged serpents, and these were the terror of old and young alike. The winged serpents were described as very beautiful. They were coiled when in repose, and "looked as if they were covered with jewels of all sorts. Some of them had crests sparkling with all the colours of the rainbow". When disturbed they glided swiftly, "sparkling all over," to their hiding places. When angry, they "flew over people's heads, with outspread wings, bright, and sometimes with eyes too, like the feathers in a peacock's tail". Locals had killed some of them, for they were as bad as foxes for poultry, and the extinction of the winged serpents was due to the fact that they were "terrors in the farmyards and coverts."[16]

The Gwiber of Penmachno

The Welsh word *gwiber* used to stand for a limbless wyrm or serpent that could fly.[17] The following legend tells of how Y Wibernant near Penmachno in Gwynedd (Britain) obtained its name.

The *gwiber* of Gwibernant near Penmachno was a deadly threat to the local communities. Not only would it eat fish and livestock, but people were sometimes killed if they ventured too far into its territory. Because it was adept in the air, water, and land, it was difficult to hunt down.

In a desperate effort to rid themselves of the dangerous *gwiber*, the people

---

15. Conradi Gessneri, *Historia Animalia*. Lib V. *De Dracone*, pp. 55, 56. ("Anno Domini 1543 audiui in sinibus Germanicae prope Stiriam subitò multos serpentes apparuisse, quadrupedes, lacertorum instar, alatos, morsu irremediabili.")
16. Trevelyan, M. 1909. *Folk-Lore and Folk Stories of Wales*. (Cit. Bill Cooper, *After the Flood*. p. 132.)
    "Penllin" is now spelled Penllyn.
17. The gwiber is related to dragons and wyverns, as well as the addanc or afanc.

pooled their resources and offered a large reward to anyone who could kill the creature. A young man named Owain ap Gruffydd[18] accepted the challenge. Before he went however, he decided to seek a local wizard named Rhys Ddewin ("Rhys the wizard") to gain some insight into his forthcoming fight with the *gwiber*.

Owain told Rhys about his quest. The wizard told him that the *gwiber* would bite him. Owain went home perplexed at the news. He soon realized that he was not satisfied with the foretelling and went back the following day to ask again. Owain disguised himself and after he told the wizard of his quest he got a different answer in that he was told he would break his neck. Owain went home frustrated and decided to return the following day to ask again. He disguised himself in yet a different manner and told Rhys of his quest, in which he got a different answer than the previous two. Rhys predicted that he would drown. In anger Owain revealed who he was and asked the wizard why he was given three different answers foretelling his death? Rhys simply replied, "We shall see. Time will tell."

Disregarding the wizards' inconsistent predictions of doom, Owain set out to kill the *gwiber*. While he was looking for the creature, he was situated on a steep rocky ledge with the Gwibernant valley below. Upon seeing the intruder, the *gwiber* swooped down and bit Owain on the neck. Owain fought back by swinging his sword, but as he did so, he slipped off the ledge and fell, breaking his neck on a rocky outcrop beneath him. He then fell into the river at the valley floor and drowned.

His body was soon found downstream by his friends who swore vengeance against the *gwiber*. After arming themselves, about two dozen men set out to vanquish the beast. After an hour into the search they discovered the *gwiber* sleeping near the river bank. They all shot the beast with arrows, severely wounding it. With a scream, the *gwiber* flew away and then dove into the river, from which it was never seen again. Due to these events, the valley where the *gwiber* lived was eventually called Y Wibernant (literally "Vale of the Flying Serpent"), and is still called that today.[19]

Qualities of a Chimera

The Nordic poetic Edda: *Völuspá* described a flying dragon as both gleaming and feathered. The Vikings called it a (Niðhöggr) "Nithhoger" (one who strikes ferociously). "Then comes flying a dark dragon, a shining serpent, coming down from Nidafjöll; He bears corpses on his feathers - as he hovers over the plain; Nidhöggr"...[20] Today, paleontologists indicate that some dinosaurs may have had feathers, or proto-feathers. This is consistent with other dragon descriptions in that some were not

---

18. Not to be confused with Owain Gwynedd ap Gruffydd, who was King of Gwynedd; from 1137 until his death in 1170. This king was known as Owain Gwynedd to distinguish him from yet another contemporary Owain ap Gruffydd, ruler of part of Powys who was known as Owain Cyfeiliog.
19. Dyfed Lloyd Evans. *Welsh Legends and Folk-tales*. And: *The Gwiber of Penmachno*, by Mike Heffernan, online article.
20. *The Poetic Edda: Völuspá* (The Old Woman's Prophecy). A collection of ancient Norse poems primarily preserved in the Icelandic medieval manuscript Codex Regius.

entirely covered in scales, but some had hair, or feathers too. The deadly Mesoamerican serpent-god *Quetzalquatl* ("feathered/bird snake"), for example, is described in much the same manner as the Nithhoger in that it too had scales and feathers.

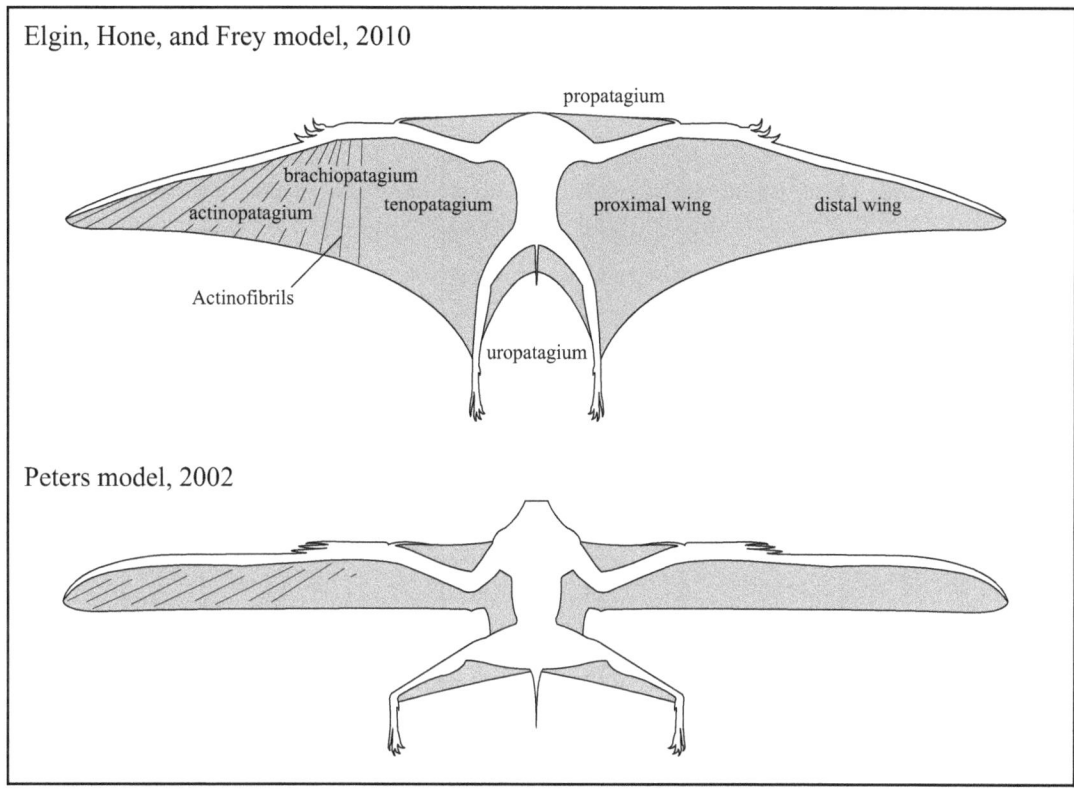

Figure 10: Two opposing portrayals of pterodactyl wing configuration.[21] Note that it is believed that contour feathers developed from actinofibrils in the bat-like membrane.

Thunderbirds

For hundreds, if not thousands of years, native North Americans, from the Atlantic to the Pacific, have passed along oral legends of thunderbirds. These large flying creatures are believed to have supernatural power and strength and are an integral part of their history and culture. The thunderbird got its name through the common belief that by beating its huge wings it would cause thunder and wind. If such a large flying creature existed, this name is appropriate since it would be natural to describe it in this fashion, especially if one were directly beneath it as it flew overhead or swooped down to capture its prey! Large eagles and cranes today make quite a sounding stir as they take off; how much more for a larger 'bird'?

Thunderbirds are given specific names by different tribes. For instance, the Ojibwe, Algonquin, Ottawa, and Shawnee tribes refer to the thunderbird specifically

---

21. Diagram simplified from *The Pterosaur Heresies - The myth of the bat-wing pterosaur.* David Peters.
See: http://pterosaurheresies.wordpress.com/2011/07/17/the-myth-of-the-bat-wing-pterosaur.

as "animikii", and also as "binesi" or "Waputhi".[22]

Like some dragons which are consistently described throughout Europe and Asia[23], the thunderbird is also consistently described throughout North American indigenous cultures. Not only was it consistently described as a large bird that could make the sound of thunder and cause wind gusts with its large wings, but it was thought to be able to actually bring or cause thunderstorms or cause rainfall as it flew. Since it is now known that large birds take advantage of warm updrafts that precede a storm, perhaps this was the reason that gave eyewitnesses the false impression that stormy weather was created by the thunderbirds. At this point the similarities to Asian (and some European) descriptions of dragons having a relationship with stormy weather should be obvious. Nevertheless it is easy to understand why the indigenous people associated the physical characteristics of thunderbirds with the weather.

Furthermore, in ceremonial masks and wood carvings, the thunderbird is also depicted as being brightly colored, with horns *or a crest* on its head, and sometimes with teeth in its beak. No other flying creature that comes close to the size of the thunderbird, having a crest on its head and teeth in its beak is known *except for* pterodactyls. It is even depicted as being multi-colored which is consistent with several other European reports about flying dragons.

In similar respects to the dragon in other cultures, thunderbirds were associated with the spirit world. One native tribe of the Pacific Northwest (Nuu-chah-nulth) believed that the thunderbird was the servant of the Great Spirit and lived on a tall mountain, observing all below. It was also understood that if one were to make the thunderbird angry it would bring disaster!

Of particular interest is that of the Sioux tribe (among others), who believed that in ancient days thunderbirds would come and kill reptilian monsters called the *unktehila*. These horned snake-like creatures were very large and were associated with water. The description of the *unktehila* has striking similarities to the *lindworm*[24] in Europe, and the *näga* in Asia.

Wyverns

Wyverns are portrayed (generally in bestiaries and heraldry) as having two legs, a dragon's body and head, wings, and a barbed tail. It was known to have a venomous bite or being able to belch fire. (The term *wyvern* was not used before the 1600's as meaning a "winged two-legged dragon". However, the Latin variant that it is derived from was associated with a poisonous viper.)[25] Here again is a creature that is consistently described that matches no other animal known, that is, except for a type of pterodactyl.

---

22. See: www.native-languages.org/animikii.htm.
23. For example, see the section entitled *The Serpents of Sussex* in the previous chapter.
24. aka: *lindorm* (Scandinavian), or *wyvern* (French).
25. *The American Heritage® Dictionary of the English Language*, Fourth Edition.

Specific Similarities of the Pterodactyl and Basilisk

The equivalent words in the Septuagint[26] for the Egyptian and Hebrew word "saraph" (indicating a flying reptile from Isaiah 14:29) are *ófeis petómenoi* (ὄφεις πετόμενοι) and have no variants. There are variants, however, of similar flying creatures, but they each have qualifying words (i.e., *aspídon petoménon* from Isaiah 30:6) to distinguish them. One such variant is *basilisk* from the Symmachi[27].

During the middle ages, the (Greek) *basilisk* (Latin *basilic*) was described as a dangerous flying serpent with a head crest, like a crown. It was considered to be the "King of the serpents" despite being comparatively small. The word *basilisk* also seems to be a variant of *basileu,* which means king in Greek.[28] Consider the following consistent reports by various reputable persons.

Prosper Alpin, a European scientist who wrote several works on the natural history of Egypt during 1581-1584, recorded and collated a large amount of eyewitness accounts regarding the dangerous creature:

> ... there is nothing for sure about the basilic, but we have heard talk, nevertheless, that there is a small serpent, as long as a palm branch, and thick like a small finger. It has a small piece of skin, like a crest, on its head and, in the middle of the back, two scales placed on one side and the other which serve as wings in order to advance more quickly. Large numbers of people have said that these serpents live in large quantities close to certain lakes in which the Nile has its source. People don't travel close to those lakes because of the well-known danger these serpents represent... That is what is said by the Egyptians who travel in Ethiopia and in Nubia.[29]

Similar to the account told by Herodotus of how Arabians used smoke to drive flying serpents away, Prosper continues:

> But the natives, who have a premonition of the arrival of the savage beasts prepare a fire of a plant the very Great and very Good God has abundantly grown in that region, as a remedy. Also by virtue of the smell of the fumes, they are prepared and escaped those reptiles and preserve the province from their incursions. The youngster told me that this plant was short and robust, having a leaf similar to that of the basilic and exudes a very unpleasant odor.[30]

---

26. The *Septuagint* is an ancient Greek translation of the Hebrew Bible. It continues to serve as the Eastern Orthodox Old Testament.
27. Symmachus (late 2nd century) was the author of one of the Greek versions of the Old Testament. It was included by Origen in his *Hexaplorum*.
28. John Goertzen, *The Rhamphorhynchoid Pterosaur Scaphognathus crassirostris: A "Living Fossil" Until the 17th Century*. An Article for the 1998 Midwestern Evangelical Theological Society Conference held at GRBS, Grand Rapids, MI.
29. Prosper Alpin, *Histoire Naturelle de l'Egypte*, p. 407. Cited by Goertzen, *The Rhamphorhynchoid Pterosaur*.
30. Alpin, *Histoire Naturelle de l'Egypte*, p. 409. Cit. Goertzen.

Almost exactly one hundred years earlier, Felix Fabri, a Dominican theologian, also visited Egypt. Though he did not give a physical description, he indicated that the *basilic* was a dangerous animal that he saw during the day in the very hot regions of upper (southern) Egypt.[31]

Edward Topsell[32] was an English naturalist and zoologist of exceptional reputation during the 16th century. Though Topsell may have borrowed from another reputable individual (Conrad Gesner), the following accounts are presented in John Ashton's book, *Curious Creatures in Zoology,* and lend a consistent description.

> Among the *Pyrenes*, too, there is a cruell kinde of Serpent, not past foure foot long, and as thicke as a man's arme, out of whose sides growe winges, much like unto gristles.
> *Gesner* also saith, that in the yeere of our Lord 1543 there came many Serpents both with wings and legs into the parts of Germany neere *Stiria*, who did bite and wound many men incurably. *Cardan*[33] also describeth certaine serpents with wings, which he saw at Paris, whose dead bodies were in the hands of *Gulielmus Musicus*; hee saith that they had two legges, and small winges, so that they could scarce flie, the head was little, and like to the head of a serpent, their colour bright, and without haire or feathers, the quantitie of that which was greatest, did not exceede the bignes of a Cony, and it is saide they were brought out of India...

> ... Topsell says it is the same as the Cockatrice, depicts it as a crowned serpent, and says:— "This Beast is called by the Græcian *Baziliscos*, and by the Latine, *Regulus*, because he seemeth to be the King of Serpents, not for his magnitude or greatnesse: For there are many Serpents bigger than he, as there be many foure-footed Beastes bigger than the Lyon, but, because of his stately pace, and magnanimious mind: for hee creepeth not on the earth like other Serpents, but goeth halfe upright, for which occasion all other Serpentes avoyde his sight. And it seemeth nature hath ordayned him for that purpose; for, besides the strength of his poyson, which is uncurable, he hath a certain combe or Corronet uppon his head, as shall be shewed in due place." [34]

As a side note on the cockatrice (aka *basilisk*), it is mentioned that "... though the cockatrice be venomous without remedy, while he is alive, yet he loseth all the malice when he is burnt to ashes. His ashes be accounted good and profitable in working of Alchemy, and namely in turning and changing of metals."[35]

Megasthenes (300 BC), wrote an account of his trip to India and briefly mentioned dangerous flying reptiles.

> In some parts of tho country there are serpents two cubits long which

---
31. Felix Fabri, *Voyage en Egypte de Felix Fabri, 1483*. Cit. Goertzen.
32. Edward Topsell, *The Historie of Foure-Footed Beasts*, 1607. (collected from the writings of Conrad Gesner and others). W. Iaggard, London.
33. See: Girolamo Cardano, *De Rerum Varietate*. 1557.
34. John Ashton, *Curious Creatures In Zoology*, London. p. 305, 318.
35. Robert Steele, *Mediaeval Lore from Bartholomew Anglicus*. p. 56.

have membranous wings like bats. They fly about by night, when they let fall drops of urine or sweat, which blister the skin of persons not on their guard, with putrid sores.[36]

Bochart (1650 AD.) was an outstanding scholar, competent in multiple languages. He wrote what is considered to be one of the most outstanding studies of Biblical animals ever produced. He was convinced that the flying serpents (*"est hydra volans"*) of Isaiah 14:29 and 30:6 were still living to some degree and were the same reported creatures as those mentioned in Arabia; and that they had pointed membranous wings (*appearing to be made of cartilage*) like bats.[37] Referring to the ancient Hebrew work *Porta Coeli*, Bochart mentioned how "the flying saraph sets fire to the air, corrupting [or poisoning] all that is near it."[38]

> To what extent the flying snakes are... remaining is confirmed by many of our generation: and in fact in France itself toward the Pyrenees Bigerrones there is a genus of serpents usually hiding, with pointed wings spread out appearing to be made of cartilage.
> And Odoardus Barbosa from mountain territory who separated them into Malabar [apparently from the Latin word mala meaning "jaws of death"] and Narsinga [apparently derived from the Latin naris which means "nose"].
> If on your travels you encounter the serpent with wings who circles and hurls himself at you, the flying snake, hide yourself because of its reputation. Lie down when the snake appears and guard yourself in alarm for that snake's manner is to go away calm, considering it a victory (the Malabar I believe).
> There are winged and flying serpents that can be found who are venomous, who snort, and are savage and kill with pain worse than fire, their reputation is (the Narsinga I believe).[39]

The French explorer, Vincent Le Blanc (~1553-1633), will be used as a closing witness in this chapter. In the 25th chapter of his book ("Of the kingdoms of Malaca and Siam, with a prodigious history of serpents"), he also described flying serpents.

> At the eastern lakes of Chiamay there are large forests and vast swamps, and there among them is danger: there are serpents who are very degenerate and, just as it becomes evening, they fly rising over the land, and rest on the end of their tail, rapidly going into motion. They are set in motion around that location at times in large numbers in a desolate area of the province.[40]

---

36. J. W. McCrindle, *Ancient India As Described By Megasthenes and Arrian.* (Fragment. XII. Strabo, XV. i. 37, p. 703. *Of some Wild Beasts of India.*) 1876-1870.
37. Samuel Bochart, *Hierozoicon sive bipartitum opus de animalibus sacrae scripturae.* Volume I.
    For one example (of several in the work) see Index, p. 42. *Saraph volans.* (Upper right-hand column).
38. Bochart, *Hierozoicon.* p. 215.
39. Bochart, *Hierozoicon.* Cited from Goertzen, *The Rhamphorhynchoid Pterosaur Scaphognathus crassirostris.*
40. *Les voyages du sieur fameux Vincent Le Blanc.* pp. 157, 158. Cited from Goertzen, *Rhamphorhynchoid.*

With so many consistent cross-cultural descriptions of these flying serpents, the literary evidence seems to indicate that pterodactyls were alive and well up until relatively recently. These descriptions, made before the term *pterodactyl* came into being, described creatures with morphological features that can be found nowhere else in the animal kingdom *except* for the pterodactyl and therefore cannot be explained except through authentic eyewitness observation. The descriptions of the *basilisk* in particular are so specific that some have narrowed it down to the *Scaphognathus crassirostris*.[41]

Author	Date	Location	Predator	Threat
(Moses)	~1400 BC	Sinai		poisonous
Isaiah	700 BC	Sinai/Egypt		poisonous
Herodotus	500 BC	Arabia/Egypt	black ibis	dangerous
Aristotle	300 BC	Nubia		
Mela	100 AD	Egypt	ibis	poisonous
Josephus	100 AD	Nubia	ibis	dangerous
Solinus	300 AD	Arabia/Egypt	ibis	poisonous
Aelianus	300 AD	Arabia/Egypt	black ibis	dangerous
Ammianus	400 AD	Arabia/Egypt	black ibis	poisonous

Figure 11: Correlation of written accounts (selected examples) of flying reptiles.[42]

---
41. John Goertzen, *The Rhamphorhynchoid Pterosaur Scaphognathus crassirostris: A "Living Fossil" Until the 17th Century.* 1998.
42. Chart modified from Goertzen, *The Rhamphorhynchoid Pterosaur Scaphognathus crassirostris.*

6: Monsters of the Deep

Serpents of the South Pacific

Taniwha (generic for monsters / dragons) have been reported for centuries by the Maori people of New Zealand. Though seen as supernatural creatures, taniwha were considered part of the natural environment. They used to inhabit the waters in and around the large island. The taniwha hid in lairs called *rua taniwha*, which could be deep pools, caves, or waterways. Some of those dwelling in the ocean had similar features to sharks but were much more gigantic in size, while those in or near fresh water lakes looked like giant lizards.

These dragons took on different roles accordingly in various legendary tales. Some were loyal protectors of mankind, like faithful guard dogs. Others were very dangerous, attacking anyone they happen upon, dragging their victims down to a horrifying watery grave. For instance, consider the following legendary account.

People who travelled on a road between two villages began to go missing. The men in one village began to think that the men in the other village were to blame for their disappearance. As the men set off to attack the other village, a giant taniwha attacked them instead, killing most of the gang. The survivors ran back to their village in fright and reported what happened. A man named Pitaka then came up with a plan to kill the taniwha. He took some rope and a number of men to hunt down the beast. When they got near the lair, they tied one end of a rope to a tree and made a noose out of the other end. While Pitaka bravely lured the dragon out, the other men looped the noose around the taniwha's tail and another noose around its neck. As the dragon thrashed around, it strangled itself on the rope. Pitaka then cut open the taniwha's stomach and found the remains of the missing people.

Some time after that, another tribe called on Pitaka to help rid them of a dangerous river-dwelling taniwha. Pitaka had the villagers make a large basket and got in it with some rope and a few other men. They were lowered into the deep river where they saw the taniwha sleeping at the bottom. Pitaka carefully tied a noose around the dragon's neck and then tugged on the rope as a signal for all the villagers who were waiting back on land. They began to pull on the rope and laboriously hauled the taniwha ashore. The villagers attacked the half-choked taniwha, beating it to death with clubs. Pitaka gained the reputation for being a dragonslayer.[1] Other South Pacific island cultures, like those of Papua New Guinea, depict similar monstrous creatures in their folklore.

The Mighty Mirreeulla

For centuries, the Dharuk people have spoken of the mighty "Mirreeulla," whose home is the Hawkesbury River near Sydney.[2] Sightings of plesiosaur-like creatures in this river have continued to modern times, with some estimating the creature(s) at up to 15 metres (50 feet) long."[3] Unrelated eyewitnesses consistently describe the creature as having a snake-like head on a long neck, a large body with two sets of flippers, and a long eel-like tail.[4] As will be demonstrated, this general description is consistent with other water-dwelling monsters throughout the world. In addition, local rock engravings made by the Aborigines, some dated approximately 3,000 years old, match no other known animal *except* for the plesiosaur.[5]

Transition

The remainder of this chapter will present some (out of many!) historical reports of sea and lake monsters. Like the pterodactyl, modern science does not technically classify prehistoric sea creatures as (land dwelling) "dinosaurs", despite them being considered as such by the general population. In like manner, eyewitnesses in the past considered large reptilian sea and lake dwelling creatures as also being dragons or related serpents.

With commentary kept at a minimum, this chapter is mainly a list of quotes by various eyewitnesses through the course of history. Keep in mind that an officer of a ship risked his career by mentioning such sightings. Also notice the descriptive similarities between unrelated reports. Some of the bodily forms described are consistent with several "prehistoric" sea creatures, like the elasmosaur or basilosaurus. The following eyewitness accounts speak for themselves.

---

1. Joseph A. McCullough, *Dragonslayers from Beowulf to St. George*. p. 76.
2. Mirreeulla = "giant water serpent". The Hawkesbury River is 45 feet deep and 75 miles long.
3. Rebecca Driver. *Australia's Aborigines ... Did They See Dinosaurs?* Answers in Genesis. 1998. Online article.
4. Rex Gilroy, who coined the name "Hawkesbury River Monster", spent over 45 years researching the Mirreeulla and has collected hundreds of reported sightings.
5. See chapter 8 for a mirreeulla petroglyph.

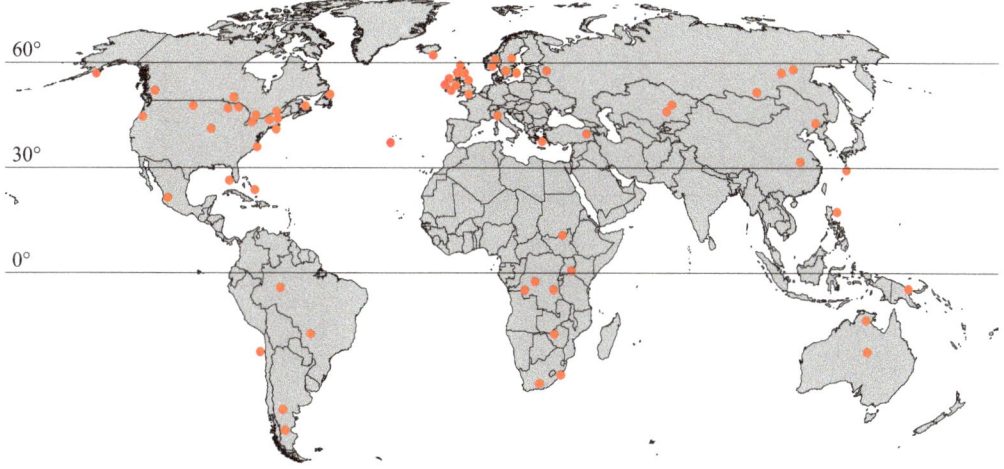

Figure 12. General overview map of major sea and lake monster sightings. Most are found between 30° and 60° North Latitude.

Sea Dragons

"Jerome saith, that the dragon is a full thirsty beast, insomuch that unneth he may have water enough to quench his great thirst; and openeth his mouth therefore against the wind, to quench the burning of his thirst in that wise. Therefore when he seeth ships sail in the sea in great wind, he flieth against the sail to take their cold wind, and overthroweth the ship sometimes for greatness of body, and strong rese against the sail. And when the shipmen see the dragon come nigh, and know his coming by the water that swelleth ayenge him, they strike the sail anon, and scape in that wise."[6]

"In Libya, according to all accounts, the length of the serpents is something appalling; sailors spin a yarn to the effect that some crews once put ashore and saw the bones of a number of oxen, and that they were sure that the oxen had been devoured by serpents, for, just as they were putting out to sea, serpents came chasing their galleys at full speed and overturned one galley and set upon the crew."[7]

In his authoritative work (eng.) *History of the Northern Peoples* (1555 AD), Olaus Magnus gave the following report (among others) of a sea serpent that haunted the Norwegian sea coast. "Seamen who work aboard ship along the shores of Norway, either in merchandise or fishing, all consistently give an astounding testimony of a serpent, vast in size; being over two hundred feet long and twenty feet in thickness. It

---

2. Bartholomaeus Anglicus, *De Proprietatibus Rerum*, book 18, 13th century CE. Cited in *Mediaeval Lore from Bartholomew Anglicus*. By Robert Steele. Chapter VII. 2004. (First published in 1905).
3. Aristotle, *History of Animals*, 8:28. p. 243. Kessinger Publishing, Jun 1, 2004.

lives in the cavernous cliffs along the coast of Bergen. On clear nights in the summer, it would come on land to devour calves, lambs, and pigs, or it wandered out to sea to feed on octopi, lobsters, crabs, and other marine creatures. The serpent was described as having arm-length hair hanging from its neck, with sharp dark-colored scales and flaming red eyes. This sea serpent would lift itself up out of the water like a tall column and would attack ships, swallowing some of the crew."[8] It is interesting to note that when this sea serpent was seen it was considered to be a bad omen, indicating the fate of the nobility or of approaching war.

On a very stormy day, there was a sighting off Cape Ann, Massacheusetts on June 26, 1639; the first sighting of a sea-serpent mentioned in North America.

"At this time we had some neighbouring gentlemen in our house, who came to welcome me into the country; where amongst variety of discourse they told me... of a sea-serpent or snake, that lay coiled up like a cable upon a rock at Cape-Ann: a boat passing by with English aboard, and two Indians, they would have shot the serpent but the Indians disswaded them, saying, that if he were not kill'd out-right, they would be all in danger of their lives."[9]

In the *Journal of Obadiah Turner*, on September 5, 1641, he also describes what seems to be the same, or similar serpent, along with the exaggerated tales of the Native Americans regarding its size:

"Some being on ye great beache gathering of clams and seaweed which had been cast thereon by ye mightie storm did spy a most wonderful serpent a shorte way off from ye shore. He was as big round in ye thickest part as a wine pipe; and they do affirme that he was fifteen fathom or more in length. A most wonderful tale. But ye witnesses be credible, and it would be of no account to them to tell an untrue tale. Wee have likewise heard it at Cape Ann ye people have seene a monster like unto this, which did there come out of ye sea and coile himself upon ye land much to ye terror of them yet did see him. And ye Indians doe say yet they have manie times seene a wonderful big serpent lying on ye water, and reaching from Nahauntus to ye greate rock which we call Birdes Egg Rocke; which is much above belief for yet would be nigh upon a mile. Ye Indians, as said, be given to declaring wonderful things, and it pleaseth them to make ye white peeple stare. But making all discounte, I doe believe yet a wonderful monster in forme of a serpent doth visit these waters."[10]

Hans Egede, a Danish protestant missionary who became known as the Bishop of Greenland, gave what is considered to be the first physical description of a sea

---

8. Olaus Magnus (Archbishop of Uppsala), *Historia de gentibus septentrionalibus...* Chapter: *De magnitudine Noruagici Serpentis, & aliorum.* Cap. XLIII. p. 771. My translation, from Latin and English versions.
9. John Josselyn, *An Account of Two Voyages to New England.* 1865. p. 22. (Some text updated for clarity)
10. Cited in *Some Annals of Nahant. Chapter XI - The Sea Serpent.* By Fred A. Wilson. 1928. (Some text updated for clarity). A fathom is 6 feet.

serpent that was given by the primary eyewitness. If the creature described was an elasmosaur or plesiosaur, it would be consistent with the serpentine shape, broad flippers, and ability to raise its head high above of the water.

"As for other sea monsters... none of them have been seen by us, or any of our time that ever I could hear, save that most dreadful monster, that showed itself upon the water in the year 1734, off our colony in 64 degrees. The monster was of so huge a size, that coming out of the water, its head reached as high as the mast-head; its body was bulky as the ship, and three or four times as long. It had a long pointed snout, and spouted like a whale-fish; great broad paws, and the body seemed covered with shell-work, its skin very rugged and uneven. The under part of its body was shaped like an enormous huge serpent, and when it dived again under water, it plunged backwards into the sea, and so raised its tail aloft, which seemed a whole ship's length distant from the bulkiest part of its body."[11]

"By this time the Dutch and the British were energetically slaughtering the bowheads off Greenland and Baffin Island for their baleen plates and oil, so Egede must have been familiar with whales. He had Pastor Bing draw a picture of the monster that was reproduced in his *Perlustration* (published in English as *A Description of Greenland* in 1745), and since Egede was known to be a sober, reliable observer, the picture thus became one of the earliest illustrations of a sea monster based on a reliable eyewitness account."[12]

Bishop Erik Ludvigsen Pontoppidan of Bergen, author of *The Natural History of Norway* (1755), took the deposition of Captain von Ferry, who claimed to have encountered a "sea-snake" that passed his ship in August of 1746. Captain von Ferry ordered his ship about in order to get a closer look at the serpent. Accordingly, he was able to get a good description, which he gave in an official letter upon the bishop's request; written to the court of justice at Bergen. (Note the dark color of the body and hairy mane that are similar features to those expressed in Olaus Magnus' work).

"The head of this sea-serpent, which it held more than two feet above the water, resembled that of a horse. It was of a greyish color, and the mouth was quite black and very large. It had large black eyes, and a long white mane, which hung down to the surface of the water. Besides the head and neck, we saw seven or eight folds, or coils, of this snake, which were very thick, and as far as we could tell, there was a fathom's distance between each fold."

Another eyewitness mentioned in the bishop's work (*Natural History*) was Governor Benstrup, who also claimed to see a sea serpent. Though his physical description was different in several aspects, he did describe the creature as having

---
11. Hans Egede, *Det gamle Grønlands nye Perlustration*. 1741.
12. Richard Ellis, *Monsters of the Sea*. Globe Pequot, 2006. p. 44.

several bends in the body like "a string of buoys".[13]

In 1789, while stationed on Penobscot Bay, the crew of the American gunship *Protector* had an unusual encounter with a semi-aquatic serpent. One of the eyewitnesses was Edward Preble, an 18-year-old ensign, who would later become a commodore and notable figure in U.S. naval history. Keep in mind that common snakes typically do not raise their heads above the water when they swim.

"In later years, when Edward Preble and Midshipman Luther Little, brother of George Little, were in a reminiscent mood about their Revolutionary War adventures, they used to relate an incident which they insisted really happened while the Protector was anchored in Broad Bay (now Muscongus Bay). One afternoon someone saw a great black snake emerge from the underbrush opposite the Protector's anchorage, enter the water, and swim past the frigate. Perhaps 40 feet long, thick as a man's body, and able to lift his head six feet out of the water; that was how Luther Little remembered the serpent. George Little told Midshipman Preble to take the ship's barge and follow the snake - an assignment huntsman Preble found congenial, if he did not suggest it himself. The boat's crew snatched up some arms and may have put a swivel in the barge, too. Off across the bay they went, Preble driving his oarsmen on and taking occasional shots at the serpent. At the sound of each shot, the snake submerged, and the boat was not fast enough to overtake it. When the serpent had been chased for perhaps a mile and a half, it ran up on Louds Island and disappeared into the woods. Preble and his men returned disappointed to the ship with only the story to show for their efforts."[14]

Printed in *Silliman's American Journal of Science and Arts* (Vol. II, 1820), and the original later found in the possession of John Q. Adams, Abraham Cummings wrote the following letter:

"Sullivan, Aug. 17th. 1803.

My Dear Sir,

With peculiar pleasure I comply with your request, though the urgency of my affairs must excuse my brevity. It was sometime in July 1802 that we saw this extraordinary sea monster, on our passage to Belfast, between Cape Rosoi and Long Island. His first appearance was near Long Island. I then supposed it to be a large shoal of fish with a seal at one end of it, but wondered that the seal should rise out of water so much higher than usual; but, as he drew nearer to our boat, we soon discovered that this whole appearance was but one animal in the form of a serpent. I immediately perceived that his mode of swimming was exactly such as had been described to me by some of the people of Fox Islands, who had seen an animal of this kind before, which must confirm the veracity of their report. For this creature had

---
13. Ellis, *Monsters of the Sea*. p. 44, 45. (The monster described was over 50 feet long).
14. Christopher McKee, *Edward Preble: A Naval Biography, 1761-1807.* pp. 13, 16.

not the horizontal but an ascending and descending serpentine motion. This renders it highly probable that he never moves on land to any considerable distance and that the water is his proper element. His head was rather larger than that of a horse, but formed like that of a serpent. His body we judged was more than sixty feet in length. His head and as much of his body as we could discover was all of a blue colour except a black circle round his eye. His motion was at first but moderate, but when he left us and proceeded towards the ocean, he moved with the greatest rapidity. This monster is the sixth of the kind, if our information is correct, which has been seen in this bay within the term of eighteen years. Mrs. Cummings, my daughter and Mss. Martha Spring were with me in the boat all that time, and can attest to the above description. I continue yours in christian affection

Abraham Cummings.

Rev. Alexander Mc. Lean."[15]

After his letter was submitted, Cummings answered those who were skeptical about his claim:

"Sullivan, Jan. 18th. 1804.

Rev. and Dear Sir,

I can recollect nothing material which could render my description of that animal more convincing. I am not sure that this motion was ascending and descending; all we can say is, it appeared so to us (for he was seen not only by me, but by three other persons). His real motion might be horizontal. Perhaps his nearest distance from us was ten rods. The sea was then very smooth, and very little wind, but still there was such a constant rippling of the water over his body, that I could not distinctly observe the magnitude or colour of any part but his head and neck. The degree of his rapidity I cannot explain. But certain I am that he had a serpent's head, of a colour as blue as possible, and a black ring round his eye. The head was three feet in circumference at least. Who ever saw fifty or sixty porpoises moving after each other in a right line, and in such a manner that those who formed the rear were no larger than haddock and mackerel, and none but the foremost shewed his head? Who ever saw a serpent's head upon porpoise or a whale? We saw him swim as far as from Long Island to the Cape before he disappeared. His head and neck all the time out of water. Now who ever saw a porpoise swim so great a distance without ever immerging at all? This is the best information which you can obtain from

Your Friend and Servant

Abraham Cummings.

Rev. Alden Bradford.

P.S. The head and neck of the animal were of the same colour."[16]

---

15. Antoon Cornelis Oudemans, *The Great Sea Serpent*. 1892. p. 121. (Much of this chapter is indebted to this authoritative and extensive work. Over 160 accounts by reputable persons (many under oath) are listed, including scholarly analysis of such reports regarding sea serpents). Loren Coleman. Cosimo Classics. 2009.
16. Oudemans, *The Great Sea Serpent*. Cosimo Classics. pp. 121, 122. A rod is 5½ yards (16½ feet).

Furthermore, in a letter from the Rev. Mr. William Jenks, of Bath, to the Hon. Judge Davis, of Boston, dated September 7, 1818, and published in the Report of 1817, the following was written in regards to the unusual motion of the serpent:

"June 28, 1809. Mr. Cummings observes that a Mr. Crocket saw two of them together about twenty years since"... 'One of those seen by Mr. Crocket was smaller than that seen by Mr. Cummings, and their motion in the sea appeared to be a perpendicular winding, and not horizontal."[17]

And finally:

"Two young men of Fox Island, intelligent and credible, saw an animal of this kind about five years since, as they then informed me. They told me, that the serpent which they saw was about sixty feet long, and appeared to have an ascending and descending motion."[18]

Here is a report from Captain George Little of the frigate *Boston*:
"Marshfield, March, 13th., 1804.
Sir,
In answer to yours of 30th. of January last, I observe, that in May, 1780, I was lying in Round Pond, in Broad Bay, in a public armed ship. At sunrise, I discovered a large Serpent, or monster, coming down the Bay, on the surface of the water. The cutter was manned and armed. I went myself in the boat, and proceeded after the serpent. When within a hundred feet, the mariners were ordered to fire on him, but before they could make ready, the Serpent dove. He was not less than from 45 to 50 feet in length; the largest diameter of his body, I should judge, 15 inches; his head nearly of the size of that of a man, which he carried four or five feet above the water. He wore every appearance of a common black snake. When he dove he came up near Muscongus Island—we pursued him, but never came up within a quarter of a mile of him again.
I have the honor to be sir
Your friend and humble servant
Geo. Little."[19]

For three days in mid-August of 1817, Solomon Allen III, along with approximately 25 other persons, witnessed a sea-serpent from both the shore (using an eyeglass) as well as from a boat. Though each situation provided different degrees of visibility, Solomon was able to determine that the creature was rough and scaly during a follow-up interview. Here is his initial report.

"I, Solomon Allen 3d. of Gloucester, in the County of Essex, shipmaster, depose and say; that I have seen a strange marine animal, that I believe to be a sea-serpent, in the harbour in said Gloucester. I should judge him to be between eighty and ninety

---
17. Oudemans, *The Great Sea Serpent*. Cosimo Classics. p. 118.
18. Oudemans, *The Great Sea Serpent*. Cosimo Classics. p. 120.
19. Oudemans, *The Great Sea Serpent*. Cosimo Classics. p. 117.

feet in length, and about the size of a half barrel, apparently having joints from his head to his tail. I was about one hundred and fifty yards from him, when I judged him to be of the size of a half barrel. His head formed something like the head of a rattle snake, but nearly as large as the head of a horse. When he moved on the surface of the water, his motion was slow, at times playing about in circles, and sometimes moving nearly straight forward. When he disappeared, he sunk apparently directly down, and would next appear at two hundred yards from where he disappeared, in two minutes. His colour was a dark brown, and I did not discover any spots upon him."[20]

On June 6, 1819, a report was given by Hawkins Wheeler, a commander of the sloop *Concord*. [The ship's mate, Gershom Bennet, saw the same creature but from a different vantage point, and also filed an official report.] Among other details regarding this sea serpent sighting, Mr. Wheeler stated that he "had a fair and distinct view of the creature, and from his appearance am satisfied that it was of the serpent kind. The creature was entirely black; the head, which perfectly resembled a snake's, was elevated from four to seven feet above the surface of the water, and his back appeared to be composed of bunches or humps, apparently about as large as, or a little larger than a half barrel; I think I saw as many as ten or twelve... I considered them to be caused by the undulatory motion of the animal–the tail was not visible, but from the head to the last hump that could be seen, was, I should judge, 50 feet." [21]

August 19, 1819. A report was given by the reputable Samuel Cabot (upon request of Col. T. H. Perkins), who saw, along with hundreds of others, a sea serpent off the shores of Nahant (near Boston). Of the many eyewitnesses on that day, several additional reports by persons of high standing were made that gave a consistent account of the creature. The following is a portion of Cabot's report.

"... my attention was suddenly arrested by an object emerging from the water at the distance of about one hundred or one hundred and fifty yards, which gave to my mind at the first glance the idea of a horse's head... I perceived at a short distance eight or ten regular bunches or protuberances, and at a short interval three or four more... I was now satisfied that the sea monster was before me, and after the first moment of excitement produced by the unexpected sight of so strange a monster taxed myself to investigate his appearance as accurately as I could... the Head... was serpent shaped, it was elevated about two feet from the water, and he depressed it gradually, to within six or eight inches as he moved along. I could always see under his chin, which appeared to hollow underneath or to curve downward. His bunches appeared to be not altogether uniform in size, and as he moved along some appeared to be depressed,

---

20. Oudemans, *The Great Sea Serpent*. Cosimo Classics. p. 134. (Interview is on p. 135).
21. *Silliman's American Journal of Science and the Arts, Vol. II*, Boston 1820. Cited in Oudemans, *The Great Sea Serpent*. Cosimo Classics. pp. 160, 161.
 ["undulatory": a wave-like motion (vertical); compare with a common snake's side-to-side (horizontal) motion].

and others brought above the surface, though I could not perceive any motion in them. ... (His length) could not be less than eighty feet long.

My first reflection after the animal was gone, was, that the idea I had received from the description you gave of the animal you saw at Gloucester, in 1817, was perfectly realized in this instance; and that I had discovered nothing you had not before described. The most authentic testimony given of his first appearance there seemed to me remarkably correct; and I felt as if the appearance of this monster had been already familiar to me.

(After several hours went by without seeing the serpent, Cabot had a second opportunity to view the creature). ... At this time he moved more rapidly, causing a white foam under the chin, and a long wake, and his protuberances had a more uniform appearance. At this time he must have been seen by two or three hundred persons on the beach and on the heights each side, some of whom were very favorable situated to observe him."[22]

In a follow-up report given on October 13, 1820, Col. T. H. Perkins wrote the following details regarding the same account at Nahant.

"... many persons of my acquaintance had a fine sight of him, and all agreed in their account of him in the principal particulars. They all agreed as to the rapidity of his movements, being very much beyond anything living they had ever seen. The apparent bunches on his back they consider as arising from the construction of his body, and that the movement was vertical and not horizontal... From fifteen to twenty three bunches... were counted by the different persons who saw him, and his size round they thought to be that of a common firkin or half barrel.

... The greatest length given to him was one hundred feet and no one who had a good sight of him thought him less than eighty feet in length... They all agreed, too, as to the colour being quite dark, approaching black."[23]

On June 16, 1826, the American ship *Silas Richards* was passing St. George's Bank (by Nova Scotia) at 6:30 PM. Henry Holdrege (the captain), and a passenger named William Warburton, were the first to see a long multi-humped serpent swimming past the ship. Mr. Warburton quickly attempted to tell the other passengers who were below deck, but only a handful came up to see. Warburton recalled, "The remainder refused to come up, saying there had been too many hoaxes of that kind already."[24] Several reports were written that gave many details of the creature. The overall event is summarized in the following:

"It was about ten rods from the ship, the sea perfectly calm, and that part which appeared out of water about sixty feet in length. The head and protuberances were

---
22. Oudemans, *The Great Sea Serpent*. Cosimo Classics. p. 167.
23. Oudemans, *The Great Sea Serpent*. Cosimo Classics. p. 168.
   A firkin = a nine gallon round container. A half barrel (aka: kilderkin) = an 18 gallon round container.
24. Oudemans, *The Great Sea Serpent*. Cosimo Classics. p. 184. (Figure 13 sketch from the same page).

similar to the representations which have frequently been given to him by persons who had seen him near Cape Ann. He was going at a very slow rate, and appeared unmindful of the ship. He was visible about seven minutes to the passengers and crew, who were on deck at the time. A certificate has been drawn up and signed by the passengers, which, with a drawing made by one of the gentlemen, gives a minute description of the serpent as seen by them. The number and credibility of the witnesses, place beyond all doubt the existence of such an animal as a sea-serpent."[25]

Two days later, on June 18th, the same (or similar) creature was seen by another vessel sailing off Cape Cod, approximately 200 miles from where the crew of the Silas Richards saw it. The descriptions of the creature (by unrelated eyewitnesses) were very consistent with those mentioned only days earlier.[26]

Figure 13. The sketch of the sea serpent as seen by the crew and passengers of the *Silas Richards*. The humps on the back were described by Warburton as resembling "in size and shape those of the dromedary" (camel).

On August 6, 1848, captain M'Quhae and the crew of the *Daedalus* were on their way back to England from the East Indies. As eyewitnesses, they gave what is now considered to be one of the most famous sea-serpent reports of all time.

The *Times* gave the initial public report: "... between the Cape of Good Hope and St. Helena, her captain, and most of her officers and crew, at four o'clock one afternoon, saw a sea-serpent... Its head appeared to be about four feet out of the water, and there was about sixty feet of its body in a straight line on the surface... it propelled itself at the rate of 15 miles an hour. The diameter of the exposed part of the body was about sixteen inches; and when it extended its jaws, which were full of large jagged teeth, they seemed sufficiently capacious to admit of a tall man standing upright between them.".

Inquiring into the truth of the matter reported in the *Times*, the Admiralty demanded an official statement from the captain, who replied with an affirming detailed report.

"... at five o'clock... something very unusual was seen by Mr. Sartoris, midshipman, rapidly approaching the ship... The circumstance was immediately reported by him to the officer of the watch, Lieutenant Edgar Drummund, with whom and Mr. William Barrett, the master, I was at the time walking the quarterdeck...

---

25. Oudemans, *The Great Sea Serpent*. Cosimo Classics. p. 183.
26. Oudemans, *The Great Sea Serpent*. Cosimo Classics. p. 185.

On our attention being called to the object, it was discovered to be an enormous serpent with head and shoulders kept about four feet constantly above the surface of the sea, and as nearly as we could approximate by comparing it with the length of what our main-topsail yard would show in the water, there was at the very least sixty feet of the animal *à fleur d'eau*[27], no portion of which was, to our perception, used in propelling it through the water, either by vertical or horizontal undulation. It passed rapidly, but so close under our lee quarter, that had it been a man of my acquaintance, I should easily have recognized his features with the naked eye; and it did not, either in approaching the ship or after it passed our wake, deviate in the slightest degree from its course to the S.W., which it held on at the pace of from 12 to 15 miles per hour, apparently on some determined purpose.

The diameter of the serpent was about 15 or 16 inches behind the head, which was, without any doubt, that of a snake, and it was never, during the 20 minutes that it continued in sight of our glasses, once below the surface of the water; its color a dark brown, with yellowish white about the throat. It had no fins, but something like the mane of a horse, or rather a bunch of seaweed, washed about its back. It was seen by the quartermaster, the boatswain's mate, and the man at the wheel, in addition to myself and officers above mentioned.

I am having a drawing of the serpent made from a sketch taken immediately after it was seen...

Peter M'Quhae, Captain.

To Admiral Sir W. H. Gage, G. C. H., Devonport."[28]

Lt. Edgar Drummond, mentioned above, confirmed M'Quhae's account in all details except for what M'Quhae had described as a mane; Drummond called it a dorsal fin. Other eyewitnesses aboard ship also gave consistent reports of the unusual creature.

The Tresco Encounter

The following lengthy and detailed account (here condensed) was given by Joseph Ostens Grey, Second Officer of the *SS. Tresco*, and documented in the *Wide World Magazine: An Illustrated Monthly of True Narrative*... vol 12.

"I know that the very word "sea-serpent" is the signal for joking, ridicule, and utter incredulity. While many reports have been brought to land, no sea-serpent, small or large, and no fragment of head or fin have ever been subjected to study by any recognized scientist; and yet such a creature confronted the steamship *Tresco* when on

---
27. (visible on the) "surface of the water"
28. Oudemans, *The Great Sea Serpent*. Cosimo Classics. pp. 209-213.

her last outward voyage from the United States.

We left the port of Philadelphia, in Pennsylvania, on May 28th, 1903, for Santiago deCuba... The *Tresco* is a large cargo-steamer... her length is three hundred and eight feet...

On this trip it so happened that, instead of the *Tresco* being heavily laden with a return cargo, she was going out in water ballast; the ship was therefore very light. She rose well out of the water, her rail some twenty feet above it...

Our skipper is Captain W. H. Bartlett... I am the second officer—Joseph O. Grey. We had twenty six men on board—good, able fellows...

Whatever the danger of mutiny may be, however, no firearms are at hand on an English ship; it is contrary to law. The *Tresco* has no guns, either...

We were two days out, some ninety miles south of Cape Hatteras. All was going smoothly on board... the weather was calm, the sea smooth, and the sky slightly obscured, but the air was clear as crystal. On this particular morning... it was my watch... It being my watch, the first mate had gone below, and the captain was in his state-room. No duty demanding his attention, he was taking a morning nap.

About ten o'clock I saw, on our port bow, something creating a vast amount of disturbance in the water...

Whatever was approaching the vessel, the water was surging about some large fish which presently I discovered were not porpoises, but sharks... It seemed to me a phenomenonal departure from anything I had heretofore observed in regard to these voracious and savage creatures. They were not attracted to the vessel by anything thrown overboard, but held steadily on their way...

From the time we sighted them until they disappeared, they kept their course, as if making all speed. What impelled them to travel at such a rate I could not imagine; nor could I offer any explanation for their assembly in such a solid mass...

The passing of the sharks had made me unusually on the alert. About an hour later I espied a fresh object in the water on our port bow. It was some distance away... exactly the direction from which the sharks had appeared. It was floating low, and it looked black. I thought it must be a derelict...

The man at the wheel beside me on the bridge thought so too as we headed for it, wondering how much of a hulk it would prove to be, or what we should ascertain of its history...

During the twenty minutes we were steering toward it I was decidedly puzzled. It seemed to me that this low-lying, dark object was moving toward us, as well as we toward it. It did not look like the hull of a vessel; nor could it be a raft. Neither would move so swiftly toward us... With a conviction that grew deeper, and ever more disquieting, we came to know that this thing could be no derelict, no object that hand of man had fashioned...

Now, swiftly, with a terrible uprising, a mighty and horrible head came out of the water, surmounting a tall, powerful neck that had the thickness and strength of a cathedral pillar, yet spindly in comparison with the huge and awful head that it supported.

All this time Leon, the quartermaster... He and I could see it well, and both of us looked at it aghast, not daring to believe our eyes.

I felt cold, with an unknown, overmastering horror. But I stood at my post on the bridge looking at that immense, dragon-like head, reared high on the long, powerful neck. It must be a sea-serpent—what else could it be?—coming towards us, and now so near.

Figure 14. A refined illustration of the *Daedalus* serpent sighting that is consistent in form with the sketches mentioned in the captain's report. Captain M'Quhae himself reviewed the illustration and was satisfied with it. Artist unknown. *Illustrated London News.*[29]

The others on deck, as well as the helmsman and myself, saw the monster... After the first inertia of fear a regular panic took place on board. All work, all duty, all discipline, were forgotten. It was every man for himself. Of our twenty-six men nearly all were below, and the few who were on deck tumbled down to their quarters in desperate, mad haste; and I longed to follow.

What they thought, or said, I do not know. My mind was completely absorbed

---

29. Gould, *Mythical Monsters*. 1886. pp. 292, 293. And A.C. Oudemans, *The Great Sea Serpent.* p. 214.

by the object in the water. I felt that I must run somewhere, anywhere, to get away; and yet the weird and awful thing, there before us, held my gaze in the one direction.

At length I recovered some measure of my self-possession.

"Jump, Leon; jump down into the wheel-house!" I shouted. "Steer down there. Let's get out of this fellow's road!"

The man obeyed with alacrity; and I, only too gladly, followed him...

I could see it steadily and well from the chart-room port-hole. I looked and tried to notice every possible thing about it, yet wondering anxiously all the while how we should escape... To me it was sickening and horrifying, and Leon had seen quite enough before he fled from the bridge...

The creature, assuredly, was enraged. So enormous was its size, so vast its strength, that even a steamer like the *Tresco* would be in danger of some kind... The rail of the ship, it was true, was twenty feet above the water; but the head and neck of the serpent were already elevated to a height of fifteen feet. It could easily come aboard...

But far more serious to contemplate was the problem of its mere weight. That alone was a menace to the ship's safety. As I have said, we were going out in ballast, very light. Such a weight on one side would inevitably list the vessel, for the centre of gravity was so high that any heavy, ill-placed burden meant the gravest danger.

There that evil thing remained, the body motionless, the tail undulating vertically. As it lashed the water with the long, snake-like tail the head all the time was reared high... It looked for all the world like some fantastic Chinese dragon become a living reality; or a page from a scientific work picturing some ancient saurian monster, neither reptile nor beast wholly, but both in part...

We needed no binoculars... the serpent was so near that even untrained eyes could have distinguished the most minute details of its appearance.

I estimated the length of the creature at about one third that of the *Tresco*, or one hundred feet...

I judged it to be about eight feet in diameter in the widest part of its body, and so about twenty feet in circumference. The body was not cylindrical at all. It had a noticeable arch toward the top, and the hump of the back sloped downwards to the neck as well as toward the tail. It was widest at the forward end, rapidly tapering backward from the hump above the shoulders.

There was something unspeakably loathsome about the head, which was five feet long from nose to upper extremity. Such a head I never saw on any denizen of the sea. The neck, eighteen inches in diameter, was slender by comparison. Underneath the jaw there seemed to be a sort of pouch, or drooping skin; there may have been a slight bulge there. The neck was smallest half-way between the head and where it joined the body.

The nose, like a snout upturned, was somewhat recurved. It was rather pointed in its general formation, but blunt at the end. I can remember no nostrils or blow-holes. The lower jaw was prognathous, and the lower lip was half projecting, half pendulous. Presently I noticed something dripping from the ugly lower jaw. Watching, I saw that it was saliva, of a dirty drab colour, which dropped from the corners of the mouth.

While it displayed no teeth, it did possess very long and formidable molars. There were two, curving down and backward like walrus's tusks, about eighteen inches in length, at the very back of the mouth. They were of a dirty ivory hue. If it had teeth or tongue it did not show them, but we saw that its mouth was red.

Its eyes were also of a decided reddish colour. They were set high in the head, like serpent's eyes, or those of water-fowl. There were elongated vertically, not lateral, were slightly elliptical rather than round, and were large in proportion to the head. Their greatest length was about seven inches and their extreme width four inches. No pupil was visible. The entire cast of the eyes appeared to be red, of the shade of maroon...

Below the eyes some scales appeared, which dragged backward, becoming larger and larger until, on the body, they were great plates, or protuberances like the denticulated ridges of an alligator's hide. They did not glisten like the scales of a fish. The smallest of the scales, near the eyes, measured about three inches in diameter... the largest of the scales... were some eight inches long... their apex being a distinct ridge.

The hide, in the general tone of its colour, could be compared to nothing but antique bronze, showing the distinct light green hue of the oxidized metal. The tone of the colour was lightest upon the back and sides. As it shaded toward the almost wholly submerged belly it became dull, dark green, deepening its hue with the decrease in the size of the plates or indurations constituting the creature's defensive armour.*

[* *Our readers will find it interesting to compare this description with that of the monster seen by Captain Thomson, of the Sydney (N.S.W.) steamer Nemesis, and Captain Grant, of the ss. Perth, off Cape Naturaliste, West Australia. This appeared in our issue for March, 1901.*]

It held itself in the same relative position to the ship during all the time the impressions I have enumerated were photographed indelibly on my brain. Its side fins, extending one-third of the way from the shoulder to the beginning of the tail, and broadest—about a foot—near the shoulder, worked like fans in swift agitation of the water.

As I gazed, fascinated with the horror of the thing, it raised its dorsal fin, obviously in wrath. And then a thing happened which, strange as it may appear after the recounting of the fearsomeness of the serpent's dreadful front, was more appalling, more sickeningly terrifying, than anything I had yet beheld. Suddenly, at the back of the head, a great webbed crest uprose, and from the eyes, hitherto so dull save for the glow smouldering in their depths, a scintillating glare appeared, as if the creature felt the moment had come for attack. The crest was a foot in height at its forward extremity, where it was supported by a sharp pointed spine.

The undulations of the tail increased in violence... it came no nearer...

It was going to turn away from us...

Its great body turned, as if on a pivot, inward in a circle, followed by its long tail. With astonishing ease for so huge a bulk it made the sweeping evolution. And only then did it lower its ugly head, that had so long confronted us in open antagonism.

Only at that moment did I think of Captain Bartlett... I wanted him to see the monster...

Springing up instantly he was ready to follow. He comprehended that something unusual was near, yet he was astonished at such a report from an excited mate. Five seconds more and we two stood together... where we could have a clear view...

Captain Bartlett stood transfixed. A moment and he found his voice:—

"Good heavens! What was that?"

"I take it, sir," I replied, "to be a sea-serpent."

"I believe you're right," he rejoined...

Now that the terrifying thing was gone we could talk and compare our observations and ideas concerning it. As I have said, I did not notice any nostrils; but I believe it was a breathing animal, endowed with lungs. While no sound reached my ears as we approached it... Captain Bartlett thought he heard distinctly... a noise which came from the creature that was in the nature of a snort or, to be exactly correct, a hoot...

The men who had fled so hastily, and the others who came at their call, looked out fearfully at the serpent from the forecastle ports... Those who did not see it... can testify to the general excitement and the facts elicited by the subsequent discussion among the men who did...

I wished we possessed powerful guns which could tear a hole in that appalling head or through the armoured body, so that we could secure the carcass as a trophy and settle once for all the controversy concerning the sea-serpent...

We have carefully collated all the facts. Our conclusion is that the creature was, without a doubt, a mammal... although more like a reptile in appearance.

At Santiago I prepared a report for the Press of Philadelphia, to be presented on my return. Although I made it out carefully, it drew forth the usual jests in several quarters, but it was credited in others..."[30]

Post Darwinian Sea Serpent Sightings

Two British scientists aboard the oceanographic research vessel *Valhalla*, on a scientific cruise 15 miles off the mouth of the Parahiba river in Brazil, saw an unusual

---

30. *The Wide World Magazine: An Illustrated Monthly of True Narrative, Travel, Customs, and Sport.* Vol 12. pp. 147 - 155.

animal in the water at about 10:15 AM on December 7, 1905. The naturalist E.G.B. Meade-Waldo wrote the following: "I looked and immediately saw a large fin or frill sticking out of the water, dark seaweed-brown in colour, somewhat crinkled at the edge. It was apparently about 6 feet in length, and projected from 18 inches to 2 feet from the water." As he reached for his field glasses, he said that a "great head and neck rose out of the water in front of the frill; the neck did not touch the frill in the water, but came out of the water in front of it, at a distance of certainly not less than 18 inches, and from 7 to 8 feet was out of the water... the head and neck were all about the same thickness. Meade-Waldo clearly saw that the head was "turtle-like". He plainly viewed the line of the mouth, which only came around a little way, not past the eyes, which were also visible. The head and neck moved back and forth in a "peculiar manner", he reported. The color of the head and neck was dark brown above and whitish below, indeed, "almost white", or "dirty white"."

The entomologist Michael J. Nicholl confirmed Meade-Waldo's report, though his use of descriptive terms varied slightly. He stated in a follow-up interview, "This creature was an example, I consider, of what has so often been reported, for want of a better name, as the 'great sea serpent'. I feel sure, however, that it was not a reptile that we saw, but a mammal."[31] This conclusion was mainly due to the line of the mouth not going beyond the eyes.

During the 1920's and 1930's a rash of reports of a sea serpent off the coast of British Columbia were made. Occasional sightings had occurred in the past, going back to at least 1897, but the Loch Ness uproar gave water monsters a revived interest. Soon the Canadian animal was given the name Cadborosaurus, which combined Cadboro Bay, on Victoria Island's southeast coast, and *saurus*. Cadborosaurus soon became "Caddy."

The first widely publicized sighting took place on October 8, 1933, and involved a witness of high repute: Maj. W. H. Langley, a barrister and clerk of the British Columbia legislature. Sailing his sloop past Chatham Island early in the afternoon, he spotted a greenish-brown-colored serpent with serrated body, "every bit as big as a whale but entirely different from a whale in many respects." He estimated its length at eighty feet.[32]

Sea Serpent Comparisons

Like the common belief that the Chinese have only one type of snake-like dragon in their culture, yet in reality they have many different kinds, the evidence indicates the same for sea-serpents, that there are several different kinds. This has

---

31. Loren Coleman, *Field Guide to Lake Monsters, Sea Serpents, and Other Mystery Denizens of the Deep.*
    See: "Type: Waterhorse; Category: Long neck" section.
32. Jerome Clark. *Unexplained!: Strange Sightings, Incredible Occurrences & Puzzling Physical Phenomena.*
    See "The twentieth-century serpent" section.

caused many skeptics to arise who only considered a small sampling of varied reports, giving the impression that the witnesses were making things up due to so-called inconsistencies. However, the many descriptions are indeed reasonably consistent when grouped accordingly. This alone is evidence that many reports are credible since they do not describe a single creature, but several types consistently.

"In the last chapter of *In the Wake of the Sea-Serpents*, at the end of a detailed recitation and searching analysis of every sea serpent report, credible or otherwise, known through 1966 (587 in all, of which he judged 358 authentic observations of unknown animals),[33] ...Bernard Heuvelmans parted company with nearly all of his predecessors. He bluntly conceded the futility of trying to force-fit from these sightings a description of a single species of animal... [he also found that their descriptive] features reappeared so often that they had to be taken into consideration. And if they were, they suggested that "sea serpent" is a generic term covering several unrecognized marine animals."[34]

Witness	Length	Color	Head	Scales	'Coils'	Undulation
Egede	4x > ship			Yes		
Magnus	200'	dark		Yes		
Cummings	60'	blueish	serpent-like			Vertical
Allen III	80'	dk brown	serpent-like			Vertical
Grey	100'	bronze/green	dragon-like	Yes		Vertical
Wheeler	50'	black	serpent-like		12	(Vertical)
Cabot	80'	black	serpent-like		13-14	Vertical
Pontoppidan		greyish	horse-like		8	
M'Quhae	60'	dk brown yellow/white	serpent-like			No
MeadeWaldo		dk brown white	turtle-like			
Langley	80'	brown/green		Yes		

Figure 15. Comparative chart of the basic components of several well-known sea-serpent descriptions.

Lake Monsters

Throughout the world, dragons and monstrous serpents have been largely associated with bodies of water. Comparing the number of reports, lake monster sightings outweigh those from the sea. This is a foregone conclusion since mankind frequents land areas (particularly those near water sources) far more than he does

---
33. Reported sightings ranged from 1639 to 1966.
34. Jerome Clark. *Unexplained: Strange Sightings.* See "The varieties of sea-serpent experience" section.

the ocean. Here are a few prime examples, out of *thousands* of historical eyewitness accounts, of lake monsters around the world.

Nicknamed "Nessie" since the 1940's, the large serpentine creature that inhabits Scotland's Loch Ness is perhaps the best known cryptid associated with a prehistoric animal, namely the plesiosaur. The *Vita Columbae* ("Life of Columba"),[35] contains a story that is considered to be the first reference to the monster of Loch Ness. According to Adomnán (aka: Eunan, the ninth Abbot of Iona), Columba encountered a group of Picts near the river Ness, which flowed out of Loch Ness. They were burying a man who had been killed by a particular monster that was living in the river. Wanting to encourage them and demonstrate God's authority, Columba instructed one of his disciples to swim to the other side of the river. The monster, lying at the bottom of the river, came up in pursuit of the swimmer. Reminiscent of Saint Martha and other European saints, Columba made the sign of the cross and commanded the monster, "Thou shalt go no further, nor touch the man; go back with all speed." Surprised by the command, the monster abruptly stopped its pursuit (as if being pulled by ropes), and quickly retreated in terror. Upon seeing this, the Picts glorified Columba's God. Documented sightings of a large creature (or creatures) inhabiting Loch Ness (and other Scottish Lochs) have been recorded ever since, up to this very day.

In North America, in the state of Vermont, for centuries there have been numerous sightings of a creature that inhabited (and still inhabits) Lake Champlain. Named "Champ", descriptions of this long-necked creature are similar to those that inhabit Loch Ness. Local Native Americans called it *Tatoskok*.[36]

Many are led to believe that the first documented sighting of Champ by Western eyes was by the French explorer Pierre de Champlain (the founder of Québec), in 1609. However, no such official report has been found. This unsupported claim originated in a 1970 article by the late Marjorie L. Porter in the Summer issue of *Vermont Life*.

A brief but sufficiently detailed report in 1819 entitled, "Cape Ann Serpent on Lake Champlain", gave the account of Captain Crum who encountered an enormous serpentine monster at about 8:00 a.m. one Thursday morning. The description was consistent with most sea monster sightings:

"... an unusual undulation of the surface of the water, which was [*bothered?*] by the appearance of a monster rearing its head more than fifteen feet and moving with the utmost velocity... (It was) about 187 feet long, its head flat with three teeth, two in the under and one in the upper jaw, in shape similar to the sea horse—the color black, with a star in the forehead and a belt of [*color?*] around the neck—its body about the size of a hogshead with bunches on the back as large as a common potash barrel—the eyes large and the color of pealed onion—He continued to move with astonishing rapidity towards the shore for about a minute, when suddenly he darted under water

---
35. Adomnán of Iona. *The Life of Columba*. See Book 2, chapter 28. 565 AD.
36. Also known as *Gitaskog* by the Abenaki and Iroquois tribes.

and has not since been seen, altho' many fishing boats have been on the look out." [37]

Another reputable sighting of the Lake Champlain monster occurred in 1883. While standing on the shore, Sheriff Nathan H. Mooney reported seeing a "…gigantic water serpent about 50 yards away". He was able to see "round white spots inside its mouth" and estimated the creature's length to be approximately 30 feet. His sighting encouraged other eyewitnesses to publicly present their own accounts. Notably, Mooney's account was given about a half century prior to the initial rash of Loch Ness sightings which made its serpentine inhabitant so famous.[38]

Also in Vermont, Lake Memphremagog is home to a similar large unknown animal that is called "Memphre." Very little is known about this mysterious creature, despite having over 200 sightings reported in the past 150 years.

Other lake monsters have been reported in various places throughout North America. One brief example is given in M.F. Hetherington's work, *A History of Polk County, Florida,* in 1928. "There is a tradition that a sea serpent, or lake serpent, used to haunt Lake Clinch. The Indians many years ago insisted there was an immense serpent in this lake. In 1907 residents of Frostproof declared they had seen the monster, and that it must be 30 feet long…"[39] However, by the time of publication of his historical work, no additional sightings of the lake monster arose. This lends some strength to the argument that perhaps the creature died around this time and was simply no longer being seen. Dismissing the native American sightings and subsequent local eyewitnesses who claimed the same thing as mere folklore is overlooking one simple fact, that it would be easy to give false testimony of a "sighting" to perpetuate a hoax for tourism purposes or personal attention. However, no sightings have been made since then, but rather have all stopped at one particular point in time.

During the nineteenth and early twentieth centuries, several Western explorers managed to penetrate the Amazonian rain forest. Many returned with incredible stories of gigantic strange serpentine creatures. Predictably, their relayed stories were mocked by skeptics; yet none could deny the consistency in the reports as to general location and description of the creatures by the native inhabitants of the Amazon region. Franz Herrmann Schmidt, an employee of the Hamburg-American Company, gave an excellent account that is presented in part here.

> "So many of my friends in Brazil have besought me to make public the account I am about to write, and so many others in the United States and in Germany have laughed at the story when I told it to them, that I have hesitated for a long time about mentioning it again. It is not pleasant to be called a liar good humoredly [sic], even when one has no means of proving that he is not, but knows that he is telling the truth. If boa constrictors as thick as trees and

---

37. *Plattsburgh Republican.* July 24, 1819. (Captain Crum was in charge of a scow/flat bottom boat). Note: due to poor copying, a couple words were unreadable in the source text (in brackets).
38. Mark Chorvinsky. Nessie and Other Lake Monsters. *"Champ" of Lake Champlain.* Online article.
39. M. F. Hetherington, *History of Polk County, Florida: Narrative and Biographical.* 1928.

over one hundred feet long are common, and are admitted to exist, I do not see why the stay at home public should not believe that what I saw in the same country is really there.

Therefore I want to remark at the outset that the man who does not believe what I have to say can go up the Amazon, and, with enough patience, see the same things; or if he does not care for the hardship he can find plenty of proof that many other men besides myself have had proofs brought to them...

On October 8, 1907, Captain Rudolph Pfleng, who was well known as a sailor and trader, and myself were in Bogota, Colombia, seeking a number of concessions in the Orinoco country, but political conditions being very unquiet we failed to get them, and on the date mentioned determined to set out at once to penetrate the interior and descend some river on the other side of the watershed to the head of navigation on some branch of the Amazon. En route we hoped to find some high bars rich in gold, perhaps some fine new rubber areas or new forests of wild cacao; also both of us were anxious to keep our late presence and our mission in Colombia a secret. Had we gone out by the coastwise route the fact would have been common gossip...

[After weeks of difficult travel through the near-impenetrable jungle]... The day had been oppressively hot, and just as the sun was getting down into the west we came to a fine waterfall about ten feet wide, with a fifty foot pool below it emptying into a brook across which an active man could leap.

Just where the brook left the pool a great brown log had fallen, making a natural bridge. One of the Indians was about to cross it, seeking some light wood for the night's fire, when he gave a queer cry and came bounding back. I saw Pfleng pick up his rifle and I did likewise. The Indian led us back to the point where he had stood and showed us what a mistake he had made. The log was a great sleeping boa constrictor. The terrible, creature had caught some sort of an animal by the pool, and having eaten it, as a lump one-third of the way down the body showed, grew sleepy and remained where it was in the sunshine, stretched across the brook.

At first we thought the creature was dead, and came near enough to see that its sides were working either through respiratory or intestinal action. I was for having a shot or two into the parts of the body we could see, but Pfleng argued against it.

At least we had a fine opportunity for studying him. For fully a half hour he lay there until the shadows struck him, and then he began to draw forward slowly, and in ten minutes was gone into the jungle. I measured with my eye the thickness of the body as compared with a certain stone by which it lay. The two were the same. The thickness of the stone was twenty-two inches, yet the snake's body was thicker further up. From the spot where the head lay to where the plated tail had marked the ground when the snake started to crawl was forty-four feet, and there being two or three loops of the body in between we estimated his full length at sixty-five or seventy feet.[40]

What caused us to leave the easier river route and plunge into the forest once more were the stories we heard from the Indians. The tribes in this

---
40. There have been many eyewitness accounts (and snakeskins) of very large snakes in the Amazon and Southeast Asian regions - some reportedly reaching over 80 feet! (i.e.; reputable reports by Colonel Percy Fawcett, Father Victor Heinz, and Bernard Huevelmans, are three typical examples).

belt are the Cocamas, the Hypurinas and the Manoteris, all of them clustering along the water courses and all as like as peas, so that I could see no reason for tribal distinctions at all. By taking the direct route to the south they assured us that we would find a wonderful cacao and rubber country, but there were great swamps inhabited by animals of such size that, the boa constrictor we had seen would be a plaything for them.

At least twenty Indians were encountered who had at various times seen this huge animal of animals. Penning and I questioned [them] minutely and were puzzled to find that, while they agreed pretty well as to description, actions, etc., there was a wide divergence, as to size and as to spots in which the creatures had been encountered. At least two hundred miles apart some of those must be, yet all lay in the general southerly direction...

We simply made up our minds that we would bag one if we could and have a good look at it; perhaps it was some new kind of gigantic alligator or some huge variety of water snake. At least it would be good sport. We had three guides from the waterside who remained with us sixteen days of travel quite as difficult as that which I have described...

The valley was like any other of many we had crossed, and we should merely have detoured the swamp if Pfleng, surveying it with his glasses, had not noticed in two or three spots on the shores of the lakes some huge swathes or crushed tracks such as the Indians had mentioned. We could not inspect these from solid ground.

The only way we could get at them was from the water so we cut a tree, made a rude dugout, shaped up some paddles and the second day set it afloat, in the open water at the head of the lake. One thing we noticed at once. There was not an alligator, iguana, or even a large water snake to be seen anywhere. This in itself was queer...

There was no question but what it had been made by some enormous body being dragged from the water through the plants and mud until solid ground was reached, when a great circular wallow in a sunny spot was made. On the plants nearby were marks of waves two feet above mean level on the average and great, flaglike stocks as thick as my leg were broken off short in the track and the tops mashed into the mud, while the movement of the body had carried quantities of the soft ooze from below the water and spread it like plaster on the crushed plants.

A very large elephant or hippopotamus could have made a similar track. In making the return journey to the water practically another course had been chosen, the point of entrance being some hundred foot to the east, and a little shelving bank there having been crushed in with the small trees that grew on it, in a way that showed that many tons of weight must have rested on it. The creature that had been able to make marks like these in the course of a peaceful progress must be a terrible thing if aroused to anger.

The Indians in the dugout grew more and more frightened, and I confess that I began to watch the water and listen for movements along the shore or among the islands with feelings slightly more tinged with anxiety than I had felt before I saw these evidences.

Leaving this spot, we proceeded slowly along and soon came to an island which was evidently a favorite sunning spot, as the plants were crushed down all over it and it was plastered with mud dragged up from the bottom.

It took much time to get ahead any and it was very late in the day before we crossed one bayou about a half mile wide to examine some similar spots on the further shore. Here we found three spots where some amphibious animal had left the water and returned to it. One was very large and the other two only about half the size.

Plainly there was more than one such creature in the lake. Another thing which we had not observed previously was that vast quantities of fronds, tender green leaves and broad stretches of flag growth had been ripped off. I have seen spots in which a herd of elephants has fed, and those looked very similar. One tree had a smear of mud on it fully fourteen feet from the ground...

We approached very carefully and a thrill shot through me as I saw that the mud on the weeds and water plants was still dripping. We were close to our quarry.

With every precaution, the paddles making no noise at all, we advanced to the water line. To have left the boat would have meant going in the mud to our waists, perhaps, and yet we could see nothing but green stuff from where we were. We argued the question in a whisper and Pfleng had just announced his determination to follow the track inland if it was the very last act of his life, when a troop of monkeys was heard approaching, gathering some great blue-black berries from small trees that grew in the mud. We had just made them out when there was a sudden outcry among them, a large dark something half hidden among the branches shot up among them and there was a great commotion.

One of the excited Indians began to paddle the boat away from the shore, and before we could stop him we were one hundred feet from the waterline. Now we could see nothing and the Indians absolutely refused to put in again, while neither Pfleng nor myself cared to lay down our rifles to paddle. There was a great waving of plants and a sound like heavy slaps of a great paddle, mingled with the cries of some of the monkeys moving rapidly away from the lake. One or two that were hurt or held fast wore shrieking close at hand, then their cries ceased. For a full ten minutes there was silence, then the green growth began to stir again, and coming back to the lake we beheld the frightful monster that I shall now describe.

The head appeared over bushes ten feet tall. It was about the size of a beer keg and was shaped like that of a tapir, as if the snout was used for pulling things or taking hold of them. The eyes were small and dull and set in like those of an alligator. Despite the half dried mud we could see that the neck, which was very snakelike, only thicker in proportion, as rough knotted like an alligator's sides rather than his back.

Evidently the animal saw nothing odd in us, if he noticed us, and advanced till he was not more than one hundred and fifty feet away. We could see part of the body, which I should judge to have been eight or nine feet thick at the shoulders, if that word may be used, since there were no fore legs, only some great, heavy clawed flippers. The surface was like that of the neck. For a wonder the Indians did not bolt, but they seemed fascinated.

As far as I was concerned, I would have waited a little longer, but Pfleng threw up his rifle and let drive at the head. I am sure that he struck between the eyes and that the bullet must have struck something bony, horny or very tough, for it cut twigs from a tree higher up and further on after it glanced. I shot as Pfleng shot again and aimed for the base of the neck.

The animal had remained perfectly still till now. It dropped its nose to the spot at which I had aimed and seemed to bite at it, but there was no blood or any sign of real hurt. As quickly as we could fire we pumped seven shots into it, and I believe all struck. They seemed to annoy the creature but not to work any injury. Suddenly it plunged forward in a silly, clumsy fashion. The Indians nearly upset the dugout getting away, and both Pfleng and I missed the sight as it entered the water. I was very anxious to see its hind legs, if it had any. I looked again only in time to see the last of it leave the land—a heavy blunt tail with rough horny lumps. The head was visible still, though the body was hidden by the splash. From this instant's opportunity I should say that the creature was thirty-five feet long, with at least twelve of this devoted to head and neck...

I should say that I have been asked to locate the region and so have worked the matter out as carefully as I can. It is about five degrees thirty minutes south and seventy degrees five minutes west, and can be most easily reached by ascending the Solimoes River.

Fort Wayne, Indiana, *Weekly Sentinel*, Feb. 8, 1911.[41]

There are four particular items mentioned that should not be overlooked in regards to supporting the authenticity of this report and its consistency with others:

a) the tapir-like snout (discussed in chapter three);

b) the virtually impenetrable armor; similar to the *leviathan* (Appendix C);

c) they dragged their bodies along the ground, similar to those mentioned in some European tales and specifically in Marco Polo's account;

d) Mr. Schmidt openly invited people to go and verify his story and gave the coordinates of where the encounter occurred.

The following claim is from an 1883 letter to *Scientific American* called "A Bolivian Saurian". Other than it having three dog-like heads[42], the description of the creature is similar to the previous *Weekly Sentinel* report as well as others.

Sir,—The 'Anglo-Brazilian Times,' March 24th, 1883, says that the Brazilian Minister at La Paz, Bolivia, has remitted to the Minister of Foreign Affairs in Rio photographs of drawings of an extraordinary Saurian killed on the Beni after receiving thirty-six balls. By order of the President of Bolivia the dried body, which had been preserved at Asuncion, was sent to La Paz. It is 12 metres long from snout to point of the tail, which latter is flattened. Besides the anterior head, it has, 4 metres behind, two small but completely formed heads rising from the back. *All three have much resemblance to the head of a dog. The legs are short, and end in formidable claws. The legs, belly, and lower part of the throat appear defended by a kind of scale armour, and all the back is protected by a still thicker and double cuirass, starting from behind the ears of the anterior head, and continuing to the tail. The neck is long, and*

---
41. *Prehistoric Monsters in Jungles of the Amazon.* See: www.strangeark.com (Historical Reprints section).
42. See "Two Heads are Deadlier than One" section in chapter 4.

the belly large and almost dragging on the ground. Professor Gilveti, who examined the beast, thinks it is not a monster, but a member of a rare or almost lost species, as the Indians in some parts of Bolivia use small earthen vases of identical shape, and probably copied from Nature.[43]

Water Panther

One of the most prominent lake-dwelling creatures for the Northeastern Native American tribes is the water panther.[44] It is also referred to as the "Great under-water wildcat." In their mythologies, water panthers are described as water-dwelling god-like monsters that are in eternal opposition to thunderbirds. Water panthers live in the deepest parts of lakes and rivers, and are believed (like those in Asia) to cause storms. They are even known to roar during such tempests. These sharp-clawed quadrupeds are depicted on petroglyphs as being serpentine in form; having long tails, dorsal spines, and horns. To some Native American tribes, the creatures were believed to be benevolent, while other tribes saw the water panther as a deadly and malevolent beast. Despite their views of the creature, tribesmen would often give some sort of offering (i.e., a dog or tobacco) to the water panther in exchange for a safe passage across a lake.[45] Furthermore, the taking of copper from particular lake regions was considered taboo due to the water panther being guardian over it.

Mistaken Identities

To be fair, besides the number of hoaxes there have been many misidentified sea creatures. More specifically, periodically there have been various dead sea animals washed up on shore that appear to be the carcasses of sea serpents. On closer examination, however, many have proved to be nothing more than the remains of a beaked whale, or other large denizen of the deep. Basking sharks in particular are frequently mistaken as being sea serpents. Due to the physical makeup of basking sharks, when they die, the lower portion of the head and jaw (among other portions of the body) decompose completely, leaving behind a skull-like lump on the end of a lengthy spine. The deceptive appearance of the decomposed and deformed remains cause it to look similar to a plesiosaur skeleton. The following two sensational reports are prime examples of such mistakes.

On April 25, 1977, the fishing vessel, *Zuiyo-maru*, of the Taiyo Fishery Co. Ltd., caught an unusual carcass that was widely publicized by the media as the possible remains of a plesiosaur. However, it was later determined through scientific examination to be a basking shark. The salvaged tissue sample (elastoidin) matched

---
43. "A Bolivian Saurian," *Scientific American*, **49:3**, 1883. (italics added for emphasis)
44. Also known as *Mishipeshu* or *Mishibijiw* in Ojibwe. *Mishipeshu* translates into "The Great Lynx."
45. W. A. Fox. *Dragon Sideplates from York Factory*. Manitoba Archaeological Journal Vol 2. pp. 27-31.

that of a basking shark as well as the number of cervical vertebrae (7) and skull shape. (Pliosaurs, aka: "Short-necked" plesiosaurs, have about 13 vertebrae while basking sharks have about seven. Basking shark 'skulls' are rounded and blunt, while plesiosaur skulls are triangular and elongated—like a snake). The disappointing scientific results were published, but with greatly reduced fanfare, leaving many to believe that an actual plesiosaur carcass was temporarily acquired.

In 1925, on Moore's Beach (about 2 miles north of Santa Cruz), a large unusual carcass was washed up on shore. After its discovery, numerous newspapers began to circulate various descriptions of the creature, causing many from surrounding regions to come see the strange serpent-like monster. It was essentially described as being about 40 feet long, with a long thin neck, duck-shaped head, and a whale-like tail. Many came to the conclusion that it was some sort of prehistoric animal, like a plesiosaur.

> ... it is little wonder local interest in the mystery of the monster continued to run at fever pitch... officials from the California Academy of Sciences (who officially claimed the body of the mammal for scientific study) carefully inspected the creature's skull, and announced to the waiting world that the mysterious monster of Moore's Beach was a North Pacific type of beaked whale. This creature was described as being so rare that no name, except its Latin one, Berardius bairdi (given to it by Leonhard Stejneger in 1883), had ever been bestowed upon it!
>
> With the mystery monster "officially" tagged with a name, and with further reports stating such things as the dual effects of decomposition and high seas had separated the body from the skin, which in turn had rolled up on itself to create the illusion of a long neck... most bay area residents nodded in agreement and readily accepted the Academy's findings... [regardless] there were also those who refused to believe the creature was a member of the whale family, and steadily clung to the belief that the Moore's Beach monster was of unknown origin..., perhaps a throwback to prehistoric times.[46]

These mistaken identities do not disqualify or account for the large amount of consistent reports given by unrelated persons (many of high repute and experience) around the globe throughout history. Besides, many misidentifications (and hoaxes) are a *result* of previous sightings and do not typically arise as original stories. Furthermore, just because there have not been any scientifically identified "true" sea serpents does not mean that they do not currently exist. Even large land animals are still being discovered in our modern age that were once thought to be extinct![47] Before they were discovered, rumors of these rare animals were also considered hoaxes or misidentifications.

---

46. Randall A. Reinstedt, *Shipwrecks and Sea Monsters of California's Central Coast.* p. 162.
47. Examples given in Appendix A.

Place	Country	Name
Loch Ness	Scotland	Nessie
Loch Lochy	Scotland	Lizzy
Lake Okanogan	British Columbia	Ogopogo
Lake Champlain	United States, Vermont	Champ
Lake Iliamna	United States, Alaska	Illie
Lake Erie	United States and Canada	South Lake Bessie
Lake Ikeda	Japan	Issie
(a deep gorge)	China, Hubei province	Chan ("toad")
Lake Tian-chi	China, Changbai Mountain	Lake Tian-chi monster
Lake Van	Turkey, Ankara	Lake Van monster
Lake Kariba	Zimbabwe, Mahombekombe	Nyaminyami
Mzintlava River	South Africa (near Mt. Ayliff)	Mamlambo
Howick Falls	South Africa, Kwa-Zulu-Natal	Inkanyamba
Lake Koskol	Kazakhstan	"Koskolteras Rhombopterix"
Lake Brosno	Russia	Brosno dragon

Figure 16. Partial list of various lake monsters.

Tian-chi 天池

Unconfirmed sightings of strange long-necked monsters living in remote lake Tianchi ("heavenly lake"), located in the Changbai mountains, in northeastern Jilin province (near North Korea), date back for more than a century. Some local records reported that in 1903, a creature, resembling a huge buffalo with a loud roar, sprang out of the water and attempted to attack three people standing near the shore. One of the men shot it in the belly six times. The beast roared and retreated back into the lake. A more recent sighting compared the creature's head to that of a human, except it had big round eyes, a protruding mouth, and a neck about 4 to 5 feet long. The creature also sported a white ring at the base of the neck and it had smooth, grey skin.[48]

According to the *Beijing Youth Daily*, on the morning of July 11, 2003, several Chinese government cadres saw a group of mysterious large creatures swimming in the volcanic lake. Provincial forestry bureau vice-director Zhang Lufeng said, "Within about 50 minutes, the monsters appeared five times. At times there was one, at times there were several. The last time, there were as many as about 20." He continued by stating that due to their distance from them, the creatures appeared only as white or black spots on the lake's surface. But from the wakes trailing in the water, he and others determined the spots were "living beings".[49]

---
48. Compare with the Kiao Lung, described in chapter 3 (*Detailed descriptions* / Kiao Lung section).
49. The Sydney Morning Herald. *China's 'Loch Ness Monster' resurfaces*. July 16, 2003.

On September 10, 2007, the *People's Daily Online*[50] reported that Zhuo Yongsheng (an employee for a local TV station run by the administration office of the nature reserve at Mount Changbaishan, Jilin) had taken both video and photos of the strange lake monsters to Xinhua's Jilin provincial bureau. One of the photos was of the creatures swimming parallel in three pairs while another photo showed them together in a group, leaving a wake behind them. Zhuo said, "I went on top of the southern slope of the mountain with two local guides at 5:05 am hoping to shoot the sunrise. I was not able to do that because it was cloudy." After waiting about twenty minutes (5:26 am), a clear view of Tianchi Lake was available. "Du Baiqing, one of the guides, suddenly pointed to the lake and yelled in amazement that a stone had emerged from nowhere." While Zhou focused his lens on the moving dark object in the center of the lake, five other forms emerged from the deep water. Zhou and the guides watched the six seal-like, finned creatures swimming in the lake for about an hour and a half until they submerged from sight at about 7:00 am. "They could swim as fast as yachts and at times they would disappear under the water. It was impressive to see them all swimming at exactly the same pace, as if someone was giving orders," he said. "Their fins - or maybe wings - were longer than their bodies." Zhuo admitted that he did not believe in legends about lake monsters until this event. "But I believed what I saw with my own eyes."

The video taken of these creatures from a distance can be found online. It is particularly interesting that the fins were, due to their size, considered by Zhou as potential wings. Thus, in addition with previous eyewitness reports, these descriptions are strikingly similar to those of the "dragon horse" mentioned in ancient Chinese writings (detailed in chapter 3). These intriguing modern sightings, with consequent video of many large living creatures in lake Tianchi, prepare us for the next chapter.

---

50. *People's Daily Online*. "Tianchi monster' caught on film". Source: Xinhua's Jilin provincial bureau. September 10, 2007.

7: Modern Accounts

This chapter covers the reports of land, air, and water dwelling dragons that were given by eyewitnesses after the term "dinosaur" was coined in 1842. Before dismissing these reports as mere fantasy, bear in mind that there have been many large animals (once thought to be legendary or mythical beasts) that have only been recently found by the scientific community. It is a wonder how such large creatures could elude notice for so long!

One example would be the large "fighting elephants" of Nepal. These giant Asian elephants were initially thought to be descendant of the wooly mammoth due to their size and double-domed head, but that belief was later found to be false. Rumors of these animals were considered legendary by the West for decades, that is, until 1992. An expedition of the *Scientific Exploration Society* discovered two of these enormous elephants in Bardia Park, Nepal. Since then, more have been found, though they are an extremely endangered species. Other large animals have been only recently found. Animals like the okapi (that are the size of a small deer), and the giant squid (archatheusis), were also thought to be legendary beasts before their physical discovery in modern times.

To reiterate, many strange reports describing unusual and unknown animals are easily disregarded, particularly by the scientific community. Naturally, no one wants to be known as being gullible, or taken for a fool. Yet time and time again, creatures that were once dismissed as mythological are now commonly known. For example, albeit not a recent discovery, the platypus was thought to be a hoax – even when the physical animal was brought in for examination!

> The platypus has perplexed scientists since its discovery by Europeans
> in the late 18th century. Here is a creature that has a furry body like most

mammals, webbed feet and a bill like a duck, and a reproductive system that involves young being hatched from eggs before suckling from their mothers. In fact, when the first platypus specimen reached England in 1799 (it was long dead), it was regarded as a hoax, a "high frolic practised on the scientific community by some colonial prankster". Experts of the day could not reconcile the fact that a duck-billed mammal with webbed feet and claws and a beaver-like tail could really exist. One zoologist, sure it was fraudulent, tried to remove the "duck's bill" from the pelt; his scissor-marks can still be seen on the original, in London's British Museum of Natural History.[1]

Before these "legendary" creatures were discovered, explorers and sailors alike were ridiculed for their claims by skeptics. The same holds true today for those claiming to encounter dragon-like animals around the world. Though hoaxes abound, there are many eyewitness reports that withstand scrutiny. Some modern reports and subsequent evidence are so consistent and compelling that various scientific teams have made expensive and treacherous trips to exotic locations in hopes of finding such elusive creatures.[2] To the dismay of skeptics, many of these expeditions gather additional evidence instead of finding a lack thereof. Nevertheless, the credibility of the following reports are yet to be determined and are presented here as *potential* evidence only.

Indian Mud Monsters

A hidden valley in the sub-Himalayan region in North East India was home to a strange creature, known only by the local villagers until the mid 1900's. Despite the altitude, the very isolated valley sports a humid, subtropical climate with extremely heavy rainfall and is home to many large animals like rhinoceros, bears, and elephants. The Apatani and Dafla tribes also live there. Both call the peculiar creature the *Buru*.

Charles Stonor, an English zoologist and agricultural officer, was the first Westerner to explore this region in 1945. His detailed reports are considered the best records of the area to date. When he initially heard the reports of the *Buru*, Stonor was puzzled, but became convinced of the creature's existence due to the consistency of the descriptions given by over 30 individuals. They told Stonor that though the *Buru* liked to keep to themselves, they could become aggressive. The Apatani told a few stories where humans were attacked. One in particular was about a hunter who, after threatening a *Buru's* young, drowned after being struck by the mother's tail. It was also mentioned that the *Buru* stayed in the recesses of the swamp during dry periods, and only came out when the swamp filled during the rainy season.

The following description of the *Buru* was given by the leading tribesmen of

---
1. Paula Weston, *The Platypus – Still More Questions Than Answers for Evolutionists*. 2002.
2. For example, see: *The Last Dinosaur*. History Channel's "Monster Quest" series. Season 3, Episode 18.

several villages in the valley. They were carefully interviewed separately by Ralph Izzard, who returned to the valley in 1948 in search of the *Buru* after hearing about Stonor's earlier expedition. Izzard had hoped that he would be able to provide actual physical evidence of the *Buru* when returning from his expedition.

The tribesmen consistently described the *Buru* as being approximately 12 to 15 feet long, with skin like a fish that had no scales. The skin color is a mottled bluish black, with a pale white underbelly. The *Buru* had three rows of short, blunt spines running down its sides and back. Its head was narrow and had a large snout that was flattened at the end. The teeth were similar to human teeth except the front upper and lower pair of teeth that were pointed like a boar's. It also had a forked tongue. Though its legs were short, being about 20 inches long, it had feet that were heavily clawed. Its tail was powerful and was approximately 5 feet in length and armored with rows of bony plates. The *Buru* was nearly completely aquatic and lived in the muddy lakes. They occasionally put their heads out of the water and made a loud, hoarse bellow. According to the local tribesmen, the *Buru* would wave their neck and head from side to side while they sifted through the muddy banks with their snout.

Stonor and Izzard realized that the Apatani spoke about the *Buru* in the past tense. Apparently, the creatures became extinct (about a generation or so before Stonor's initial expedition to the region) due to the growing Apatani population. As the people needed more food, the swamps were drained for cultivation. Consequently, the *Buru* retreated to a few remaining pools and eventually died off due to the loss of their habitat.[3] Other sightings of animals similar to the *Buru* have been seen in Bhutan, where even the king claimed to have seen one many years ago.

In an attempt to match the *Buru* with a dinosaur fossil, the *scelidosaurus* has most of the same physical characteristics of the *Buru*, as described by the Apatani and Dafla tribes. There are also varieties of stegosaurids that are found in nearly every continent in the world that are similar to the *Buru*. Some have large bony plates running along the entire back, while others, like *kentrosaurus*, have smaller plates mixed with spikes (thagomizers), and other variations.

Figure 17. Assumed silhouettes of a *kentrosaurus* (left) and *scelidosaurus* (right).

To this day, paleontologists do not know for certain how the plates along the back of some stegosaurids (like the well-known *stegosuarus stenops*) were arranged.

---

3. George M. Eberhart, *Mysterious Creatures: A Guide to Cryptozoology*, Vol 1, p. 77.
See also: Ralph Izzard, *The Hunt for the Buru*, Craven Street Books, 1951.

The common method is to show them in a "zig-zag" pattern, though they may have been positioned side by side. In this case however, the only discernible difference between a *scelidosaurus* and a *Buru* are the boar-like front teeth; *scelidosaurus* fossil skulls do not indicate such dentition. Perhaps this single discrepancy can be explained by means of morphological adaptation?

A common example of morphological adaptation can be seen in "Darwin's finches".[4] Darwin noticed that finch beaks changed in shape and size between generations depending on certain environmental changes and consequent food sources on the Galápagos Islands, verifying micro-evolution. However, Darwin then made a leap of logic and theorized that these adaptations were indicative of macro-evolution, that the finches would ultimately change into something else in due time.

Leelanau Lake Monsters

It is common knowledge that some creatures living today have body shapes that look just like other things in nature, like the walking stick insect (Phasmatodea) and leaf insects (Phyllium bioculatum), for example. As postulated in chapter three, there are some ancient reports about dragons that seem to indicate that some had a type of camouflage. Though less frequent today, similar eyewitness reports still occur.

One such account of a camouflaged lake monster occurred in the following manner. In the late 1800's, a dam was built on Lake Leelanau, Michigan. This was done to provide power to the Leland Sawmill. As a consequence, the dam sealed off the largest outlet and raised the lake's water level, turning much of the surrounding area into a swamp with dead, standing trees.

Shortly afterwards in 1910, a young teenager named William Gauthier was fishing for perch from his rowboat along the shallow shores of what was then called Carp Lake. William decided to row further out into the lake due to not catching anything for some time. As he proceeded out, he passed several dead cedar trees that were still standing in the water. William decided to tie his boat to one of the trees in order to continue fishing in that area where he had never fished before. He approached one of the trees that was in a convenient spot and as soon as his rope touched it, two eyes quickly opened and glared at William! The startled creature and the frightened boy stared at each other for a few seconds. Immediately after what seemed to be an eternity for William, the creature dove under the boat and swam with rapid undulation. As the creature's head rose out of the water on the far side of the boat, William noticed that the creature's tail remained out of the water on the opposite side. He determined the creature had a neck about 5 feet long and about 6 inches in diameter, and the water was about seven feet deep.

---

4. The term "Darwin's Finches" was first used by Percy Lowe in 1936, and also in 1947 by David Lack in his book *Darwin's Finches*.

In telling of this event, William admitted to having been quite terrified from the encounter and did not go out on the lake for many years afterward. William Gauthier was well educated and came from a prominent family in the area. He knew of others who also saw the creature, but were afraid to admit it publicly due to ridicule. Since the creature was apparently able to hide itself in plain sight, it coincides with the fact that there were few reports about the creature since it was seldom seen, if not recognized. A few other informal reports of this strange creature were given around this time, supporting Gauthier's claim, but discontinued after a while, leading researchers to believe that the creature may have since died.[5]

A more recent account was presented to Lon Strickler[6] at the end of 2012, which described a different lake monster inhabiting the same lake. Though the description is quite different than the creature described in 1910, it will become evident that this animal is strikingly similar with other lake monster sightings.

> I received the following email this morning (Monday). I spoke to the witness later in the day:
> Hello - I found your email address on Google and decided to write you. I live in Kalamazoo, MI and have lived in the area for most of my life. North of me is Lake Leelanau, a place where I have camped and fished for many years. I know the lake very well and have been on it hundreds of times.
> In June of this year, my wife and I took our RV to Leelanau Pines for a week. This campground is in the lower west side of the lake. On the last day of our trip I was heading back to the boat launch after an hour or so on the lake when I noticed something sticking out of the water. It was about 300 ft. from shore. It looked like a long thick piece of black rubber until it suddenly dove back into the water. I cut the motor and sat and watched.
> A few minutes later I noticed surface movement about 50 ft from me. It looked like a very thick black snake. It shimmered in the sunlight as it skirted across the water. The head was broad like a viper but about 10 inches wide. The body was about 5 foot long. It didn't seem to have any appendages. The body tapered to a lizard-like tail. I watched it for about 20 seconds until it plunged back into the depths.
> The head looked like that of a pit viper but it was definitely not a snake. The body at it's *(sic)* widest point was about 20-25 inches across with a slight ridge running down the back. I thought that it may be a large turtle at first but as I watched it I soon realized that this was something entirely different.
> Can you give me an idea what this was? I have asked a few friends who are also outdoorsmen and they are stumped. I appreciate your help. SN (name and personal information was removed from the original email).
> NOTE: I contacted SN and received a quick response. We later talked by phone. I believe SN truly witnessed something unique. Does anybody have an opinion to what this was? I later learned that there was an obscure 'monster' encounter at Lake Leelanau in 1910. I dug up what I could find... there wasn't

---

5. See: www.unknownexplorers.com/leelanau.php and www.leelanau.com/blog/the-lake-leelanau-monster.
6. Lon Strickler is the author and publisher of the syndicated 'Phantoms and Monsters' blog. Also a co-host at 'Beyond the Edge Radio'.

much to offer. – Lon[7]

Kulta

The oral histories and knowledge of the Australian Aboriginal peoples (Kooris) is known as Dreamtime. Most in the West consider these tales as mere myths and legends since many of these stories feature very strange large animals. However, the Aborigines insist that some of their oral traditions describe real flesh-and-blood creatures that either once existed or are still alive today.

Australian Aborigines (Kooris) describe the *kulta* as a giant herbivorous serpent that once lived in the (now nonexistent) swamps. The *kulta* was described as having a small head at the end of a long serpentine neck, a large body that was supported by four powerful legs, and a long, pointed tail. This description is similar to others in Australia, like those regarding the serpentine *Kooleen* and *Myndie*. The Kooris maintain that through the course of time the swamps dried up and the land became a desert, thus causing the ultimate demise of the *kulta*.[8] This is consistent with the drastic environmental changes and unmatched extinction rates Australia has endured compared to all other countries, particularly during the past few centuries.

Bunyip and Burrunjor

In July 1845, the *Geelong Advertiser,* of Victoria, Australia, (following a previous report in June) reported the finding of an *unfossilized bone* that formed part of the knee joint of an unknown giant animal. The bone was shown to an intelligent Aboriginal, who immediately identified it as being a *"bunyip* bone", which he then declared he had seen. "On being requested to make a drawing of it, he did so without hesitation."[9] The article continued with a story of an Aboriginal woman being killed by a *bunyip*[10] as well as that of Mumbowran, a man "who showed several deep wounds on his breast made by the claws of the animal"; offering the "most direct evidence of all". The article provided the following description:

> The Bunyip... is represented as uniting the characteristics of a bird and of an alligator. It has a head resembling an emu, with a long bill, at the extremity of which is a transverse projection on each side, with serrated edges like the bone of the stingray. Its body and legs partake of the nature of the alligator. The hind legs are remarkably thick and strong, and the fore legs are much longer, but still of great strength. The extremities are furnished with long claws... When in the water it swims like a frog, and when on shore it

---

7. Lon Strickler, *Cryptid Encounter on Lake Leelanau.* Nov. 5, 2012. Phantoms and Monsters / PM Network.
8. Rebecca Driver, *Australia's Aborigines ... Did They See Dinosaurs? Creation Ex Nihilo* magazine. Vol. 21, Issue 1. pp. 24-27.
9. *Wonderful Discovery of a New Animal.* Geelong Advertiser and Squatters' Advocate. July 2, 1845. p. 2.
10. Modern Aboriginal Australians translate bunyip as meaning "devil" or "evil spirit".

walks on its hind legs with its head erect, in which position it measures twelve or thirteen feet in height.

Figure 18. Professional illustration of the bunyip[11] [left] (based on Aboriginal descriptions) compared with skeletons of a trachodon.[12] [right] The physical dimensions and unusual nose shape are strikingly similar to some hadrosaur fossils, which are found in North/South America and Asia.

Despite this report, *bunyip* descriptions vary across the continent. *Bunyips* are associated with water and are sometimes referred to as a "water spirit". Because they are usually hidden in waterways and cause dread among Aboriginals, they often have trouble describing the *bunyip* consistently.

Like the *bunyip*, stories of the *burrunjor* persist among the Aborigines from ancient times. The mere mention of the *burrunjor* often invokes fear from any Aboriginal, especially those who claim to have seen it. They are not the only people who maintain to have seen these beasts however. Many Europeans and various residents of remote areas claim to have seen the *burrunjor* too.

Land inhabited by the *burrunjor* extend throughout northern Australia's tropical region to as far south as the "Red Centre". It is described as being a dark-colored bipedal predatorial reptile with long arms and large three-toed feet, standing approximately 20 to 25 feet tall. It has been suggested that the *burrunjor* could be a surviving remnant of the (believed to be) extinct giant monitor lizard (Megalania prisca), which grew to a similar size. The similarities end there however, for giant monitors may walk on their hind legs for short distances, but the *burrunjor* appear to be completely bipedal. Thus, theropod dinosaurs match the description best. Consider the following case-histories documented in *Burrunjor! The Search for Australia's Living Tyrannosaurus,* and *Out of the Dreamtime The Search for Australasia's Unknown Animals*.[13]

In 1950, near the border between the northern Territory and Queensland, cattlemen found that some of their livestock were mutilated over a wide area. The

---
11. *Creation Ex Nihilo* magazine. Volume 21, Issue 1. pp. 25. Referencing the *Geelong Advertiser*. April 27, 1991.
12. William Diller Matthew, *Dinosaurs - With special reference to the American Museum Collections*. Photo by A.E. Anderson. Chapter VII. "The Beaked Dinosaurs" (Continued), Fig 28. (Image in public domain / www.gutenberg.org).
13. Authors/researchers: Rex and Heather Gilroy. (Selected paraphrased accounts from quoted online sources that reference these two books).

half-eaten bulls and cows were killed by an unknown beast. In an effort to find the beast, those searching on horseback found reptilian tracks of a large biped. Following the three-toed tracks with their dogs, the footprint trail led them through some rough jungle terrain and eventually entered a swampland. The cattle dogs became uneasy and ran away. The horses were also uneasy and resisted going through the swamp. Determined to catch their quarry, two cattlemen broke off from the others and continued on foot with their rifles in hand. They reached the opposite side of the swamp and came across more tracks in an open field. While one man was searching nearby, the other briefly saw the dark figure of some huge creature moving far off in the dense woods and estimated it to be about 30 feet in height! Realizing the potential danger, both men left the area in haste.

In 1961, Johnny Mathews, a part-Aboriginal tracker, claimed he saw a 25 foot tall bipedal reptilian creature moving through some scrub near Lagoon Creek on the Gulf Coast. Almost a decade later (1970), he explained that hardly anyone outside his own people believed his story, though he was sure of what he witnessed.

> Campfire stories substantiating Aboriginal claims are commonplace across the far north. Back in 1978, a Northern Territory bushman and explorer, Bryan Clark, related a story that had taken place some years before. While mustering cattle in the Urapunji area, he became lost in the remote wilderness of that part of Arnhem Land. It took him three days to find his way out of the region and back to the homestead from where he originally set out.
>
> He had not known at the time, but his footprints had been picked up and followed by two Aboriginal trackers and a mounted policeman. On the first night of their search they camped on the outskirts of the Burrunjor scrub, even though the two trackers protested strongly against doing so. The policeman hobbled his horse, cooked their meal, then climbed into his swag[14] and went to sleep.
>
> Old stories of the mesa country say that one or more Burrunjor reptilian monsters would emerge from this particular area as darkness fell, to raid cattle stations, dragging off stock in their powerful jaws to devour, leaving the remains scattered about the area of their huge tracks as they returned to their lair. It is a region to avoid for Aborigines.
>
> Later that night the two Aborigines, shouting unintelligibly and grasping for their packs and saddles, suddenly woke him up. The policeman also realized at this moment that the ground appeared to be shaking. Hurriedly getting to his feet, he too gathered up his belongings, and shortly afterwards, the three galloped away. As he told Bryan Clark later at the Urapunji homestead, he had also heard a sound, somewhat like a loud puffing or grunting noise, certainly loud enough to be coming from some large animal. When asked if he intended to include this incident in his report, he replied he would not because he feared no one would believe him.
>
> The policeman warned Bryan never again to return to that area, because if he got lost there again he'd be "on his own", as no one would come

---

14. A sleeping bag or bedding.

looking for him! The region's cave art, thousands of years old, depicts these monstrous animals. Many Aborigines believe these monsters wander back and forth across the Gulf country and Cape York to this day.[15]

In 1985, the Askey family were in their 4-wheel drive vehicle on a back road sightseeing while heading for Roper River Mission. While on this desolate backroad, the whole family saw two bipedal reptilian creatures moving together across an open plain some distance away. They estimated the creatures were 20 feet tall and described them as being greyish-brown and having a dinosaur-like appearance. The father, Greg Askey, said that they did not wait around!

Continuing their investigations in July and August 2006, Rex and Heather Gilroy acquired many other ancient Aboriginal myths and legends about the *burrunjor*. In addition, they also found that some were claiming to have had contemporary sightings by various people over a wide area of Australia's interior.

Bipedal Reptiles of North America

Since the late 1800's, large bipedal reptiles resembling theropod dinosaurs have been sighted in the states of Wyoming, Colorado, and northern New Mexico. Witnesses describe an animal that is approximately ten feet long and about five feet tall. It has a long, pointed snout filled with sharp teeth, with sharp claws on its hands and feet. It is completely bipedal and has very large eyes. Some report seeing dorsal spines. In most cases these creatures tend to be shy by avoiding humans, however some have been known to be aggressive.

Among other places, Pagosa Springs, Colorado is an area where there have been multiple outbreaks of consistent sightings.[16] However, one particular report came from Wyoming. Chad Arment (investigator and author/editor/publisher of cryptozoology books) was contacted by Anita R., who requested information about a particular strange creature she and her mother encountered one night while driving on I-80, approximately 40 miles west of Sinclair, Wyoming in April 2003. Anita explained that the prehistoric-looking creature came in front of their car. It kept its head in the shadows but it was shaped like a kangaroo head. It had large feet and short arms. The alligator-like tail was as long as her car. Despite slamming on the brakes and swerving to avoid collision, the creature leaped to a close proximity from the slowing car. Then, as the car stopped, it suddenly leaped out of sight. Anita went on to give a lengthy and detailed description of the creature, and also mentioned that she contacted a truck driver who also indicated knowledge of the unknown animal.

---

15. Rex and Heather Gilroy, *Burrunjor! The Search for Australia's Living Tyrannosaurus.* Uru Publications. 2011. p. 149. See: http://thecryptozoologist.webs.com. *"Kasai Rex, Burrunjor, And Mini-T-Rex: Evidence Of Surviving Carnivorous Dinosaurs? Part 2"*
16. See: Chad Arment, *Cryptozoology and the Investigation of Lesser-Known Mystery Animals.* (chapter by Nick Sucik summarizes many of these reports). 2006.

> While we were terrified, afraid of hitting it, we were so amazed we noticed every detail. It is gray in color, the scales being 2 shades of gray. That's the best way I know how to describe what we saw. Again I want to mention that a female truck driver online that travels that area frequently, when I asked her if she'd seen anything weird there, her comment was, 'You mean the big green dinosaur?... You should try stopping with a fully loaded trailer'... but, it isn't green. It is gray. At least what we saw and when we saw it, it was gray...
>
> She also stated that every time an alternative route was available, she took it because everyone knew how that would jump in front of your vehicle... She's the only person I've ever talked with that had seen it or heard about it. Keep in mind, I didn't tell her what we saw, I only asked if she had ever been on that stretch of I-80 and had she ever seen anything strange. Her reply was, 'you mean the big green dinosaur?' It's not green though. It is gray. So that was confirmation and corroboration.[17]

Anita and her mother still do not know exactly what it was they saw that night. Despite pouring over many photos of reptiles and image reconstructions of dinosaurs, they have found no complete match, though some dinosaur images are similar in part (i.e., the body and legs of the Parasaurolophus[18] and head of a Nanotyrannus). Chad Arment encourages a long-term regional investigation "to determine if the many sightings are based on an actual living, albeit unknown, animal."

African Water Devils

In 1776, a French priest wrote about the natural history of the Congo Basin of Africa.[19] In his book, he described how French missionaries "have observed in passing along a forest, the track of an animal which they have never seen; but it must be monstrous, the prints of its claws are seen on the earth, and formed an impression on it of about three feet in circumference. In observing the posture and disposition of the footprints, they concluded that it did not run in this part of its way, and that it carried its claws at the distance of seven or eight feet one from the other."[20]

In 1909, Lt. Paul Gratz described a creature that inhabited the swamp lands surrounding Lake Bangweulu in Northern Rhodesia (Zambia). He said he was shown a piece of *"Nsanga's"* skin on the island of Mbawala. It was a "degenerate saurian which one might well confuse with the crocodile, were it not that its skin has no scales and its toes are armed with claws."[21]

---

17. For a more detailed report see: Chad Arment, *An Account of a North American Bipedal Reptile from Wyoming.* BioFortean Review, (August 2008, No. 19). www.strangeark.com.
18. As shown in Dr. David Norman's *The Illustrated Encyclopedia of Dinosaurs.* p. 123. And the Natural History Museum of London website. (www.nhm.ac.uk)
19. Abbe (Liévain-Bonaventure) Proyart, *Histoire de Loango, Kakongo, et Autres Royaumes d'Afrique; Rédigée d'après les Mémoires des Préfets Apostoliques de la Mission française; enrichie d'une Carte utile aux Navigateurs.*
20. Translated by John Pinkerton. *A General Collection of the Best and Most Interesting Voyages and Travels in all Parts of the World: Volume 16.* 1914. *History of Loango, Kakonga, and other Kingdoms in Africa* (1776).
21. Bernard Heuvelmans, *On the Track of Unknown Animals,* 1959. p. 461.

Also in 1909, naturalist Carl Hagenbeck (Hamburg Zoo director; considered to be one of the greatest animal collectors in history) recounted in his autobiography how he received various separate reports of a strange creature living in the Congo swamps. Due to the convincing nature of these reports, Hagenbeck sent an expedition to the region to search for the creature. The expedition was ultimately ruined due to disease and hostile natives, however.

> Some years ago I received reports from two quite distinct sources of the existence of an immense and wholly unknown animal, said to inhabit the interior of Rhodesia. Almost identical stories reached me, firstly, through one of my own travellers, and, secondly, through an English gentleman, who had been shooting big-game in Central Africa. The reports were thus quite independent of each other... the natives... had told both my informants that in the depth of the great swamps there dwelt a huge monster, half elephant, half dragon... and, still more remarkable, on the walls of certain caverns in Central Africa there are to be found actual drawings of this strange creature. From what I have heard of the animal, it seems to me that it can only be some kind of dinosaur, seemingly akin to the brontosaurus. As the stories come from so many different sources, and all tend to substantiate each other, I am almost convinced that some such reptile must still be in existence.[22]

Figure 19. Artwork from, "Is a Brontosaurus Roaming Africa's Wilds?" *The New York Herald.* Feb 13th, 1910. *Caption: "Mysterious creature resembling the Brontosaurus drawn from descriptions by two natives of Northern Rhodesia."* Though this graphic shows the creature with two horns, the Rhodesian natives indicated males only had one. The horn is a feature consistent with some ancient Asian descriptions of serpentine dragons. Artist unknown.

In 1913, a German Captain (Freiherr von Stein zu Lausnitz) was directed to explore the Cameroon. He wrote about an unknown creature that inhabited the Ubangi, Sanga, and Ikelemba River regions. The local people, who feared the animal, named it *Mokele-mbembe*, which means "one who stops the flow of rivers".

---

22. Carl Hagenbeck. *Beasts and Men.* Longmans, Green, 1911. p. 96. ("brontosaurus" = apatosaurus)

The animal is said to be of a brownish-gray color with a smooth skin, its size approximately that of an elephant; at least that of a hippopotamus. It is said to have a long and very flexible neck and only one tooth but a very long one; some say it is a horn. A few spoke about a long muscular tail like that of an alligator... It is said to climb the shore even at daytime in search of food; its diet is said to be entirely vegetable... At the Ssombo River I was shown a path said to have been made by this animal in order to get at its food. The path was fresh and there were plants of the described type [a liana] nearby.[23]

In 1932, Ivan Sanderson, a Scottish explorer, and Gerald Russel, and American naturalist, were at the Mamfe Pool on the Mainyu River in Northern Cameroon. There were many caves along the cliff-like banks of the river. Some were partially filled with river water. They heard a loud disturbance that sounded like fighting beasts coming from one of the caves. Then they both saw the back of a very large creature break the surface of the water and moments later submerge. "Farther upstream near the confluence of the Cross River, they saw "vast hippo-like tracks: although there were no hippopotami in the area". Sanderson was told there were no hippos because this creature, the "*embulu-em'bembe*" (Sanderson's spelling), drove them away."[24]

In 1948, A.S. Arrey was swimming with a number of British soldiers in Lake Barombi Mbo near Kumba (northern Cameroon). Suddenly, the center of the lake was disturbed from something beneath the water. After the swimmers got out of the water in haste, two long-necked creatures broke the surface of the lake. Upon seeing them rise, some of the soldiers ran away while others stayed to watch. The neck of the first creature was estimated to be about 12 to 15 feet long, having a small head with a single horn. The second creature was similar in appearance but was slightly smaller. The natives claimed that this second creature was female since it had no horn. Typically, descriptions of *mokele-mbembe* indicate it having smooth skin, but in this case, the eyewitnesses claimed that these two creatures had snake-like scales. This matches recent reports indicating that as the mokele-mbembe mature, they develop toughened skin like a caiman. The natives in this particular region call these creatures *Jago-nini*, which means "giant diver". They also state that the creatures seldom left the water and were seen infrequently.[25]

In July 1963, at 1:00 pm., J.M. Lefebvre examined some strange animal tracks (spoor) in the muddy swamps of the Democratic Republic of the Congo. His description of these tracks are similar to those described by Marco Polo and the Nordic saga, *The Story of the Völsungs*.

---

23. Willy Ley, *Willy Ley's Exotic Zoology*. Reprinted by Bonanza Books. 1987. p. 70.
24. Roy P. Mackal, *A Living Dinosaur: In Search of Mokele-mbembe*. 1987. p. 211.
25. Karl Shuker, *In Search Of Prehistoric Survivors*. 1996. p. 20. (See also: genesispark.com/essays/behemoth-or-bust)

I first came across the spoor, in a muddy spot. It was formed by, in the center a kind of depression or farrow between 3 and 6 feet wide, similar in shape [like] one would make by dragging a bag of coal in the sand. On each side of it were footprints, 2 to 3 feet wide by 3 to 4 feet long, eggshaped with the broad side towards the front... The footprints were between 3 and 5 feet on each side of the belly mark, and the marks of the rear feet were overlapping the ones of the front one. The tall shrubs which were on the spoor were crushed like with a bulldozer.

At the sight, my trackers stopped abruptly and refused to let us go farther. Considering the size of the animal and the gauge of our guns, my friend and I decided to retreat –

On our way back, the trackers showed to us on the other side of the clearing the animal... a huge greyish mass, towering well above the grass. I estimate from 20 to 40 feet high. A long flexible neck about the size of a tree trunk and ± 30 feet long. A very small head held at a right angle from the neck.[26]

Country / Location / Tribe	Name
Camaroon / Baka tribe	Li'kela-bembe
Central African Republic / DRC / Bandas tribe	Badigui (water devil)
Central African Republic / Birao district	Guanerou
Congo (DRC) / Bantu (Lingala language)	Mokele-mbembe (stopper of rivers)
Gabon / Ogooue river	Jago-nini / Amali / N'yamala (giant diver)
Zambia / Njumbo tribe	Mbilintu
Zambia / Lake Bangweulu	Nsanga

Figure 19. List of different names used to describe sauropod-like creatures inhabiting Central Africa.

Since the 1970's to the present, as a result of these initial accounts, there have been over 20 fully-funded expeditions from various countries to the Central African regions in search of this strange animal. Professor Roy Mackal, who went on a couple expeditions to find mokele-mbembe himself, summarized the accumulating evidence:

> From discussion with over 30 Congolese (including pygmies) in the Impfondo and Epena areas we were able to confirm practically all of the detail described earlier, including the alleged food plant of the animals, the "malambo", of which we obtained a specimen and which has tentatively been identified as a species of *Landolphia*.
>
> Eyewitness descriptions establish the largest of these animals as up to 10 metres in length, long tail, reddish brown to grey in colour. The thickness of the long neck ranges from that of a man's arm to the thickness of a man's thigh. In some cases a rooster-like comb was described as being present on the head.
>
> A number of miraculous aspects were attached to the more factual

---

26. Mackal, *A Living Dinosaur*. 1987. p. 212. (some spelling updated for clarity).

descriptions, including the widespread belief that if a *mokele-mbembe* is observed nothing must be said about the event or death will follow. This belief of course contributes to the difficulty of obtaining information.[27]

Elephant Killers

In December 1919, the London Daily Mail published a letter written by C.G. James, who had lived in Northern Rhodesia (Zambia). He described a huge creature having a single ivory horn, that lived in the waters of Lake Bangweulu, Lake Mweru, and the surrounding swamp region. This unusual animal was called "*Chipekwe*" by the natives and was seldom seen. This creature is mentioned in *Far Away Up the Nile,* by John Guille Millais, and *Eighteen Years on Lake Bangweulu*, by Joseph Edward Hughes. In Hughes' book, the following account is given:

> For many years there has been a persistent rumour that a huge prehistoric animal was to be found in the waters of our Lake Bangweulu. Certainly the natives talk about such a beast, and '*Chipekwe*'... is the name by which they call it.... Mr. H. Croad, the retired magistrate...told me that one night, camped by the edge of a very deep small lake, he heard a tremendous splashing during the night, and in the morning found a spoor on the bank — not that of any animal he knew, and he knows them all.
>
> Another bit of evidence about it is the story Kanyeshia, son of Mieri-Mieri, the Waushi Paramount Chief, told me. His grandfather had said that he could remember one of these animals being killed in the Luapula in the deep water below the Lubwe.
>
> A good description of the hunt has been handed down by tradition. It took many of the best hunters the whole day spearing it with their large 'Viwingo' harpoons–the same as they use today for the hippo. It is described as having a smooth dark body, without bristles, and armed with a single smooth white horn fixed like the horn of a rhinoceros, but composed of smooth white ivory, very highly polished.
>
> ... the natives reported a hippo having been killed by a *Chipekwe* in the Lukula [river]. The throat was torn out.[28]

> Possibly, it is what a friend of Col. H.F. Fenn allegedly saw in Lake Edward, on the border between what is now the Democratic Republic of Congo and Uganda, the *Irizima* ("the thing that may not be spoken of"), described in a 1927 article in *Chambers's Journal* as "like a gigantic hippopotamus with the horns of a rhinoceros upon its head."[29]

In 1954, an article by Lucien Blancou, former game inspector in Likouala, was published in the journal *Mammalia*. It described a similar animal called the *Emela-ntouka*; a name used only by the natives in the Likouala region of the Congo.

---

27. Mackal, A Living Dinosaur. 1987. p. 301. ("Malambo"/"*Landolphia*": the fruit-bearing sand apricot-vine).
28. Hughes, *Eighteen Years on Lake Bangweulu*, 1933, p. 146. Cited by: Mackal, *A Living Dinosaur.* 1987. pp. 203, 204.
29. Jerome Clark. *Unexplained!: Strange Sightings.* See "Other dinosaurs in Africa" section. pp. 277-279, 284.

Despite it being a herbivore, it is known to attack other large animals and kill them. Consistent reports of an aggressive "beast which sometimes disembowels elephants" was reported from the areas of Epena, Impfondo, and Dongou. Blancou stated that at Dongou, it was claimed that an *Emela-ntuoka* was killed in about 1934.[30]

Similar (and possibly related) to the *chipekwe* and *emela-ntouka*, the Baka pygmies in Cameroon identify pictures of a triceratops with a creature they call the *Ngoubou*. They describe it as being as large as an ox, with one to four horns on its head, and a neck frill. Adult males are said to have the largest neck frill. The *Ngoubou* are also known to fight with elephants. They inhabit the areas along the Boumba and Dja rivers in Southern Cameroon. Though the word *ngoubou* is also used for rhinoceros, the pygmies differentiate the two by stating that this particular animal is not a typical rhinoceros, having more than two horns with a neck frill. They also indicated that there was a definite decline in the *ngoubou* population in recent years, making them more difficult to find.[31]

Näga Encounters

In 1951, Stewart Wavell went on an expedition to investigate the cultural traditions and ceremonies of the Semelai people in Malaysia. Wavell soon learned that the Semelai believed in giant cobra-like serpents, which lived in the Bera and Chini lakes (Tasik Bera / Tasik Chini). According to legend, these monstrous serpentine creatures guard a sunken ancient Khmer city. At least half of this legend has been verified by archaeologists, who have studied the ancient ruins at the bottom of the lake system. Despite many people claiming to have seen these strange creatures, the serpents have never been photographed or scientifically documented.

Though the Semelai call these huge serpents *ular tedong*, they are also referred to as the *näga*. These creatures were described as being covered in large grey scales. The *ular tedong* also sported two horn-like protuberances on the back of their heads, similar to some dragons described in ancient Chinese writings. These creatures made booming noises, were never seen out of the water and were considered peaceful, having no incidences of them attacking people.

One such creature was seen by a Malayan police officer, who was later interviewed by Wavell. The officer told Wavell that he was swimming in Tasik Bera when he saw the head and neck of a huge, silvery-grey serpent rising out of the water to about 15 feet! Though he quickly swam to shore, the *ular tedong* did not give chase.

Testing his suspicions, Wavell drew a picture of a sauropod dinosaur and showed the Semelai tribe. They were amazed that it resembled the *ular tedong*. With that confirmation, Wavell went to search for the serpents near the location where

---

30. Online article. Accessed 1-31-2014. (www.phantomsandmonsters.com/2013/04/emela-ntouka-elephant-killer.html).
31. www.genesispark.com/exhibits/evidence/cryptozoological/ceratopsian/africa

the police officer had previously seen one. While camping near the shore, he was surprised by a loud booming noise. "A single staccato cry from the middle of the lake chilled my body with fear. It was a snort: more like a bellow—shrill and strident like a ship's horn, an elephant trumpet and a sea lion's bark all in one." [32] Wavell frantically switched on the recorder and held up the microphone waiting for another booming call. Unfortunately, the sound never repeated and he left with no tangible evidence.

African Flying Dragons

Reports of a creature resembling a pterosaur, called the Kongamato ("overwhelmer of boats") have been made by the natives of the Jiundu swamps of Western Zambia, Angola, and Congo. Various European explorers claimed to have seen it too. The kongamato is consistently described as being red or black in color, smooth skin with no feathers, leathery wings spanning four to seven feet, having a beak with teeth, and claws. It is said to be a nocturnal creature having bioluminescent capability. Due to its deadly reputation of capsizing canoes, and the superstitious ability to cause death to anyone who merely looked at it (like the basilisk in European accounts), the natives reacted with dread when shown illustrations of pterosaurs by British scientists, distinguishing the kongamato from other birds and bats.

In 1923, Frank H. Melland first heard about the kongamato while working in the Jiundu region of Northern Rhodesia (Zambia). *"Muchi wa kongamato"* was a charmed potion that was supposed to protect travelers from floods caused by the creature. Intrigued by this charm, Melland asked the natives about the monster. They replied that it was "a lizard with wings like a bat." After presenting illustrations of pterosaurs to the natives, he wrote, "... every native present immediately and unhesitatingly picked it out and identified it as a kongamato. Among the natives who did so was a headman from the Jiundu country, where the kongamato is supposed to be active." [33]

In 1925, the future Duke of Windsor and G.W. Price, a reputable English newspaper correspondent, visited Rhodesia. While there on official business, a civil servant told them of a particular man who entered a swamp known in that region to be a place of "demons". Upon his return, the natives found the man on the verge of death due to a large wound in his chest. He explained how a huge "bird" with a long beak had attacked him. Wanting to identify the bird, the wounded man was shown a picture of a pterosaur by the civil servant. Upon seeing it however, the man screamed and ran from the civil servant's home in fright.

In 1988, Roy Mackal led an expedition to Namibia. While there, he gathered

---

32. Stewart Wavell, *The lost world of the East: an adventurous quest in the Malayan hinterland.* 1958. p. 170.
33. Frank H. Melland, *In Witch-bound Africa.* 1923. [pp. 238-241 ?]
    (See also: http://community.fortunecity.ws/roswell/siren/552/af_konga.html)

reports of a creature with a wingspan of up to thirty feet (comparable in size to pteranodon fossils). Eyewitnesses described it mainly as a glider, but also having the capability of true flight. It was usually seen gliding in the evenings. Mackal's expedition was unsuccessful in collecting substantial evidence. However, James Kosi, one of the members of the expedition, claimed to have seen the giant gliding creature from about 1000 feet away. He described it as being black with white markings.

In addition to the kongamato, there are modern reports of giant flying lizards from the deserts of Namibia (among other places in Africa), similar to those recorded in ancient accounts. Also, another flying creature, with reptilian-like, evenly-spaced white teeth, was encountered in the forested mountains of Cameroon by the leader of the Percy Sladen Expedition. The natives called it the *olitiau* and were in fear of it.[34]

Indonesian Pterosaurs

> An interesting letter appears in yesterday's Daily News from Mr. Smithurst, the engineer of the steamer which made the voyage up the newly discovered Baxter River in New Guinea, referred to in Sir Henry Rawlinson's address at the Geographical Society last week. The river seems to be a magnificent one, and could evidently be made navigatable to a considerable distance inland. The exploring party found the banks to consist mainly of mangrove swamps, though, near the end of the journey, high clay banks with Eucalyptus globulus were found. Scarcely any natives were seen, though there were frequent signs of their being about. Mr. Smithurst refers to a very remarkable bird, which, so far as we know, has not hitherto been described. The natives state that it can fly away with a dugong, a kangaroo, or a large turtle. Mr. Smithurst states he saw and shot at a specimen of this wonderful animal, and that "the noise caused by the flapping of its wings resembled the sound of a locomotive pulling a long train very slowly." He states that "it appeared to be about sixteen or eighteen feet across the wings as it flew, the body dark brown, the breast white, neck long, and beak long and straight." In the stiff clay of the river bank Mr. Smithurst states that he saw the footprints of some large animal, which he "took to be a buffalo or wild ox," but he saw no traces of the animal. These statements are very wonderful, and before giving credence to them we had better await the publication of the official account of the voyage. A very fair collection of rocks, stones, birds, insects, plants, moss, and orchids has been made, which will be submitted to a naturalist for his opinion. The dates of Mr. Smithurst's communication are from August 30 to Sept. 7.[35]

Among the islands of Indonesia including a portion of Australia's northern coast, isolated modern reports, mainly from the natives of Papua New Guinea and Umboi island, remain consistent with ancient descriptions of flying dragons. These

---

34. Kryptozoologie Online. *Kongamato.* Article in German. 2005.
   (www.kryptozoologie-online.de/enzyklopadie/enzyklopadie/kongamato.html).
35. *Nature,* "Giant Bird in New Guinea". (Nov. 25, 1875), V. 13, p. 76. (www.strangeark.com/reprints/ngbird.html).

large creatures are described as having long tails typically ending with a diamond-shaped tail vane, brown leathery skin, featherless bat-like wings, sporting a head crest. No other animal in the historical record has all of these features except pterosaurs. In addition, consistent with ancient Chinese accounts (among others), these nocturnal animals seem to have bioluminescent characteristics since they can be seen periodically glowing brightly at night. Furthermore, these descriptions are consistent with other modern sightings from Africa and North America.

In the remote mountain regions of Papua New Guinea, the natives around the Tawa village call them *"indava"*. In other dialects on the island they are called *"duwas"*, *"wawanar"*, and *"seklo-bali"*. The natives distinguish these animals from the large bats that inhabit the island.

> The complexity of hundreds of languages and dialects however, makes research challenging. For example, "ropen," near Wau (mainland P.N.G.) means "bird." The same word (ropen), in another area of the mainland, refers to the giant fruit bat that English speakers call the Flying Fox. Descriptions on Umboi Island differentiate the fruit bat ("byung" in the Kovai language) from what they call "ropen," for the larger creature eats fish, glows at night, has a long tail, and holds itself upright on a tree trunk, rather than upside down from a branch.[36]

Investigator Paul Nation went on several expeditions in search of the *indava*. The first two expeditions failed to find any evidence except for local tales. He was told that the creatures lived in trees but did not have a permanent colony location. On the third trip to Papua New Guinea (Nov. 2006) however, he was able to capture on video a couple bioluminescent lights flying in the night sky. The natives identified the strange lights as emanating from the indava's breast. Professional analysis of the videotape (analyzed by Clifford A. Paiva, Missile Defense Physicist, BSM Associates, and Harold S. Slusher, Professor, Physics Department University of Texas at El Paso) concluded that the lights were not faked and did not resemble any other living animal or man-made aircraft.

Many investigators believe that the *indava* are similar to the *ropen* (on Umboi island), if not the same species. Opinions as to which type of rhamphorhynchoid pterosaur they may be differ between *Sordes Pilosus* and the *Dimorphodon*.

Jonathan Whitcomb and David Woetzel are perhaps the only cryptozoologists to have published scientific papers regarding contemporary living pterosaurs in a peer-reviewed journal. In 2004, both explored Umboi Island (Papua New Guinea), in two separate expeditions, and interviewed various native eyewitnesses of the *ropen*. It was determined that over 90% of *ropen* sightings on Umboi Island are of its bioluminescent light. The bright yellowish glow typically lasts for about 5 to 6

---

36. http://creationwiki.org/ropen. (accessed February 25, 2014).

seconds at a time. The lights are frequently seen flying towards the coast during the first two hours after sundown, about 500 feet in altitude. In addition, none of those interviewed had seen a *ropen* light fly in a contrary direction (from the coast to the interior). Some investigators speculate that the bioluminescent flash helps the *ropen* orient itself to the terrain, or helps attract fish as it feeds along the coastline.

Whitcomb's scientific article *Reports of Living Pterosaurs in the Southwest Pacific*[37] stated the following:

> ...Paul Nation's late-2006 expedition resulted in video evidence of what is believed to be bioluminescence of an unidentified flying creature. This interested the producers of Destination Truth on the Sci-Fi Channel enough that they mounted a video expedition in early 2007 that recorded another instance of this unidentified light. Thanks to the broadcast of that episode in mid-2007, the public has been exposed to the possibility of living pterosaurs.

Like Paul Nation's video, two forensic experts could not explain the video evidence caught by the Destination Truth team.

Woetzel's scientific paper, *The Fiery Flying Serpent*,[38] (See Appendix C) focused on ancient accounts of potential pterosaurs.

> Over the years Biblical scholars have speculated about the nature of the creature described in the Authorized Version [of the English Bible] as "the fiery flying serpent." The nexus of modern archaeological discoveries, ancient historical accounts, and recent cryptozoological research provides new insights into the identification and characteristics of this creature.[39]

In 2004, Jonathan Whitcomb interviewed Duane Hodgkinson, of Montana, by e-mail, survey form, and telephone. The following was included in Whitcomb's article *Reports of Living Pterosaurs in the Southwest Pacific*.

> ... [Hodgkinson] and an army friend were in a jungle clearing west of Finschhafen (then New Guinea) in 1944... when something 'huge' took off into the air from the far side of the clearing. The creature ran to their left, taking six to ten steps to get airborne and ascended at an angle of about 30 degrees (similar to an air-plane taking off). It then disappeared over the dense brush but soon returned and flew over the clearing, presenting a "perfect side view" of its features before again flying out of view. The wings never stopped flapping, at one to two seconds per flap, while it flew. ... He estimated the legs to be 3–4 ft (1–1.2 m) long. The top of the back was 5–6 ft (1.5–1.8 m) above the ground just before takeoff. Although he did not notice details of the tail, he estimated it was "at least" 10–15 ft (3–4.6 m) long. ... During flight, the feet were tucked up to the body. Hodgkinson was unsure of other features. The

---
37. Published in *Creation Research Society Quarterly*, Volume 45, Number 3, Winter 2009.
38. Published in *Creation Research Society Quarterly*, Volume 42, Number 4, March 2006.
39. Both (Whitcomb / Woetzel) quotes from *CRSQ* cited at: www.livepterosaur.com/media/scientific-papers.

color was dark but not black. He took no notice of any feathers or hair, and he remembered nothing about the eyes.[40]

In 2005, Hodgkinson was also interviewed while being videotaped by Garth Guessman about the same event. Hodgkinson was a flight instructor who had owned an airplane with a wingspan of twenty nine feet. During his interview with Guessman, he said, "I would say that that pterodactyl had the approximate same wing spread as what my airplane did."

> ... "It was huge, and as it took off ... I estimated the wingflaps were maybe about one or two seconds in frequency, and the brush all below was totally swaying from the down-rush of the air from these wings. ... The creature flew out a little ways, and we were discussing what in the world was that, and here it turned around and came back and it was up probably I would say maybe fifty or a hundred feet above us, and flew right back alongside and we got a perfect side view of it. ... It had the long appendage out the back of its head, and it had a long neck, and ... it was a dark color. ... I was so fascinated with the appendage out the back of his head, and I was watching that as he flew by, and I didn't pay attention to what the end of his tail looked like." The interview (Guessman) then asked, "And you're sure it wasn't just long legs?" Hodgkinson: "No, no." Guessman: "It was a tail..." Hodgkinson: "Yes." Guessman: "What was the visibility ... between you and the creature?" Hodgkinson: "It was clear ... absolutely clear." When asked about the creature's tail length, the World War II veteran thought for awhile; he was unsure about his estimate but said, "at least ten or fifteen feet." He estimated the head length, not counting the appendage: "I don't know, but I'd say three or four feet."[41]

As recent as June, 2008, a pilot was flying a small twin-engine plane from Broome, Australia, to Bali, Indonesia. He and his copilot were both former navy pilots. Nearing the end of the flight, the pilot saw what appeared to be another airplane that was on a collision course. He soon realized that it was not a plane but rather a strange giant flying creature! He put his plane into a dive but the creature did likewise. A quick bank by the plane prevented a collision. Both the pilot and copilot referred to the creature as a "pterodactyl."[42]

American Pterosaurs

There are hundreds of reports across North America of pterodactyl-like creatures. Eyewitness sightings, though infrequent, have been occurring for over a century. The descriptions across North America are consistent with each other; and

---

40. *Creation Research Society Quarterly*, Volume 45, Number 3, Winter 2009.
41. Cited from www.livepterosaur.com/media/Hodgkinson. (accessed March 2, 2014).
42. Investigated by Jonathan Whitcomb, author of *Searching for Ropens*. http://livepterosaurs.com. (accessed 2-28-2014).

are remarkably consistent with those of the *ropen* in the South Pacific and Africa. Some of these features are also consistent with native American thunderbirds.

In 2007, Garth Guessman, David Woetzel, and other cryptozoologists, began investigations into several reports of *ropen*-like activity in North America. Eyewitnesses reporting flashes of light were coming from several undisclosed areas along the Western United States. One cryptozoologist, Scott Norman, claimed to have seen one at close range.

In 2008, making an assessment of the numerous North American sightings, Jonathan Whitcomb surmised that the behavior of these flying bioluminescent creatures seem to indicate that they catch bats in flight. He investigated a particular sighting at a wildlife refuge in Southern California and found the eyewitness to be credible. Whitcomb noted that "his reputation in his profession could only be damaged, were he to perpetuate a hoax." The overall length of the creature (head to tail) was estimated to be thirty feet. The American sightings were consistent with those in the South Pacific in that the *ropen*-like creatures were featherless and had long tails (described in over 80% of reports).[43]

Other Pterosaur Sightings

> One night in 1952, U.S. Air Force Pvt. Sinclair Taylor, on guard duty at Camp Okubo, Kyoto, Japan, said he heard a loud flapping noise. Looking up, he saw an enormous "bird" in the moonlight. When it approached, he got frightened and put a round into the chamber of his carbine. The "bird" now had stopped its flight and was hovering not far away, staring at the soldier. "The thing, which now had started slowly to descend again, had the body of a man," Taylor recalled. "It was well over seven feet from head to feet, and its wingspread was almost equal to its height. I started to fire and emptied my carbine where the thing hit the ground. But when I looked up to see if my bullets had found home there was nothing there." When the sergeant of the guard came to investigate and heard the story, he told Taylor that he believed him because a year earlier another guard had seen the same thing.[44]

In 1956, engineer J.P.F. Brown was driving from Kasenga, Zaire (DRC) to Salisbury, Zambia. At approximately 6:00 p.m., he stopped for a break at a place called Fort Rosebery (Mansa, Zambia), located west of Lake Bangweulu. It is here that he saw two prehistoric-looking creatures flying slowly and silently overhead. He estimated that each had a three to three-and-a-half foot wingspan, long thin tail, and a narrow head with a dog-like muzzle. The overall length, from beak to tail, was estimated to be about four-and-a-half feet. Mr. Brown also noticed a large number of sharp pointed teeth when one of the creatures opened its mouth.[45] Perhaps J.P.F. Brown

---
43. Jonathan Whitcomb, *Live Pterosaurs in America*. Cited in http://creationwiki.org/ropen.
44. Jerome Clark, *Unexplained!: Strange Sightings*. pp. 41, 42.
45. *Rhodesia Herald*. April 2, 1957. Cited from *"The "Kongamato" of Africa"* (www.genesispark.com).

was a modern eyewitness to what ancient East Asians referred to as "sky dogs"?[46]

An eyewitness description originally published in *Strange Magazine,* entitled, *The Flap of Pterodactyloid Wings*, has characteristics that are consistent with both the thunderbird and sky dog. Ruth Lundy sent a letter to Mr. Chorvinsky, who was writing about monsters at the time, describing an incredible creature she saw around 3:00 am while driving on the highway in Carroll County, Maryland. At first she thought it was a man, but as she got closer it resembled more like a pterodactyl, but standing upright on two feet like a man. It was brownish-grey and over six feet tall. It had a face like a man, but with a pointed chin that appeared to be beak-like. As Ruth drove closer to the creature, it began to flap its wings and then flew over her car causing it to shake from the force of the large wings. Ruth was disturbed by the sighting and though she told others about it, they thought she was making the story up.[47]

The description of it having a man-like face is intriguing in that some animals have human-like facial characteristics when seen from the front. In this case, the long beak would be foreshortened if held upright and may appear to be a pointed chin or nose upon first glance at such an angle. If the beak is held downwards, like a pelican, then the appearance of a man's face could also be described depending upon the coloring and physical features of the top portion of the beak.

Though it is consistent with other accounts and descriptions (not to mention the time in which it is seen), Ruth Lundy's story cannot be verified via a physical specimen. *However,* it is partially consistent with the fossil record in that some pteranodons have been found to have digitigrade feet[48] (i.e., an animal that stands or walks on its toes. Digitigrades include walking birds, cats, dogs, etc. They can move rather quickly and quietly). This indicates the possibility and potential of walking or standing bipedally similar to a man. More specifically, this finding means that some pterosaurs stood erect, instead of quadrupedally like a bat, as is often portrayed.

---

46. "Sky dog": 天狗 Chinese; *Tian gŏu*, Japanese; *Tengu*. Originally was a type of (unknown) large bird of prey; traditionally depicted with both human and avian characteristics. Initially, tengu were pictured with beaks, however in time this feature has been humanized as an unnaturally long nose.
47. *Strange Magazine*, Issue 7, p. 35. Also online at: www.strangemag.com/firstperson.html#pter.
48. David Peters, The Pterosaur Heresies. See: *At Least Two Flat-Footed Pteranodon Specimens.* (and) *How Did Pteranodon Walk?* https://pterosaurheresies.wordpress.com.

8: Dragon Art

Artwork of dragons were produced throughout history and on every continent (except Antarctica). Apparently, like written descriptions in ancient literature, artistic depictions of dragons are of various types. What has often been overlooked is that many of these authentic artistic representations bear striking resemblances to specific dinosaur kinds. This chapter presents a small selection of such evidence among many others found throughout the earth.

Before presenting the archeological and artistic evidence, several particular claims of ancient dinosaur art need to be addressed. The first are the famous stones of Ica Peru. Due to controversial and inconclusive issues relating to them, these stones will not be included in this book until a scientific analysis has been performed and a peer reviewed published article regarding their authenticity is made. Second, the dinosaur-like figurines of Acambaro, Mexico have every indication of simply being folk art made by the local villagers (for money), and fraudulently buried in an archeological excavation.[1] Thus they are not valid evidence. The third claim is the carving of an alleged stegosaurus at Angkor Wat (a Cambodian Hindu temple). Though the artwork is authentic, as to what the stylized creature is specifically is highly controversial. If it is a depiction of a stegosaur, then the proportions are incorrect, particularly the head. The "bumps" along its back have been claimed as being either the bony plates of the dinosaur, or simply stylized sun rays, or other artistic background feature. Some claim it is a hippo or rhino, but the depiction is not perfect for those animals either, partly due to the significant tail. Since the creature depicted is not immediately recognizable as a dragon, it too will not be considered.

Since it is beyond the scope of this book to present the hundreds, if not thousands, of archeological artifacts showing man's familiarity with dragons, only a

---

1. Charles Di Peso. The Clay Figurines of Acambaro, Guanajuato, Mexico. *American Antiquity* 18(4): 388-389.

few will be highlighted here to show some consistency. Due to certain copyright laws, permission for some intended photos were not attained at the time of publishing, therefore an outlined illustration is given in its place. The advantage of this is that elements of the artifact can be focused on, whereas the disadvantage is that the reader will need to look elswhere to see a photo of the real thing. Nevertheless, the following artistic artifacts should provide evidence worthy of consideration that man and dinosaurs co-existed.

Ceremonial Roman Sword

On September 13, 1924, Charles Manier found something on Silverbell Road northwest of Tucson that was to change the notion of Arizona history for good. The find included an array of ancient Roman artifacts, mostly made of lead. The trove, discovered in a lime kiln, included more than 30 objects... The objects were encrusted with caliche—a sheet of hard, crusty material that "grows" due to a reaction of chemicals and water in desert soils over many years. This encrustation was proof to the excavators that the objects were quite old.

In 1925, University of Tucson archaeologists working in the lime kiln outside of Tucson unearthed a short, heavy broadsword of apparent Roman manufacture. Other artifacts found at the site bore both Hebrew lettering and a form of Latin used between A.D. 560 and 900. Even though many of the Tucson artifacts were unearthed by professionals, controversy rages over their authenticity...

...The most startling of the Roman discoveries was a short, heavy broadsword with the clear depiction of a brontosaurus carved into it![2]

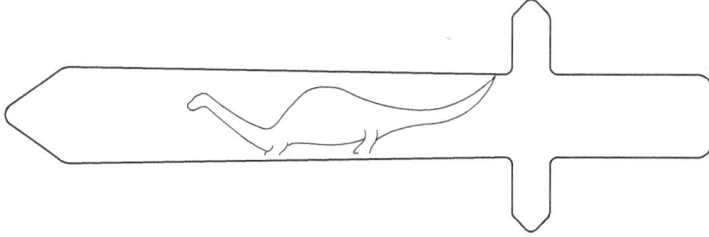

Roman sword. The Arizona Historical Society currently has the sword. A photo of the artifact can be seen at genesispark.com.

Babylonian Dragon

Originally dating to the 6th century BC., the reconstructed Ishtar Gate to the ancient city of Babylon portrays a creature known as the *mušḫuššu* (aka *sirrush*[3]). In Akkadian, *muš-ḫuššu* can be loosely translated as "splendor serpent" or "glamorous snake". Robert Koldewey, a German archeologist who discovered the Ishtar Gate in 1902, regarded the *sirrush* as a real animal, one that the Babylonians were familiar

---
2. David Hatcher Childress. *The Lost Cities of North and Central America*. 1992. pp. 293, 294.
3. The reading sir-russu ("sirrush") is an early Assyriology mistransliteration. [The Assyrian Dictionary, vol. 10 part II, p. 270].

with. He came to this conclusion based on the fact that Babylonian art *consistently* depicted the *sirrush* over many centuries, while those of mythological creatures changed dramatically in shorter periods of time. Also, the *sirrush* is shown on the Ishtar Gate along with real animals, namely, the lion and the (now extinct) auroch. The creature's front legs gave Koldewey doubt, however, since they appeared to be feline in appearance. This also caused some to think it is nothing more than a mythical hybrid. Nevertheless, some have speculated that the *sirrush* was either an iguanodon, (a dinosaur with birdlike hindfeet)[4] or a Sivatherium, (an extinct genus of giraffid).[5]

Ishtar Gate *muš-ḫuššu*. Note the forked tongue, horn and head crest. Many descriptions of dragons have some elements of hybrid characteristics. *Photo by Mark Ahsmann. (cropped). Licensed under the Creative Commons Attribution-Share Alike 3.0 Unported license. http://commons.wikimedia.org.*

Necking Sauropods

The tomb of Richard Bell, Bishop of Carlisle, 1410-1496 AD., has a narrow piece of brass that runs around the edges of the tomb. Engraved on the brass are various recognizable animals along with two serpentine creatures that match no other known animal except for a sauropod. The brass has been worn down over several centuries of foot traffic but the images are still distinguishable.

Notice that the creature on the left has spikes on the bulbous tail tip (perhaps

---

4. Bengt Sjögren *Berömda vidunder*. 1980.
5. Willy Ley. *Exotic Zoology*. 1959.

an indication of gender). This specific club-like feature (due to enlarged vertebrae) is found *only* on Shunosaurus ("Sechuan lizard") fossils, a sauropod found in Asia. It was one of the smaller sauropods at approximately 40 feet long. This engraving is therefore portraying not only a generic long-necked dinosaur, but a specific kind of sauropod! The necking behavior (like fighting giraffes) is also evidence that the artist (or the Bishop) saw these creatures alive since the same peculiar behavior is shown in other cultures.

Tomb of Bishop Bell. Portion of brass strip showing two sauropods. A photo of this can be seen in Vance Nelson's *Dire Dragons*, or various online photos.

Thousands of years before the Bishop of Carlisle, during the Uruk Period (4100-3000 BC), in Mesopotamia (Iraq), cylinder seals were commonly used. One in particular is made of jasper and coincidentally portrays the same type of sauropod necking behavior. Archaeologists refer to this "mythical" creature as a serpopard and consider it a hybrid animal representing some allegorical meaning. Despite this, ancient Egyptians are well known for their accurate depictions of animals, leading some archaeologists to consider that the serpopard may not be a mythical creature but one that existed during that period in history but is now extinct. One notable detail to support this assumption is that the whip-like tails are quite thin compared to the necks (depicted in the following figures). Coincidentally, this physical feature is consistent with many sauropod fossil skeletons (neck vertebrae are much larger/thicker than the tail vertebrae), the Apatosaurus louisae being a good example.

Jasper cylinder seal and impression. Mesopotamia, Uruk Period (4100 BC–3000 BC). Currently located at the Louvre, Department of Oriental Antiquities, Richelieu wing, ground floor, room 1a, case 2.
Photo (left - cropped) by Marie-Lan Nguyen. 2010. Photo (right - cropped) by PHGCOM. 2007. World Images.
Left photo is licensed under the Creative Commons Attribution-Share Alike 3.0 Unported license.
Right photo is licensed under the Creative Commons Attribution-Share Alike 4.0 International, 3.0 Unported, 2.5 Generic, 2.0 Generic and 1.0 Generic license. http://commons.wikimedia.org.

In England, depicted in a late fourth century Roman mosaic dedicated to Nodens, a Celtic divinity, two serpents are also necking.

Illustration of the mosaic at Lydney, Gloucestershire, England. Source from: Wheeler, R.E.M. and Wheeler, T.V., *Reports of the Research Committee of the Society of Antiquaries of London, No. IX.* The Society of Antiquaries, London, 1932. pp. 65, 66 and Plate XIX A.

The following page presents a funerary silk banner from Mawangdui, Changsha, Hunan, which was draped over the coffin of the Lady Dai (168 BC), wife of the Marquess Li Cang (186 BC), chancellor for the Kingdom of Changsha. It is one of the oldest silk paintings in existence, it portrays four serpentine long-necked dragons, two, coincidentally, having intertwined necks.

Funerary silk banner. Han dynasty (206-25 AD), Colors on silk, height 6 feet 8.5 inches. National Museum, Beijing. Photographer unknown. *Public domain.*

    The same intertwining long-necked dragon behavior is also depicted on what is called the Narmer palette. This palette, dated around 3100 BC., has some of the earliest Egyptian hieroglyphics ever found. The prominent mid-section shows two men, each holding a leash that is fastened to the creature's large serpentine necks.

Again, note the long thin tails in relation to the necks. Other palettes have been found that do not show the necking behavior, but portray the same serpentine quadrupeds along with other recognizable animals.

Narmer Palette (serpopard side).
Photographer unknown. *Public domain. http://commons.wikimedia.org.*

Ceremonial Palette from Hierakonpolis. Photo by Jon Bodsworth. 2010.
Licenced as Copyrighted Free Use. http://commons.wikimedia.org.

Manshaat Ezzat Palette (First Dynasty).
See *National Geographic*. January 2003. p. 78 for photo taken by Kenneth Garrett.

Four Dogs Palette. (Cosmetic palette). Louvre. Department of Egyptian Antiquities, Sully, room 20.
Guillaume Blanchard, July 2004. (Cropped. Sauropod-like animal at bottom upside down)
Creative Commons Attribution-Share Alike 1.0 Generic license.

Crocodile Leopards

The Nile Mosaic of Palestrina was created in approximately 100 BC and is well preserved despite being moved and restored several times. "The Nile Mosaic originally covered the floor of a partly artificial grotto in the mountainside on which the town of Praeneste was built."[6] It has been on exhibit at the Museo Nazionale Prenestino since 1953. It represents Ptolemaic Egypt along the Nile river and portrays over 40 kinds of animals and over 12 kinds of plants, many of which are labeled.

Nile Mosaic of Palestrina. Two dragon-like creatures (encircled in black) are depicted alongside various other identified animals. Two other odd creatures appear to be extinct mammals (encircled in white) and may be some type of *entelodont*, and the other may be a *camelops*?[7]
Photo by WolfgangRieger. *Public domain. http://commons.wikimedia.org.*

Among the many recognized animals in the scene are some that are not easily identified today. A few have characteristics of extinct fauna. The dragon-like *KROKODILOSCHERSAIOS* ("land crocodile"[8] or "large crocodile lizard"[9]), and the *KROKODILOPARDALIS* (literal "crocodile leopard"), are of particular interest.

---
6. Paul Meyboom, *The Nile Mosaic of Palestrina: Early Evidence of Egyptian Religion in Italy.* 1995. p. 8.
7. http://s8int.com/articles/315/Dinosaurs-in-Literature-Art-History-Page-57.htm (accessed May 10, 2014).
8. Meyboom, *The Nile Mosaic of Palestrina. pp. 26, 27.* Mayboom's definition.
9. "KROKODILOSCHERSAIOS" Septuagint etymology: a large lizard, i.e., a monitor or thorny-tailed lizard.

Though these two creatures are similar in appearance and name, it has been suggested that both of them are representations of the extinct giant lemur. This does not make sense in light of the practical naming convention, which is descriptive of both the reptilian characteristics (i.e., the mouth extends beyond the eyes, etc.) and (supposed) agility of the animal. Nile monitor lizards have also been proposed, but these two creatures have long sharp teeth. The top creature has what appears to be ears, so the thorny-tailed lizard is not an option. Nor are they simply crocodiles either since they are distinguished from those that are represented in the lower left corner of the mosaic, not to mention the ability to turn their heads dramatically. Thus these two cannot be identified with any known living creature, but coincidentally have features similar to some dinosaurs.

Mosaic Detail. Top: KROKODILOSCHERSAIOS ("large crocodile lizard"). Bottom: KROKODILOPARDALIS ("crocodile leopard").

New World Pottery

The handle on a Mesoamerican pottery object matches no other known creature except a sauropod dinosaur. Made by Mississippi Caddo Indians in approximately 1200 AD. This artifact (below left) is currently housed at the Creation Evidence Museum in Texas.

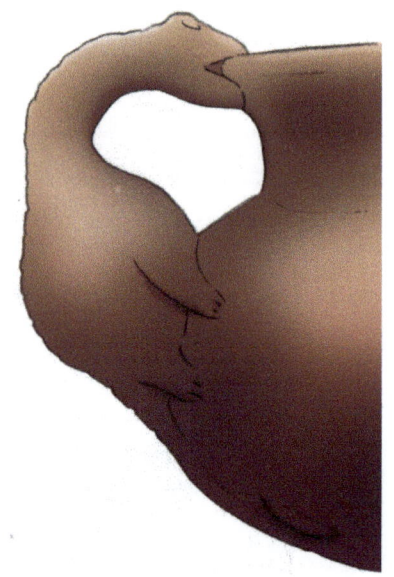

Illustration of Mississippi Caddo Indian pottery.
Photo source: www.genesispark.com.

Illustration of Mayan bowl with lid.
Photo source: The Gardiner Museum.

A placard for a peculiar pottery bowl featuring an unknown bird (above right) in the Gardiner Museum states:

> This object is a Mayan incised lidded bowl, Early "Classic Period", with ring foot, cylindrical sides, surmounted on the top by a conical-shaped lid with "avial" head as handle. The "bird" has a wide notched beak, ridged eyes and crest, domed sides incised with outspread wings. The entire object is in black with traces of red pigment.
> Earthenware (Blackware), traces of red pigment Classic period, AD 250-450. The object is Mayan and is from the country of Guatemala.[10]

There are several short-crested pteranodons and a few pterodactyls that would fit this carved depiction well.

---
10. Cited from http://s8int.com/dinolit16.html. The Gardiner Museum is located in Toronto, Canada.

In the fossil record, ornithocheiridae were among of the largest flying animals ever discovered. Among other odd features, *some had a premaxillary crest on the snout that distinguished them from all other flying creatures*, including pelicans.

Ornithocheiridae have been found in South America, relatively close to where this Mayan funerary vase was found, in a tomb at Dzibanche (Yucatan peninsula). Though ornithocheiridae have been known since the mid 1800's, the vase is dated to about the time when the city of Dzibanche was at its height, from 200 to 618 AD. The creature shown on the vase may have been a relative of the *caulkicephalus* or *ornithocheirus*.

Illustration of a Mayan funerary vase. Source from www.latinamericanstudies.org/ceremonial-vessels.htm.

Asian art

Here is a copy of an ancient Chinese bronze sculpture of what appears to be a bipedal theropod-like dinosaur. Some suggest that this may be an artistic representation of a type of *therizinosaur*. The original bronze sculpture is on display at the Glendive Dinosaur and Fossil Museum in Glendive, Montana. It is dated to the Han Dynasty (206 BC -220 AD) and is over 2,000 years old.

The following two illustrations show Tang Dynasty (618 AD – 907 AD) "running dragons" made of solid gold. Compare these small figures to the dragon portrayed on the Babylonian Ishtar gate (see beginning of this chapter). The Ishtar dragons preceed these golden figures by one thousand years and they share consistent features, like the wavy horns and thin scaly bodies. Coincidentally, the dinosaur *massopondylus* also bears a striking resemblance! If the following quote is correct, that *massospondylus* wandered in herds, then it would make sense why the artist made so many figures. (Compare with Leviticus 11:29,30 in Appendix C).

> Fossil concentrations have suggested that Massospondylus was a herd animal, perhaps wandering through the ancient landscape of what is today South Africa – as well as the rest of Africa – like modern wildebeest. It was certainly widespread. Remains of Massospondylus have also been found in North and South America, China and India.
> – www.primeorigins.co.za/young_minds/massospondylus.htm[11]

---
11. Cited from http://s8int.com/WordPress/tag/living-dinosaurs

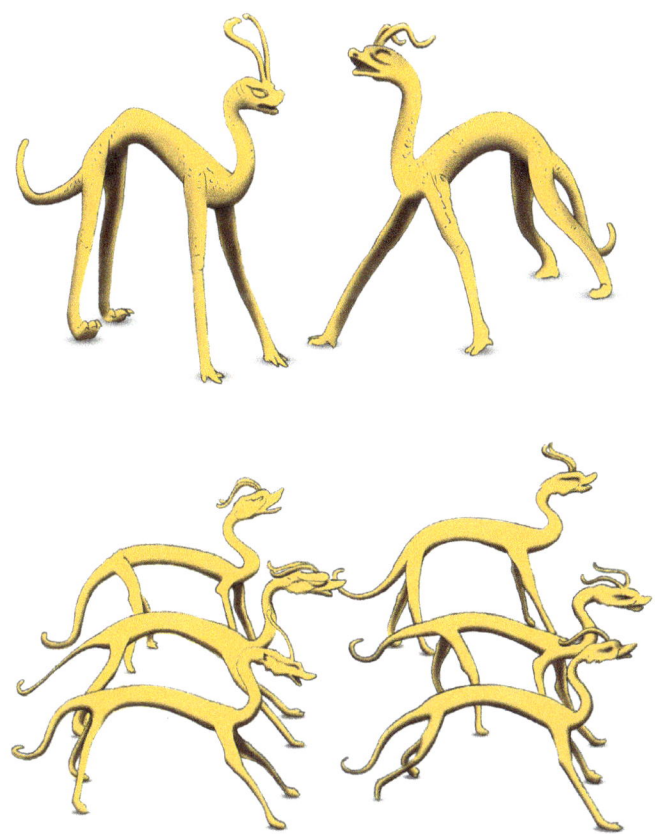

Illustrations of dragon figures on display at the Shanghai Museum.

One of the cultures of ancient China (3500 - 3000 BC) were the Hongshan. The Hongshan culture stylistically carved many kinds of recognizable animal pendants on various types of stone.[12] The following two dragon carvings have been expertly verified by third-parties as being authentic and depict no other known animal *except* a type of ceratopsian (i.e., *protoceratops*). Notably, protoceratops fossils are some of the most prevalent in Northern China and Mongolia region.

Illustrations of the Hongshan, bloodstone and turquoise figures.

---

12. See Vance Nelson's *Untold Secrets of Planet Earth - Dire Dragons* for photos and more examples.

Men fighting dragons

The following rare art treasure is made of jade and was crafted during the Eastern Zhou Dynasty (1025 - 722 BC). It stands along hundreds of other ancient artifacts throughout the world that portray men, beasts, and dragons together. On the bottom half of the circular disc there is an archer shooting at what appears to be a deer-like animal, and a swordsman (center right) is fighting a recognizeable bear (lower right). The spearman (top center) is attacking what at first appears to be a panther (or other large cat), but the neck is too long and portrays a serpentine-like underside (a tiny detail that should not be overlooked), thus this appears to be a type of dragon instead of a large cat. The other recognizeable dragon in this violent scene is behind the spearman at the upper right, not to mention the similar dragon displayed on the very top of the disc.

Eastern Zhou dynasty - jade.
Photographer: Rex Su Xiang. Source: www.sunrise-art.com (background removed). *Used with permission.*

As mentioned in chapter four, St. George slaying a dragon is a very common motif in medieval art throughout Europe. Depending on the region and experience of the artist, the dragon was apparently interpreted differently. At the "Palau de La Generalitat" in Barcelona Spain, in St. George's Chapel, there is a well preserved altar cloth (made in 1600 by Antoni Sadurni) which portrays St. George slaying a dragon.

Illustration of the St. George tapestry.

What sets this particular depiction apart is the amazing similarity of the dragon to the extinct nothosaurus. Not only is the size[13] and body type almost exact to those found in the fossil record, but a remarkable and distinguishing detail is found in the gaping mouth. The dragon sports an impressive set of teeth. Those in front are large and protrude forward. In addition, the teeth suddenly are significantly smaller in the back half of the mouth. This dentition perfectly matches those of the nothosaurus. Therefore it is reasonable to conclude that a nothosaurus was living at the same time as the artist, who apparently saw one; particularly when the dragon portrayed is not your standard-looking mythical dragon.

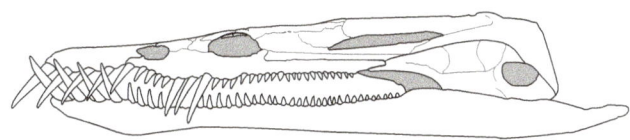

Figure 20. Nothosaurus skull. Side view, combining various reconstructions.

---

13. Nothosaurus grew to about 13 feet in length. Their fossils are found throughout Europe and Asia.
 For a detailed image of the dragon portrayed on the altar cloth, see Vance Nelson's *Untold Secrets of Planet Earth - Dire Dragons*, p. 102.

Hollow-brick earthenware tomb tile showing a stylized man fighting a dragon. China, Luoyang, Henan Province, Eastern Han Dynasty (25-220 AD).

Exhibit in the Royal Ontario Museum, Toronto, Ontario, Canada.
Public domain. Photography was permitted in the museum without restriction.

Portrayals in Stone

Due to no organic materials in the rocks themselves, it is difficult at best to accurately date when petroglyphs were made. Patination and other factors help determine their age and authenticity.

Here is an illustration of a native American petroglyph of a creature that matches no other type of animal other than a sauropod. Located under Kachina Bridge at Natural Bridges National Monument, Utah.[14] Though secular scientists agree that it is an authentic petroglyph, they are baffled by it and deny that it represents a dinosaur.[15]

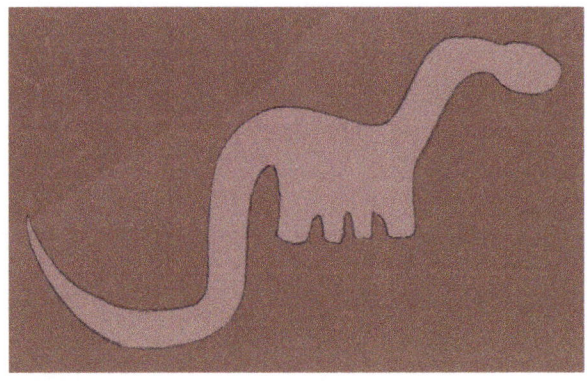

Illustration of the Kachina Bridge petroglyph.

---
14. Dr. Andy McIntosh, *Utah's Testimony to Catastrophe.* May 8, 2007. (answersingenesis.org).
15. Ishmael Abrahams, *Kachina Bridge Dinosaur Petroglyph - Still Good Evidence.* March 18, 2011. (answersingenesis.org).
   See also: Vance Nelson, Kachina Bridge Dinosaur Refuted? (www.untoldsecretsofplanetearth.com)

Black Dragon Canyon, Utah, has a pictograph that many identify as a quetzalcoatlus, partly due to the peculiar head crest and enormous wingspan. The actual pictograph has been maligned by disrespectful visitors who outlined the image with white chalk.

Illustration of the Black Dragon Canyon pictograph.

Here is a petroglyph of a Mirreeulla, also known as the Hawkesbury River Monster in Sydney, Australia. The outline is similar to a plesiosaur. This petroglyph is dated approximately 3,000 years old. (See *"The Mighty Mirreeulla"* in chapter 6).

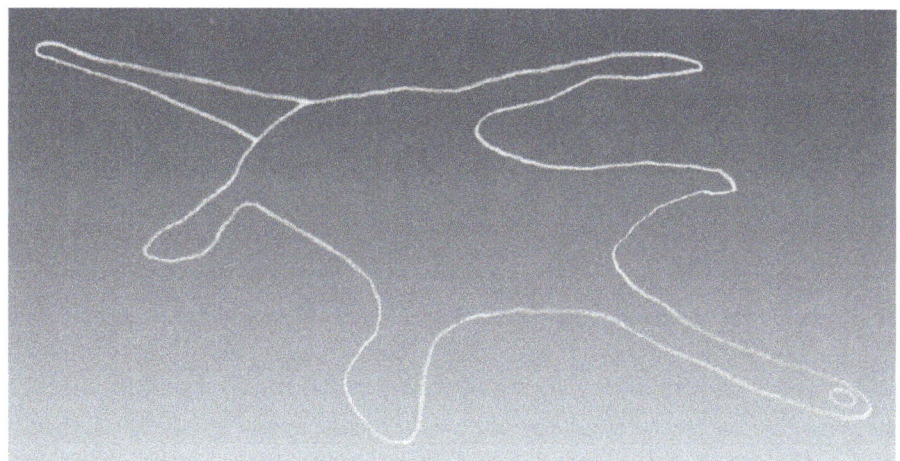

Illustration of the Mirreeulla petroglyph.

"On May 1, 2012, Vance Nelson and Harry Nibourg were on site in the Amazon rainforest in Peru documenting pictographs... [one of which] shows nine warriors hunting what appears to be a dinosaur."[16] During their two year investigation, Nelson

---

16. *Recent Dinosaurs in the Amazon News Report.* Vance Nelson. Untold Secrets of Planet Earth. Quoted from Youtube video description. (www.youtube.com/watch?v=M4yt1WoDlYQ#t=230).

and Nibourg were able to legally procure pigment samples. The samples were tested using the latest techniques of Plasma Oxidation in conjunction with AMS carbon-14 dating. The tests demonstrated that the pigments are around 3,000 years old.[17] Though the actual photo of the long necked dinosaur surrounded by warriors is not shown in this book (See "Amazon Expedition" by Vance Nelson), the pictograph itself is compelling evidence that man and dinosaurs lived together in history.

Illustration of the Amazon pictograph

---
17. Vance Nelson was contacted directly for this information. See *Untold Secrets of Planet Earth: Amazon Expedition*.

Afterward

This book has taken many years to write and was an attempt to gather a relatively comprehensive list of both circumstantial and hard evidences on the topic of dinosaurs living contemporaneously with mankind. I have presented anatomical consistencies with fossils, artistic consistencies in archaeology, and cross-cultural descriptive consistencies **(Figure 21)**. Some comparative descriptions between cultures have never been presented publically and were only discovered by myself when researching the material. In addition, scientific evidence has been briefly presented showing that life did not evolve over millions, or even billions of years from simple organisms to more complex organisms, even at the genetic level.

If the evidence has caused you to reconsider any particular views you may hold of an old earth paradigm, and has encouraged you in knowing that the Genesis account can be trusted at face value, the purpose of this endeavor has been reached. Through a lifetime of personal and formal research, I have found that the entire Bible can be trusted. More importantly, the Bible points to one historic figure, Jesus, who demonstrated and backed up his claims of being deity and the *only* savior of mankind.[1] How you respond to his question, "Who do you say that I am?"[2] will determine your eternal destiny. If you do not know Jesus and what it means to repent and obediently follow him, I encourage you to begin to seek him out by studying the Bible and regularly attend a Bible-based evangelical Christian church. "Historic Dinosaurs" would not have been possible without the dedicated work of many others who have blazed the trail before me, and for that I am very grateful.

---

1. John 14:6
2. Matthew 16:13-17

Some dragons:	Asia	Europe	Africa	Americas
Decreasing reports of land dragons as time progresses	■	■	■	■
Some ancient artwork match specific dinosaur fossils	■	■		■
Associated with water	■	■	■	■
Lived in caves	■	■	■	■
Considered dangerous	■	■	■	■
Bioluminescent	■	■	■	■
Ability of flight	■	■	■	■
Hunted by humans (for safety, valor, or medicine)	■	■	■	■
Mystical qualities assigned	■	■	■	■
Chimera-like (scales, hair, feathers...)	■	■	■	■
Emitted a chemical-like fire or poison	■	■	■	☐
Eat birds	■	■	■	
Tough scales	■	■	■	
Long necks (serpentine)	■	■	■	
Matching descriptions of color, and shape	■	■	☐	☐
Enemies of tigers, panthers and elephants	■	☐	☐	
Used for medicinal or practical purposes	■	■		☐
Excellent eyesight	■	■		
Used in some sort of divination	■	■		
Had a lump in the head that was considered valuable	■	■		

Figure 21: Partial list of descriptive consistencies between cross-cultural reports and artifacts throughout history. Keep in mind that written records in Africa and the Americas were not as prolific as they were in Asia and Europe.
■ = Consistent   ☐ = Partially consistent

Appendix A: Living Fossils

This is a *partial list* of currently common living organisms (also known as "living fossils") that have demonstrated longevity upon this Earth. Dates are given according to the mainstream geologic timeline. Their virtually unchanged existence questions the macro-evolutionary theory. Approximately 79% of terrestrial vertebrates living today are found in the fossil record (Carl Zimmer, *Insects Ascendant*, p. 30).

In addition to those listed here, several are rather large in size *and have only been discovered recently*, lending support for various eyewitness reports of previously undocumented creatures. Some examples are: the giant fighting elephants found in Nepal and the previously unknown "Riwoche" horse found in Tibet in the mid 1990's, the hairy Sumatran Rhinos recently discovered in Borneo (descendants of the Wooly rhino), and the giant squid Architeuthis. These recent discoveries give credence to other sightings of supposedly large extinct or "mythical" creatures, such as those reported by natives in Indonesia, Central Africa, and South America.

(Items in *italics* are under 65 million years, which is considered the end of the age of the dinosaurs. Dates are approximate. Ordered according to mainstream dates.)

ANIMALS

AMPHIBIANS

Chinese Hynobiidaes
300 million years ago (mya).
A type of amphibian species still found in Guiding county, near the Southwestern area of China's Guizhou province.

Hellbender
300 mya.
An amphibian.

Tailed Frog
150 mya.
Considered to be a primitive frog. They don't have a true tail but do possess tail-wagging muscles. The male's tail-like extension, in particular, serves as a copulatory organ.

Salamanders
150 mya.

A recent fossil find in China. The shocking discovery is that salamanders are virtually unchanged from what we have today.

Nasikabatrachus Sahyadrensis (Pig-nosed frog / Purple frog)
100 mya.

Dubbed a new species, but considered a living fossil, this creature is considered to be the precursor to modern-day frogs and has remained unchanged.

REPTILES

Crocodile
240 mya.

Protosuchus ("first crocodile") resembled modern-day crocodiles.

Alligator
230 mya.

They are members of the crocodile family.

Tuatara
225 mya.

A highly endangered reptile in New Zealand. It is the only survivor of a group of reptiles named Sphenodontia and has not changed in the course of time.

Gila Monster
200 mya.

A desert reptile.

Alligator Snapping Turtle
200 mya.

Having expanded ribs incorporated into their shells, a horned beak, and other features, turtles do not appear closely related to other reptiles, and their origins have puzzled mainstream paleontologists.

Rubber Boa
130 mya.

A snake.

FISH / AQUATIC ANIMALS

Atlantic Hagfish
550 mya.
Considered the most primitive of all living fishes. They are the only vertebrates whose body fluids are the same density as sea water. Because hagfishes are soft-bodied, their presence in the fossil record is poor, but found in late Precambrian strata.

Coelacanth Fish
400 mya.
This is arguably the most publicized "living fossil". These fish have remained the same for millions of years and were discovered living in 1938. There are a few population areas of these fish living in the waters outside of South Africa and Australia.

Lungfish
350 mya.
These creatures have the ability to breathe in water that is very poor in oxygen.

Horseshoe Crab
300 mya.
An annoying creature to many fisherman in the Atlantic and the Gulf of Mexico.

Sturgeon
250 mya.
These large fish have remain unchanged from the fossil record.

Sharks
180 mya.
Shark-like creatures can be seen in the fossil record approximately 450 million years ago during the Paleozoic Era. Some modern sharks date back at least 180 million years ago. Fossils of a Great White relative with 8-inch-long teeth have been found in many areas.

The Frilled Shark (Chlamydoselachus anguineus) in particular, usually inhabits deep waters between 400 and 4200 feet and is referred to as a 'living fossil', since it has not changed over time. The eel-like Frilled Shark may be responsible for some 'sea serpent' sightings. Extinct types are known from fossil teeth. Thought to be extinct itself, it was first discovered alive in Japanese waters during the 1800's. It has also been found at great depths throughout the globe.

Hydrolagus Metallanasi
150 mya.
This type of chimaera has not changed from the fossil record. It was found in the depths of the Atlantic in 2001.

Needlefish
125 mya.
Found in Morocco. Cretaceous period fossils are identical to needlefish of today.

Herring
50 mya.
These fish have undergone no changes at all from the fossil record.

Crabs
50 mya.
Virtually unchanged from the fossil record.

Stingrays
50 mya.
Remained unchanged from the fossil record.

White-flag Dolphins
30 mya.
These rare freshwater dolphins have remained unchanged from the fossil record.

Seahorse
5 mya.
Fossils found from the lower Pliocene. The genus is still extant today, living in subtropical and tropical waters in various parts of the world.

INVERTEBRATES / EXOSKELETAL

Chitons
550 mya.
Chitons are considered to be a primitive group of marine mollusks that first appeared in the Lower Cambrian Period. There are about 500 species worldwide, varying in length from a quarter inch to 13 inches. The shell consists of eight overlapping plates.

Gastropods
550 mya.
They are the most diverse of the mollusk classes. Found very early in the Cambrian period. Shells of a particular genus appeared in the Oligocene Epoch, 26 to 38 million years ago.

Graptolites
550 mya.
Recent studies have shown that *Pterobranchia* represent this ancient index fossil.

Oysters
550 mya.
Oysters are bivalves, a group of mollusks that first appeared in the fossil record in the Lower Cambrian Period. Oysters of the modern-day genus Cassostrea, appeared in the Cretaceous Period (65 to 136 million years ago).

Crinoids
550 mya.
There are about 550 living species of Crinoids still alive today. Still unchanged.

Slit Snail
500 mya.
Fossil slit snails were known long before any living specimens were found. Shells of living slitsnails are virtually indistinguishable from some of the fossil forms and even more remarkable is the anatomy of these animals. Unlike most living gastropods, they have a bilaterally symmetrical body plan that is considered to be primitive.

Velvet Worms
500 mya.
These amazing little creatures have remained largely unchanged from the fossil record.

Jellyfish
500 mya.
Also unchanged from the fossil record.

Echinoderms (i.e. sand dollars) / Star fish / Brittle Stars
500 mya.
Unchanged from the fossil record.

Neopilina mollusks
500 mya.
These mollusks are similar to those found in fossils. Although the specific genus Neopilina does not occur in the fossil record, it closely resembles the genus Pilina that does. The differences are considered negligible. In 1952, ten living specimens were discovered off the Pacific coast of Costa Rica at a depth of over 3,500 meters.

Nautiluses

500 mya.

A slow moving Cephalopod. Unchanged from the fossil record.

Bloodsucking Lamprey

360 mya.

A fossilized specimen found in an ancient South African lagoon shows that this creature hasn't changed much from the fossil record.

Triops (Tadpole Shrimp) [Triops longicaudatus] / **(and other shrimp)**

200 mya.

A freshwater crustacean of the order Notostraca, resembling a miniature horseshoe crab. Triops gets its name from its three eyes, and longicaudatus refers to the elongated tail structure. Virtually unchanged from the fossil record.

Cerith

100 mya.

Fossils of this species are found in the Jurassic Period. A similar ancestor of this gastropod, Othonema, is even more ancient. Cerith species were widespread throughout North America in the Paleozoic Era ranging from 220 to 340 million years ago.

Sea Urchins

80 mya.

Exactly the same for over 80 million years

Limpets

65 mya.

Mollusks have the most complete fossil record of any phylum in the plant or animal kingdom. Today's keyhole limpets go back more than 65 million years. Earlier relatives appear in the fossil record about 190 million years old.

Neoglyphea

60 mya.

Found living in the Coral Sea, this crustacean was thought to have been extinct. It was discovered 400 meters under water during an expedition in the Chesterfield Islands, northwest of New Caledonia.

Another specimen from the Neoglyphea group was discovered in 1908 in the Philippines by a U.S. research vessel. It remained unidentified until 1975, however. After this discovery, more were found in expeditions to the Philippines between 1976 and 1984.

Brachiopods
50 mya.
One particular brachiopod is called "Lingula", which in Latin means "little tongue". It is a genus of the family Lingulidae, which is among the few brachiopods surviving today but also known from fossils.

INSECTS / ARACHNIDS / BUGS

[Other insects and arachnids are too numerous to mention here. Even orb-web spider webs have been found (most encased in amber as well as fossils) showing that insects and arachnids have been around since the beginning and have not changed much, if at all, over time. Approximately 84% of all 'bugs' living today are found in the fossil record (*Denton. p. 189*). Here are a few...]

Millipede / Centipede
395 mya.
Millipedes and scorpion-like arachnids are found in the Devonian Period.

Bristletails / Firebrats
390 mya.
A member of a group of small, wingless, fast-running insects called bristletails (looks like a silverfish). A specific species of bristletail discovered in California is a true living fossil and closely resembles insect fossils found in Carboniferous sedimentary rocks.

Cockroaches
300 mya.
This very unpopular pest has not changed from the fossil record.

Dragonflies
250 mya.
These fast flying insects have remained largely unchanged from the fossil record. *Meganeura monyi* was the largest insect ever found in the fossil record, with a wingspan of about 76cm (30 inches) and a body length of about 45.7 cm (18 inches).

Cicadas
150 mya.
These buzzing insects have not changed in all this time.

Butterflies
130 mya.
Butterflies are represented around the globe and are unchanged from the fossil record.

Army Ants

100 mya.

These ants have remained unchanged from the fossil record.

Phyllium Celebicum *(leaf-imitating insect)*
47 mya.
These strange looking creatures have remained morphologically similar to those found in fossils.

Lice
44 mya.
Lice have been around for a long time.

MAMMALS

Platypus (a monotreme – a mammal that lays eggs)

245 mya.

This creature has not changed, which contradicts the theory that this was an "intermediate" creature between reptiles and mammals. Fossils were also found in South America, which goes against the theory that Australia was an isolated area evolving its own animals.

Shrew

125 mya.

Fossils reveal little change of this small creature.

Tree Sloth

75 mya.

Fossil remains are the same as those living today.

Opossum

70 mya.

No change from the fossil record.

Nine-banded Armadillo
55 mya.
This little creature, and its ancestors the anteaters and sloths, form a group distinguished from other living mammals by their unique vertebral joints.

Bats
50 mya.
The oldest known bat fossil, a Jamaican Fruit-eating bat from the early Eocene, was found in Wyoming.

Lemur Monkey
47 mya.
One well preserved fossil (95% complete) is considered the 'final missing link' that scientists have been looking for ever since Darwin started the theory of macro-evolution. Radiometric dating places "Ida" at 47 million years old. It is only 1 ft 9 inches long and is practically identical to modern lemur monkeys.

Mountain Beaver
40 mya.
The only living member of its family, Aplodontidae, and found only in the western United States and Canada. The Mountain Beaver is often considered the most primitive living rodent which has a very simple type of rootless molars.

Przewalski's horse
40 mya.
Thought to be extinct. Discovered in Mongolia in 1881. It is the last of the true/original purebred horses.

Kangaroo
40 mya.
Various forms of this animal, some larger and some smaller than modern kangaroos, are found in the fossil record. The various fossils are confusing to mainstream scientists evolutionary-wise.

Thylacine *(a marsupial canine)*
30 mya.
Now thought to be extinct – the last known to exist in modern captivity (Tazmanian zoo) died in 1936.

Okapi *(Okapia johnstoni)*
20 mya.
They are the closest living relative of the Giraffe. Native to the rain forests in Africa around the Congo, it was known only by the local people until 1901.

Echidna *(a monotreme – a mammal that lays eggs)*
15 mya.
No change from the fossil record.

Laotian Rock Rat
11 mya.
Once believed to be extinct until one was captured during a Southeast Asian expedition.

BIRDS

[Fossils of two 'advanced' crow-like birds (Proto-Avis Texensis) were found to exist 75 million years *before* Archeopteryx – which is about 200 million years ago. Though the rest of the examples of living birds (below) have been found in layers much more recent, these findings prove that (some – if not all) modern birds have remained practically unchanged since the Triassic Period and did not evolve from dinosaurs.]

Western Grebe
80 mya.
Grebes are the only living representatives of an ancient bird order that appears in Upper Cretaceous fossils. Today's species probably arose 25 to 35 million years ago.

Red-billed Tropicbird
50 mya.
The oldest record of the tropicbird family is an Eocene Epoch fossil found in England of a now-extinct species. There are three extant species of tropicbirds living today.

Frigatebird
50 mya.
Frigatebird fossils make their appearance in the Eocene Epoch. It was during the Eocene that nearly all of the modern orders of birds (perhaps as many as 80 percent of them), and even some of the genera that survive today, began to appear.

Chachalaca
50 million years ago
A chicken-like bird. Unchanged from the fossil record.

Hummingbirds
30 million years ago.
Some modern hummingbirds share a remarkable resemblance to those found in fossils.

PLANTS

FLOWERING

Fossils belonging to flowering plants go back 130 million years; each has the distinguishing features of all flowering plants, including female ovaries containing seeds. They are no different from present-day flowering plants.

VARIOUS

Giant Horsetail
400 mya.
A division of plants called Sphenophyta that arose in the Devonian Period. One genus called Equisetum ('horsetails') is still living today. In the Paleozoic, sphenophytes often grew to about 50' tall. Though they were the size of trees, their form has not changed from the smaller versions found today.

Psilotum (whisk fern)
400 mya.
It has no "evolutionary relative" and remains unchanged.

Tree Clubmoss
400 mya.
Lycopods are found as far back as the Devonian Period. Much of North America's coal came from decayed lycopods. Only three genera of clubmosses survive today. Ancient clubmosses would dwarf those found today – they were about 100 feet in size!

Haircap Moss
360 mya.
Mosses go back to the Carboniferous Period. A moss from East Asia has been found that is identical to fossil specimens from 60 million years ago. Although haircap mosses are considered primitive plants, they are successful enough to number about 10,000 species worldwide today.

Bracken Fern
300 mya.
In the Pennsylvanian Period ferns were the size of trees, up to 45 feet tall, with trunks 2 feet in diameter. These plants reproduce from spores.

Betula plant
60 mya.
Fossils found in Montana date back to the Paleocene epoch.

TREES

Lepidodendron (scale tree)
340 mya.
This tree has not changed over the course of time.

Whitebark Pine
300 mya.
Conifers appear in the Pennsylvanian Period and still dominate many of the forests around the world. Whitebark is considered to be the most primitive of the modern pines because its cones do not open until they begin to decay.

Ginkgo
270 mya.
The Ginkgo tree belongs to the family Ginkgoaceae. They were thought to be extinct by western science until they were discovered in Japan in 1691.

Cycads
245 mya.
Cycads and their relatives (i.e.; Conifers, Chinese ginkgo), are called gymnosperms, which means "naked seed". No fruit-like structure is formed from part of a flower called an ovary, which surrounds the gymnosperm seed. Cycads were more common during the Triassic and Jurassic periods (about 245 to 140 million years ago).

Wollemi Pine (a.k.a. the "Dinosaur Tree")
150 mya.
These pine trees were discovered in Australia in 1994.

Oak
145 mya.
The remains of oak trees, even pollen, are common in the North American fossil record. The tree has not changed.

Sassafras
100+ mya.

Dawn Redwood (Metasequoia glyptostroboides)
90 mya.
In 1948, a paleobotanist named Dr. Ralph Chaney, led an expedition in China up the Yangtze River to a fog-covered valley where many of these particular trees were growing. Though it is similar to the California redwood, the dawn redwood is deciduous and loses its leaves during the winter.

Northern Hackberry
65 mya.

A member of the elm family, hackberries were also common in North West America during the Tertiary Period, about 1.8 million years ago. The fossils of snout butterflies have been found with those of hackberries, which is their preferred food to this very day.

Giant Sequoia
65 mya.
A relative of the dawn redwood.

Sweetgum
55 mya.
Still exists today and is essentially unchanged.

American Sycamore
50 mya.
Ancestors of the sycamores are abundant in the fossil record.

Poplar
50 mya .
Fossil poplar tree leaves were found in Green River, Utah, and have not changed.

Sumac
50 mya.
Still the same.

Willow
35 mya.
Still the same.

Plane Tree
18 mya.
Still the same.

Appendix B: Toxins & Bioluminescence

This is a partial list of currently living land-dwelling creatures that lend evidence to the feasibility of the "fire breathing dragon" and support a reasonable consideration of what may have been a real creature. This list does not include the many sea dwelling animals that have a wide range of harmful, if not deadly toxins and unusual methods of subduing their prey (i.e.: the electric eel).

VENOMOUS, TOXIC, & CHEMICAL-SHOOTING LAND ANIMALS

REPTILES

Beaded Lizard
Gila Monster
Horned lizard (Not venomous - but at least four species are able to squirt an aimed stream of blood from the corners of the eyes up to 3 feet away)
Komodo Dragon (mild venomous bite)
Monitor Lizard (mild venomous bite)
Vipers and venomous snakes (i.e.; Giant Spitting Cobra)

MAMMALS

Eurasian water shrew / Various Short-tailed Shrews (venomous bite)
Pangolin [shown above] (can emit a noxious smelling acid from glands like a skunk)
Platypus (venomous spike on the back leg)
Skunk (Skunks have two glands, one on either side of the anus, that produce a mixture of sulfur-containing chemicals. Muscles located next to the scent glands allow them to spray with high accuracy as far as 7 to 15 ft. The smell aside, the spray can cause irritation and even temporary blindness)
Solenodon (a venomous shrew-like mammal)

INSECTS

Arachnids
Bombadier beetle (hydrogen peroxide and hydroquinone are stored in two separate 'compartments'; the beetle adds a catalyst to cause the explosive reaction to start)
Caterpillars (some)
Various other insects

The following list of bioluminescent organisms lend credibility for the reported 'bioluminescent' pterodactyls in Malaysia as well as the "flying fiery serpents" mentioned in the Bible, Herodotus, and other historical accounts. Note that bioluminescence is not the same as biofluorescence (the phenomenon of reflecting light as a different color), which is found in many animal kinds (too many to include here) including the critically endangered hawksbill sea turtle. Simplistically, bioluminescence emits light, and biofluorescence reflects light. The point is that several animal kinds have the capability to either emit or reflect light, giving the appearance of glowing or having fire-like qualities.

BIOLUMINESCENCE

NON-MARINE ORGANISMS

Annelids
Arthropods (some)
Centipedes (some)
Dyakia striata
Fireflies
Ghost fungus (Omphalotus nidiformis)
Glow worms
Honey mushroom
Jack O'Lantern mushroom (Omphalotus olearius)
Millipedes (some)
Mushrooms (see Foxfire)
Mycena (some)
Mycetophilid flies (some)
Panellus stipticus
Railroad worms
Terrestrial mollusc

FISH

Anglerfish
Cookie-cutter shark
Flashlight fish
Gulper eel
Marine hatchetfish
Pineconefish
Porichthys
Rattails (some)

MARINE INVERTEBRATES

Aequorea victoria (a jellyfish)
Bolitaenidae
Clams (some)
Cnidarians (some)
Colossal Squid
Coral
Crustaceans (some)
Ctenophores ("comb jellies")
Cuttlefish (not bioluminescent, but it is interesting to note that this strange creature can change its 'skin' very rapidly to match the surrounding environment, appearing radiant if needed.)
Echinoderms (some, i.e.; Ophiurida)
Krill
Mastigoteuthidae
Nudibranchs (some)
Ostracods
Octopods (some)
Sea pens
Sepiolidae
Sparkling Enope Squid
Squid (some)
Teuthida

PLANKTON AND MICROBES

Dinoflagellates
Vibrionaceae (i.e.; Vibrio fischeri, Vibrio harveyi, Vibrio phosphoreum)

Appendix C: Biblical Dinosaurs

DRAGON ("TANNIN") וְיִנַּת

The following is a partial list of Bible verses utilizing the Hebrew word for dragon. Note that in many modern English translations, *tannin* ("dragon" singular; plural: *tanninim*) has been replaced with *jackal, whale,* or other contemporary creatures that are *also* referred to as *tannin* in Hebrew. The word "dragon" in these particular verses describe (by context) an actual serpent-like creature, and in some cases the physical creature is used as an allegorical comparison with the spiritual.

Leviticus 11:29,30 (The *great lizard* and *sand reptile* are described as "swarming reptiles"; neither of which today swarm in groups nor are considered 'great'. Thus it may be describing another creature than the proposed modern thorn-tailed lizard and such; and other lizard types are described that can be identified – as opposed to the Hebrew word *tannin* used here).

> Now these are to you the unclean among the swarming things which swarm on the earth: the mole, and the mouse, and the great lizard in its kinds, and the gecko, and the crocodile, and the lizard, and the sand reptile, and the chameleon.

Nehemiah 2:13 (This verse is reference for the many documented sightings of dragons in wells in East Asia, as mainly presented in chapter 3).

> So I went out at night by the Valley Gate in the direction of the *Dragon's Well* and on to the Refuse Gate... (italics mine)

Job 7:12
> *Am* I a sea, or a sea serpent (*tannin*), That You set a guard over me?

Psalm 74:13
> Thou didst divide the sea by thy strength; thou brakest the heads of the dragons in the waters.

Psalm 91:13
> Thou shalt tread upon the lion and adder: the young lion and the dragon shalt thou trample under feet. (KJV)

Isaiah 27:1 (Correct English translation should be "sea dragon" – not a whale).

> In that day the LORD will punish Leviathan the fleeing serpent, With His fierce and great and mighty sword, Even Leviathan the twisted serpent; And He will kill the dragon who lives in the sea.

Isaiah 51:9 (Potentially; this verse can be taken as figurative for Jesus' victory over Satan, in addition to it being compared with an actual physical event).

> Awake, awake, put on strength, O arm of the LORD; Awake as in the days of old, the generations of long ago. Was it not You who cut Rahab in pieces, Who pierced the dragon?

Isaiah 43:20

> The beasts of the field shall honour me, the dragons and the owls: because I give waters in the wilderness, and rivers in the desert, to give drink to my people, my chosen. (KJV)

Jeremiah 9:11

> And I will make Jerusalem heaps, and a den of dragons; and I will make the cities of Judah desolate, without an inhabitant. (KJV)
> [see also Jeremiah 10:22; 49:33; 51:37 regarding the dwellings of dragons]

Jeremiah 14:6

> And the wild asses did stand in the high places, they snuffed up the wind like dragons; their eyes did fail, because there was no grass. (KJV)

Jeremiah 51:34

> Nebuchadrezzar the king of Babylon hath devoured me, he hath crushed me, he hath made me an empty vessel, he hath swallowed me up like a dragon, he hath filled his belly with my delicates, he hath cast me out. (KJV)

Ezekiel 29:3

> ... Thus saith the Lord GOD; Behold, I am against thee, Pharaoh king of Egypt, the great dragon that lieth in the midst of his rivers, which hath said, My river is mine own, and I have made it for myself. (KJV)

Most (if not all) other *'tannin(im)'* references in the Bible can be interpreted as *either* dragon or jackal, thus are neutral in support of a real dragon/dinosaur-like creature.

BEHEMOTH בְּהֵמוֹת

Job 40:15-24 (Behemah [plural: בְּהֵמוֹת Behemoth], is translated simply as a very large beast. However, God's description of this creature does not match the hippopotamus, elephant (*the tail in particular*), or the crocodile, as proposed by modern scholars. Each of these proposed animals are caught frequently by hunters even when the animals are "on watch". Also, the described location of both mountains and marshes that are affected by this creature is consistent with other ancient non-Biblical accounts regarding dragons).

> Behold now, Behemoth, which I made as well as you; He eats grass like an ox. Behold now, his strength in his loins and his power in the muscles of his belly. He bends his tail like a cedar; The sinews of his thighs are knit together. His bones are tubes of bronze; His limbs are like bars of iron. He is the first of the ways of God; Let his maker bring near his sword. Surely the mountains bring him food, and all the beasts of the field play there. Under the lotus plants he lies down, in the covert of the reeds and the marsh. The lotus plants cover him with shade; The willows of the brook surround him. If a river rages, he is not alarmed; He is confident, though the Jordan rushes to his mouth. Can anyone capture him when he is on watch, with barbs can anyone pierce his nose?

LEVIATHAN לִוְיָתָן

Job 3:8 / 41:1-34 (Note the repeated description of the capability of breathing fire. This creature does not fit the proposed descriptions of a whale or saltwater crocodile (even metaphorically) since they can be pierced with harpoons and spears, captured and divided for the marketplace. Thus, either God is inaccurate in his descriptions of the very creatures He made, or He is speaking of a very dangerous large reptile-like water-dwelling animal we are not acquainted with in modern times).

> Let those curse it who curse the day, Who are prepared to rouse Leviathan.

> Can you draw out Leviathan with a fishhook? Or press down his tongue with a cord? Can you put a rope in his nose or pierce his jaw with a hook? Will he make many supplications to you, or will he speak to you soft words? Will he make a covenant with you? Will you take him for a servant forever? Will you play with him as with a bird, or will you bind him for your maidens? Will the traders bargain over him? Will they divide him among the merchants? Can you fill his skin with harpoons, or his head with fishing spears? Lay your hand on him; Remember the battle; you will not do it again! Behold, your expectation is false; Will you be laid low even at the sight of him? No one is so fierce that he dares to arouse him; Who then is he that can stand before Me? Who has given to Me that I should repay him? Whatever is under the whole heaven is Mine. I will not keep silence concerning his limbs, or his mighty strength, or his orderly frame. Who can strip off his outer armor? Who can come within his double mail?

Who can open the doors of his face? Around his teeth there is terror. His strong scales are his pride, Shut up as with a tight seal. One is so near to another that no air can come between them. They are joined one to another; They clasp each other and cannot be separated. His sneezes flash forth light, and his eyes are like the eyelids of the morning. Out of his mouth go burning torches; Sparks of fire leap forth. Out of his nostrils smoke goes forth as from a boiling pot and burning rushes. His breath kindles coals, and a flame goes forth from his mouth. In his neck lodges strength, and dismay leaps before him. The folds of his flesh are joined together, firm on him and immovable. His heart is as hard as a stone, even as hard as a lower millstone. When he raises himself up, the mighty fear; Because of the crashing they are bewildered. The sword that reaches him cannot avail, nor the spear, the dart or the javelin. He regards iron as straw, bronze as rotten wood. The arrow cannot make him flee; Slingstones are turned into stubble for him. Clubs are regarded as stubble; He laughs at the rattling of the javelin. His underparts are like sharp potsherds; He spreads out like a threshing sledge on the mire. He makes the depths boil like a pot; He makes the sea like a jar of ointment. Behind him he makes a wake to shine; One would think the deep to be gray-haired. Nothing on earth is like him, one made without fear. He looks on everything that is high; He is king over all the sons of pride.

Psalm 74:14 / 104:26

You crushed the heads of Leviathan; You gave him as food for the creatures of the wilderness.

There the ships move along, And Leviathan, which You have formed to sport in it.

Isaiah 27:1 (see "Dragon" section above)

(FLYING) FIERY SERPENTS הַשְׂרָפִים

... the hapax legomenon[1] of *Nehushtan Ntwhn*, apparently a compound word of *nahash whn* (serpent) and *tan Nt* (translated 'dragon' by the Septuagint, Vulgate, ASV, and KJV). That would be an apt description of a reptilian quadruped with a snake-looking appearance...

... Isaiah then resurrected the word *saraph JrW* for the angelic creatures that he saw at God's throne (6:2). Later he would qualify the word with *m'opheph Jpvfm* when indicating mere animals (14:29 and 30:6) so the audience would know that flying reptiles were intended, not angelic beings (who are qualified by the word standing, *o'mdim Mydmf*, not flying *Jpvfm*).

Saraph JrW may be related to the cuneiform word for a "serpent;" *siru*. Archibald H. Sayce says that the Egyptian word *seref* means "flying serpent." An Egyptian origin for the word appears plausible since there is archaeological evidence and ancient accounts of the presence of flying reptiles there. Since the Israelites had lived there for many years, it is not surprising that they adopted the Egyptian name for them...

...The Hebrew word for burning is also *saraph JrW*. Scholars appear

---
1. hapax legomenon: a word occurring only once within a context, either in the written record of an entire language, in an author's work, or in a single text.

uncertain about whether the animals were named for the burning effect their poison produced or their bright color. There is support for both of those hypotheses. Certainly they were poisonous as indicated by both the Pentateuch and Isaiah.[2]

Num. 21:6-9 ("fiery serpents" would be translated correctly in English as "snakes seraphim" in the Masoretic text. Seraphim = "burning/bright ones" that can fly.)

> The LORD sent fiery serpents among the people and they bit the people, so that many people of Israel died. So the people came to Moses and said, "We have sinned, because we have spoken against the LORD and you; intercede with the LORD, that He may remove the serpents from us." And Moses interceded for the people. Then the LORD said to Moses, "Make a fiery serpent, and set it on a standard; and it shall come about, that everyone who is bitten, when he looks at it, he will live." And Moses made a bronze serpent and set it on the standard; and it came about, that if a serpent bit any man, when he looked to the bronze serpent, he lived.

Despite the origin myths of the rod of Asclepius and the Caduceus symbol, they both seem to be related to the Biblical description of a flying fiery serpent on a pole for healing purposes. It was later called Nehushtan and was used for idol worship (2 Kings 18:4), which may be the true source for secular origin myths.

Deut. 8:15 (Distinction is made between 'serpents' and 'fiery serpents' in the original Hebrew and is reflecting on the "snakes seraphim" event in Numbers 21:6-9)

> He led you through the great and terrible wilderness, with its fiery serpents and scorpions and thirsty ground where there was no water; He brought water for you out of the rock of flint.

Isaiah 14:29 (New King James)

> Do not rejoice, all you of Philistia, because the rod that struck you is broken; For out of the serpent's roots will come forth a viper, and its offspring will be a fiery flying serpent.

Isaiah 30:6 (New King James)

> ... Through a land of trouble and anguish, from which came the lioness and lion, the viper and fiery flying serpent...

---

2. John Goertzen. The Bible and *Pterosaurs*. Article. 1998. Italics added.

Appendix D: Corrections and Notes

While doing research for this book, the following repeated false claims and careless citations by both leading Christian and secular organizations were found in various sources:

1. *"Marco Polo wrote that the chariot of the Chinese Emperor was pulled by dragons."*
Other Chinese historians indicated this (as mentioned in chapter 3), but not Marco Polo.

2. *"In A.D. 67 Roman Historian Octavus Livy wrote that he personally witnessed a battle between the eighth Roman Legion (led by General Scipio Regulus) and a great Heraldic Dragon in what is now Lybia and which lasted for almost a week. Over three thousand Roman soldiers were killed in the battle, which finally ended with the remaining Romans building siege engines and cornering and crushing it to death it in a canyon."*
The (correct) Roman historian, Titus Livius Patavinus, aka: "Livy", was not alive at the time to personally witness the event. Livy was born approximately in 64 BC and died in 17 AD.
The persons named "Octavus (Octavius?) Livy" and "Scipio Regulus" could not be found in other ancient manuscripts except in the passage above.
The amount of slain soldiers and method of killing the serpent are not indicated in Livy's work, though Leonardo da Vinci, commenting on the same event, mentions that the serpent was killed by a catapult.
No reference was given in any of the articles where this particular claim was found.
The actual battle with a huge serpent was described historically as taking place in 256 BC by the army of Marcus Attilius Regulus during the first Punic war.

3. *Clarification (from chapter 4, pg 90)*: Many sources claim that Ulysses Aldrovandus ascribed a *winged* bipedal dragon to the account of the Italian herdsman killing a small dragon by striking its head (see pg. 402 of *Serpentum, et draconum historiae libri duo*). This is not correct in that winged bipedal dragons were described later in the same work (pp. 419 – 423) as coming from Ethiopia and other regions, whereas the particular dragon killed in Italy apparently did not have any wings, as illustrated on p. 404 of *Serpentum, et draconum historiae libri duo*.
Note: similar sketches of the various dragons presented in Ulysses' work were also included in Athanasius Kircher's *Mundus Subterraneus Vol 2.*, 1678; pp. 96 – 100.

4. *"In the end of November and beginning of December last, many of the country people observed dragons appearing in the north and flying rapidly towards the east; from which they concluded, and their conjectures were right, that...boisterous weather would follow."* ("Flying Dragons at Aberdeen," A Statistical Account of Scotland, 1793, p. 467.)

This quote is presented as a word-for-word quote with no mention of text modification. The reference is partially given in many articles where the above quote is used, and the title "Flying Dragons at Aberdeen" is not used in the source material.

The actual text is a footnote found in *A Statistical Account of Scotland*, volume VI, by Sir John Sinclair, Bart., 1793 (p. 467), and reads as follows:

"In the end of November and beginning of December last, many of the country people observed very uncommon phenomena in the air, (which they call dragons), of a red fiery colour, appearing in the N. and flying rapidly towards the E. from which they concluded, and their conjectures were right, a course of loud winds, and boisterous weather would follow."[1]

The following two clerical errors were discovered in the original manuscript and the errors have been duplicated in all subsequent copies found:

Mythical Monsters, by Charles Gould.
In Appendix II it is written as, "Book II, chapter 16", whereas it should be: "Book XII, chapter 16". (pg. 381, in reference to *De Natura Animalium*, by Aelian).

The final sentence in this particular section (pg. 382); "The masculine sex also seems to be privileged by nature among brutes, inasmuch as the male dragon is distinguished by a crest and hairs, with a beard." should be referenced as: Book XII, chapter 26.

The following widely used quotes have yet to be found. Current status is "to be determined" (TBD).

1. *"In 900 A.D. Irish writings record an animal with iron nails on its tail and a head similar to a horse. It also had thick legs and strong claws. These details match the features of dinosaurs like the Kentrosaurus and Stegosaurus"*
Unsupported claim. No actual source given or found – TBD.
The following two specifically referenced "sources" that make this claim do not indicate the original source of the quote:
The Great Dinosaur Mystery and the Bible, by Paul S. Taylor.
Ancient Secrets of the Bible, by Charles Sellier and Brian Russell.

---

1. The old-fashioned use of the letter "*f*" has been modernized to "s" for clarity.

2. *"Konrad Gesner published an encyclopedia entitled Historiae Animalium. In it he indicated that 'Dragons are extremely rare and smaller in the 1500's.'"*

Searching through an online (university) Latin copy (translating almost line by line) of Gesner's *Historiae Animalium,* focusing on the 5th book (Lib V. Serpents), and chapter *De Dracone*, this statement, *"Dragons are extremely rare and smaller in the 1500's."* (in Latin) was not found. Thus this claim is TBD.

The following is the reference for this quote that is supposedly somewhere within Gesner's 4500+ page encyclopedia:

Konrad Gesner, *Historiae Animalium*

(Tigvri: C. Froschovervm, 1551-1587). Verrill, p.224.

Cited by Jorge Luis Borges, *The Book of Imaginary Beings* (NYC: Dutton, 1969), p.240. The specific "Verrill" version noted here was not found.

3. *"An encounter between Jaques Cartier and his crew with a "giant finned snake" that moved through the water like a "caterpillar", using its side fins to propel itself forward; including the unsuccessful attempt at capturing it."*

As much as could be found, all articles and books that make this claim do not indicate a specific source location, other than *"one entry in his journal..."* TBD.

4. "1113 AD: *A group of churchmen from Laon in France were going from town to town in Wessex, England, bearing with them relics of the Virgin Mary, which they used to perform miracles of healing. At the coastal town of Christchuch, they were astonished to see a dragon come out of the sea, "breathing fire out of its nostrils.""*

As much as could be found, all articles and books that make this claim do not indicate a specific source location. TBD.

5. *1937. Alfred Peterson, a nurse aboard a British troopship in the China Sea, spotted what at first he thought was a big tree floating in the sea. A few minutes later he noticed it was still there, keeping pace with the ship. This peaked* [*sic.* piqued] *his interest and he took a closer look. What he saw was a 25-foot long, gray-black, body with a head shaped like a giraffe.*

This quote is widely mentioned in the context of sea serpents but no source information has been found. TBD.

6. Genesis Park (genesispark.com) and Dragons of Genesis (http://truedinos.webnode.com) generically state that the Nazcan pottery (dated between 400-700 AD), with what appears to be a long-necked dinosaur (see below), is on display at "the museum of Lima". An attempt was performed by Dragons of Genesis to locate it after a request was made. In addition, the Museo Nacional de Arqueología, Antropología e Historia

del Perú (National Museum of Archaeology, Anthropology and History of Peru) was contacted since it appeared to be the most logical choice out of many museums in Lima, Peru, and they made a search, respectfully replying promptly that the item was not in their collection. The authenticity of this artifact is questionable since the museum that has it is currently unknown. In addition, the head and neck portion appear to be not original (white arrow in the photo below shows a potential discrepancy in the media). Dennis Swift is a possible owner (to be verified) since he presented it on various shows. TBD.

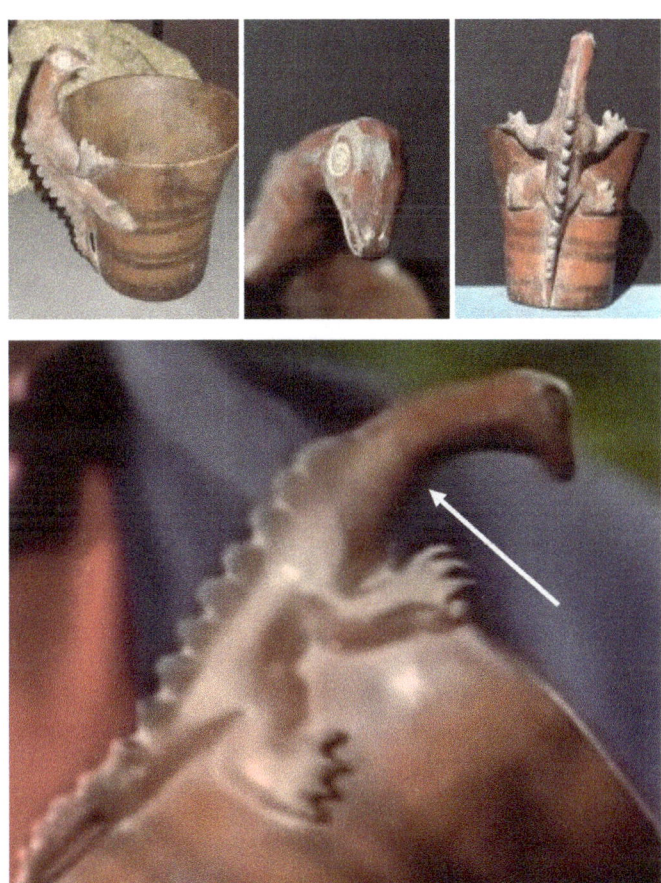

References

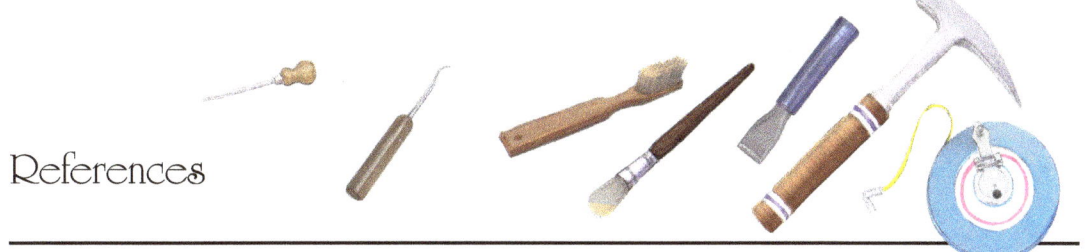

Introduction

Sarfati, Jonathan. *Refuting Evolution.*
Master Books, Green Forest, AR. 1999.

Stark, Rodney. *For the Glory of God, How Monotheism Led to Reformations, Science, Witch-hunts, and the End of Slavery.* Princeton, NJ. Princeton University Press. 2003.

Surtees, Marc. *Did Birds Evolve from Dinosaurs?*
Web article. 2006. (www.truthinscience.org.uk)

Chapter 1 - Opposing Views

Allen, Lad (Director). *Unlocking the Mystery of Life.* Special Edition.
67 minutes. Illustra Media. 2002.

Arp, Halton. *Doppler toppler? A review of: Seeing Red: Redshifts, Cosmology and Academic Science.* Apeiron, Montreal, Canada, 1999. First published: Technical Journal (now Journal of Creation) 14(3):39–45, December 2000. By Michael Oard.

Bigalke, Ron J. Jr. *The Genesis Factor - Myths and Realities.*
Master Books, Green Forest, AR. 2008.

Brown, Walt. *In the Beginning – Compelling Evidence for Creation and the Flood.*
8th ed. Phoenix, AZ.: Center for Scientific Creation, 2008.

Cadwallader, Mark. *May, 2015 Newsletter.* Creation Moments, Inc.
P.O. Box 839, Foley, MN 56329.

Chaffey, Tim and Lisle, Jason. *Old Earth Creationism on Trial - The Verdict is In.*
Master Books, Green Forest, AR. June, 2008.

Hodge, Bodie. *Biblically, Could Death Have Existed before Sin? Satan, the Fall, and a Look at Good and Evil.* Answers in Genesis online article. March 2, 2010.

Jeanson, Nathaniel T., Ph.D. *New Genetic-clock Research Challenges Millions of Years.* Acts & Facts Magazine. Volume 43 Number 4. April 2014.
Published by Institute for Creation Research. (www.icr.org)

Lisle, Jason. *The Ultimate Proof of Creation resolving the origins debate.*
Master Books, Green Forest, AR. 2009.

Lisle, Jason. *Anisotropic Synchrony Convention—A Solution to the Distant Starlight Problem.* Answers Research Journal 3 (2010): 191–207. September 22, 2010.
(www.answersingenesis.org/articles/arj/v3/n1/anisotropic-synchrony-convention)

McDowell, Josh. *The New Evidence that Demands a Verdict, Evidence I & II.*
Nashville.Thomas Nelson Publishers, 1999.

Michael J. Behe. *Darwin's Black Box - The Biochemical Challenge to Evolution.*
Free Press Publishers, 2006, Second Ed.

Morris, Henry M. and John D. *The Modern Creation Trilogy, Volume One.*
Master Books, Green Forest, AR. 2004.

Mortenson, Terry, Ph.D., and Ury, Thane H., Ph.D. (Editors) *Coming to Grips with Genesis - Biblical Authority and the Age of the Earth.* Master Books. 2008.

Mortenson, Terry. *The Great Turning Point.*
Master Books, Green Forest, AR. 2004.

Science X (phys.org), May 21, 2018. Far from special: Humanity's tiny DNA differences are 'average' in animal kingdom.
The Rockefeller University. 1230 York Avenue. New York, NY 10065.
(https://phys.org/news/2018-05-special-humanity-tiny-dna-differences.html)

Sharon Begley. *Science Finds God.*
Newsweek, July 20, 1998, p. 44.

Van Bebber, Mark and Taylor, Paul S. *Creation and Time: A report on the Progressive Creationist Book by Hugh Ross.* Eden Communications. 2nd ed. 1995.

Chapter 2 - Geologic Evidence of a Catastrophe

Acts & Facts. August 2014. Vol 43, No 8. "Original-Tissue Fossils: Creation's Silent Advocates". By Brian Thomas, M.S. Published by Institute for Creation Research.

Acts & Facts. May 2015. Vol 44, No 5. "Settling the Dinosaur Weight Debate". By Tim Clarey, Ph.D., and Jeffrey P. Tomkins, Ph.D. Published by Institute for Creation Research.

Acts & Facts. Feb 2016. Vol. 45, No 2. "Duck-Bill Dinosaur Blood Vessels". By Brian Thomas, M.S. Published by Institute for Creation Research.

Austin, Steven A. *Origin of Limestone Caves.* Acts & Facts. 9(1). 1980.

Batten, Don. *The creation music man (who makes dinosaurs).* Creation ex nihilo, vol. 19(3), pp. 49-51. June 1997.

Brown, Walt. *In the Beginning – Compelling Evidence for Creation and the Flood.* 8th ed. Phoenix, AZ.: Center for Scientific Creation, 2008.

Carpenter, Kenneth. *Dinosaur Eggs and Babies.* Cambridge University Press. 1994.

Craig, William Lane. *Reasonable Faith - Christian Truth and Apologetics.* Crossway Books, a division of Good News Publishers. 1994.

Davis, Buddy; Liston, Mike; Whitmore, John. *The Great Alaskan Dinosaur Adventure.* Master Books, Green Forest, AR. 1998.

Discovery News. *T.Rex fossils yield soft tissue.* Discovery News, Mar 24, 2005. (http://news.discovery.com/dinosaurs/t-rex-fossil-soft-tissue-found.html).

Froede, Carl R. *Geology by Design - Interpreting Rocks and their Catastrophic Record.* Master Books, Green Forest, AR. 2007.

Halls, Kelly Milner. *Dinosaur Mummies - Beyond Bare-Bone Fossils.* Darby Creek Publishing, 2003.

Ham, Ken. *The Great Dinosaur Mystery Solved!.*
Master Books, Green Forest, AR. 2009.

Helder, Margaret. *Fresh Dinosaur Bones Found.*
Creation ex nihilo, vol. 14(3), p. 16. 1992.

Horner, Jack. *Jack Horner: Where are the baby dinosaurs?* TEDxVancouver. Nov. 2010. 18 minutes. (www.ted.com/talks/jack_horner_where_are_the_baby_dinosaurs)

Kitchen, Kenneth. *Ancient Orient and the Old Testament.*
Chicago. InterVarsity Press. 1966.

Maclachlan, Renton. *Tarawera's Night of Terror.*
Creation 18(1): 16–19. December 1995.

Meyers, Stephen and Doolan, Robert. *Rapid Stalactites.*
First published: Creation 9(4):6–8. September 1987.
(www.answersingenesis.org/creation/v9/i4/stalactites.asp).

Morris, John D. *The Polystrate Trees and Coal Seams of Joggins Fossil Cliffs.*
El Cajon, Ca.: Institute for Creation Research. 1999.
(www.icr.org/article/polystrate-trees-coal-seams-joggins-fossil-cliffs).

Mortenson, Terry, Ph.D., and Ury, Thane H., Ph.D. (Editors) *Coming to Grips with Genesis - Biblical Authority and the Age of the Earth.* Master Books. 2008.

Nilsson, Heribert. *Synthetische Artbildung (The Synthetic Origin of Species).*
C.W.K. Gleerup in Lund, 1953.

OOPARTS & Ancient High Technology -- *Evidence of Noah's Flood?.*
(http://s8int.com).

Oard, Michael. *Rapid cave formation by sulfuric acid dissolution.*
First published: TJ (now Journal of Creation) 12(3):279–280. December 1998.

Parker, Gary and Mary. *The Fossil Book.*
Master Books, Green Forest, AR. 2005.

Petersen, Dennis R. *Unlocking the Mysteries of Creation – The Explorer's Guide to the Awesome Works of God.* El Dorado, CA.: Creation Resource Publications. 2002.

Romer, Alfred S. *Vertebrate Paleontology.*
University of Chicago Press, Chicago. 3rd ed. 1966.

Schweitzer, Mary, and Staedter, T, *The Real Jurassic Park.*
Earth Magazine. June 1997.

Wesson, Robert. *Beyond Natural Selection.*
Massachusetts Institute of Technology Press. 1991.

Wieland, Carl. *Fast fossils – Billions of well-preserved fossil fish clash with popular belief.* (http://creation.com/fast-fossils).

Wieland, Carl. *Dinosaur soft tissue and protein—even more confirmation!.*
May, 2009. Found at:
(http://creation.com/dinosaur-soft-tissue-and-protein-even-more-confirmation).

Woodmorappe, John. *Noah's Ark: A Feasibility Study.*
Institute for Creation Research. July 1996.

Van Heerden, Andre (Director). *Dragons or Dinosaurs? - Creation or Evolution?.*
75 minutes. Cloud Ten Pictures. Release date, April 6, 2010.

Chapter 3 - Eastern Historic Dragons

Aston, William George, C.M.G. *Nihongi: Chronicles of Japan from the earliest times to A.D. 697, Volume 1.* 1896. London. Published by Kegan Paul, Trench, Trubner & Co., Ltd. Harvard University Library. Feb. 7, 1961.

Bakker, Robert T. Ph.D. *The Dinosaur Heresies - New Theories Unlocking the Mystery of the Dinosaurs and Their Extinction.*
William Morrow and Company, Inc. New York. 1st ed. 1986.

CBS News.com. *Dino Nose Job Needed.*
CBS Worldwide Inc. February 11, 2009 9:23 PM
(www.cbsnews.com/stories/2001/08/02/tech/main304665.shtml).

De Groot, J. J. M. *The Religious System of China. Vol. VI.*
E. J. Brill, editor, Leiden. 1910. Volume VI, 414 pages, + illustrations.
Reprinting by Literature House, Ltd. Taipei. 1964.
Supplemented edition: December 5, 2007, à Chicoutimi, Québec.

De Visser, Marinus Willem. *The Dragon in China and Japan*. Published by Amsterdam, J. Müller. 1913. Cornell University Library. New York. 1918.

Firdawsi, Abolqasem. *Shahnameh: The Persian Book of Kings*. Translated by Dick Davis. New York, NY, USA: Penguin Group. 2006.

Fung, L. P. *A Dual-Purpose Chinese Dictionary*. Published by Ta Chia Publishers Ltd. Hong Kong. (issue date not given).

Gould, Charles. *Mythical monsters*. Printed by W. H. Allen and Co. 13 Waterloo Place. S.W. Publishers to the India Office. 1886.

Legge, James, D.D., LL.D. *The Chinese Classics, Vol. V, Part II*. Hong Kong: Lane, Crawford & Co. London: Trübner & Co., 60, Paternoster Row. London Missionary Society. 1872. (Harvard University Library).

Legge, James (translation), Confucius. *The Confucian Analects, the Great Learning & the Doctrine of the Mean*. Dover Publications, Inc. 1971.

Li Shih-Chen. *Chinese Medicinal Herbs*. Translated and Researched by F. Porter Smith, M.D. and G. A. Stuart, M.D. Georgetown Press. San Fransisco. 1973.

Martin, Hallie D. *Paleoartists See Bones and Make Dinosaurs*. Science in Society. Northwestern University. June 11, 2008. (http://scienceinsociety.northwestern.edu/content/articles/2008/medill-reports/june/dino-art/paleoartists-see-bones-and-make-dinosaurs).

Parker, Chris. *Tracking the Sauropod Dinosaur Through the Art of Ancient Peoples: Part 2*. Self published online via Calaméo. 2009. PDF format.

Rhys, Ernest. *The Travels of Marco Polo the Venetian*. London: Published by J. M. Dent and Sons Ltd. and in New York by E. P. Dutton and Company. 1908.

Zhao, Gang. *Man and Land in Chinese History: an Economic Analysis*. Stanford Univ Press. November 1986.

Chapter 4 - Western Historic Dragons

Aberdeen Bestiary. 12th Century. Translation & Transcription Copyright 1995. © Colin McLaren & Aberdeen University Library. (www.abdn.ac.uk/bestiary).

Adams, Frank Dawson. PH.D. *The Birth and Development of the Geological Sciences.* Waverly Press, Inc. December, 1938

Aelian, Claudii. *De Natura Animalium.*
(Latin translation by Friedrich Jacobs. Frommann edition. Jena. 1832).

Aelian, Claudii. *On Animals.* [See: *On Animals*, Volume III: Books 12-17. Loeb Classical Library. Translated by A. F. Scholfield. Harvard University Press. 1959.

Aldrovandus, Ulysses, and Ambrosini, Bartolommeo. *Serpentum, et draconum historiae libri duo.* Published by Bononiae : apud C. Ferronium. 1640.

Anglicus, Bartholomaeus. *De Proprietatibus Rerum.* Book 18. 13th century.

The Anglo Saxon Chronicle Part 2: A.D. 750 - 919.
Online Medieval and Classical Library Release #17.
(http://omacl.org/Anglo/part2.html).

A.R. *True and Wonderfull - A Discourse relating A Strange and Monstrous Serpent, or Dragon, Lately Discovered and yet living to the great Annoyance and divers Slaughters both Men and Cattell, by his strong and violent Poyson. In Sussex, two Miles from Horsam, in a Woode called St. Leonards Forrest, and thirtie Miles from London, this present Month of August, 1614.* Printed at London, by John Trundle. 1614.

Aristotle. *Historia Animalium* (The History of Animals). Written 350 B.C. Translated by D'Arcy Wentworth Thompson. The Internet Classics Archive by Daniel C. Stevenson, Web Atomics. World Wide Web presentation is copyright © 1994-2000. (http://classics.mit.edu/Aristotle/history_anim.mb.txt).

Beowulf - an Anglo-Saxon Epic Poem. Translated from the Heyne-Socin text.
by JNO: Lesslie Hall, Ph.D. (J.H.U.). D.C. Heath & Co., Publishers. Boston, New York, Chicago. 1892. Project Gutenberg (http://www.gutenberg.org).

Cooper, Bill., B.A. (Hons). *After the Flood - The early post-flood history of Europe traced back to Noah.* New Wine Press. West Sussex, England. 1995.

Belon, Pierre. *Portraits d'oyseaux, animaux, serpens, herbes, arbres, hommes et femmes d'Arabie et d'Egypte, observez par P. Belon du Mans, le tout enrichy de quatrains, pour plus facile cognoissance des oyseaux et autres portraits...*
Méjanes library [France]. 1557.

Bostock, John, M.D., F.R.S. H.T. Riley, Esq., B.A. *The Natural History. Pliny the Elder.* Taylor and Francis, Red Lion Court, Fleet Street. London. 1855. (www.perseus.tufts.edu).

de Folieto, Hugo. *Elephants, Dragon, and Mandrake.* (Sloane 278, folio 48v). British Library MS, Druce translation. 13th century.

de Voragine, Jacobus. Archbishop of Genoa. *The Golden Legend* (Latin: *Legenda aurea* or *Legenda sanctorum*). Compiled (approximately) 1270 A.D.

Ashe, Geoffrey, et al. (contributors). *Folklore, Myths and Legends of Britain.* Reader's Digest Assoc., N.Y. 1973. 552 pages.

Frith, Roger. *Dragons in Essex.*
The East Anglian Magazine, Vol.21. Nov. 1961 – Oct. 1962.

Giles, J. A., D.C.L. *Old English Chronicles.*
George Bell & Sons. London. 1906.

Gilmer, James Edward, Ph.D. *100 Year Cover-Up Revealed – We Lived With Dinosaurs!* Revised Ed. Published by AuthorHouse. 2012.

Gould, Charles. *Mythical Monsters.*
London, W.H. Allen and company. 1886.

Grammaticus, Saxo ("Saxo the Learned"). *The Danish History, Books I-IX.*
fl. Late 12th - Early 13th Century A.D. (Text based on *The Nine Books of the Danish History of Saxo Grammaticus*, translated by Oliver Elton, Norroena Society, New York, 1905).

Greek Mythology - Heroes and Creatures.
Wikimedia Foundation. e-book / .pdf. Nov. 14, 2010.

Harley Manuscript 3244 (Bestiary). British Library. London, England. c 1255-1265.

De Hortus Sanitatis. Printed by Jacob Meyderbach. (1491 - 1497?)

Isidore of Seville, *Etymologies* (book 12, 4:29). c 560 - 636.

Livius, Titus. *The History of Rome, Vol. 1. Books I - XX.* Literally translated, with notes and illustrations by D. Spillan, A.M., M.D. New York. Harper and Brothers, Publishers, Franklin Square. 1887.

Livius, Titus. *The History of Rome.* Book XLI, Chapter 9.
William A. McDevitte, York Street, Covent Garden, London. Henry G. Bohn. John Child and son, printers, Bungay. 1850. (www.perseus.tufts.edu).

Lucan, *Pharsalia* (book 9:848). c 61.

The Mabinogion. From the Welsh of the Llyfr Coch O Hergest (The Red Book Of Hergest). In the Library of Jesus College, Oxford. Translated, with notes by Lady Charlotte Guest. London: Bernard Quaritch, 15 Piccadilly. 1877. (Scanned at sacred-texts.com. February, 2004. John Bruno Hare, redactor. This text is in the public domain).

McAdams, William. *Records of Ancient Races in the Mississippi Valley: Being an Account of Some of the Pictographs, Sculptured Hieroglyphs, Symbolic Devices, Emblems, and Traditions of the Prehistoric Races of America, with Some Suggestions as to Their Origin.* 1887. Cornell University Library. September 22, 2009.

Milàn, Jesper. *New theropod, thyreophoran, and small sauropod tracks from the Middle Jurassic Bagå Formation, Bornholm, Denmark.* Bulletin of the Geological Society of Denmark, Vol. 59, pp. 51–59. ISSN 0011–6297. © 2011.

The Anglo-Saxon Version from the Historian Orosius. By Alfred the Great (King of England). London. Printed by W. Bowyer and F. Nichols. MDCCLXXIII (1773).

Philostratus, Flavius. *The Life of Apollonius of Tyana.* (approximately 230 AD.) Translated by F.C. Conybeare. Published in 1912. Loeb Classical Library - No 16.

Pliny the Elder (Secundus, Plinius). *Natural History.* c 77 - 79.

Pliny the Elder (Secundus, Plinius). *The Historie Of The World. Commonly Called, The Naturall Historie of C. Plinius Secundus.*
Translated by Philemon Holland. Doctor in Physicke. 1601.

Richter, Jean Paul (compiler/editor). *The Literary Works of Leonardo da Vinci, Volume 2.* London. Sampson Low, Marston, Searle and Rivington. 188 Fleet Street. 1883.

The Story of the Volsungs, (Volsunga Saga) - With Excerpts from the Poetic Edda. Project Gutenberg. Author: Anonymous. October 25, 2009. www.gutenberg.org. Text based on "The Story of the Volsungs", translated by William Morris and Eirikr Magnusson. Walter Scott Press, London, 1888.

Trokelowe, John, and Blaneford, Henry. *Chronica et Annales.* Translated and reproduced in the *Rolls Series*. Edited by Henry Thomas Riley. London: Longmans, Green, Reader, and Dyer. 1866.

Völuspá, The Poetic Edda (*The Old Woman's Prophecy*). A collection of ancient Norse poems primarily preserved in the Icelandic medieval manuscript *Codex Regius*. Late 13th Century.

Chapter 5 - Flying Fiery Serpents and Thunderbirds

Alpin, Prosper. *Histoire Naturelle de l'Egypte.* L'institut Francais D'Archaeologie Orientale, Caire, translated from Latin to French by R. de Fenoyl. 1979.

The American Heritage® Dictionary of the English Language. Fourth Edition. Houghton Mifflin Company. September 2000.

Anglicus, Bartholomaeus. *De Proprietatibus Rerum.* 1240 AD.

The Anglo-Saxon Chronicle. Part II. 750–919 AD. Translated by Rev. James Ingram (London, 1823), with additional readings from the translation of Dr. J.A. Giles (London, 1847). The text of this edition is based on that published as "The Anglo-Saxon Chronicle" (Everyman Press, London, 1912). (http://omacl.org/Anglo)

Ashton, John. *Curious Creatures In Zoology.* (*With 130 Illustrations throughout the Text*). London. John C. Nimmo. 14, King William Street, Strand. 1890.

Barney, Stephen A.; Lewis, W. J.; Beach, J. A.; Berghof, Oliver. *The Etymologies of Isidore of Seville.* Cambridge University Press, New York. 2006.
The first complete English translation of the Latin *Etymologies of Isidore*, bishop of Seville (560–636 AD).

Bochart, Samuel. *Hierozoicon sive bipartitum opus de animalibus sacrae scripturae.* 2 volumes. London. 1663. Libraria Weidmannia, Lipsiae. 1793-1796.

Cardano, Girolamo. *De Rerum Varietate, libri XVII.* 1557.
Cooper, Bill., B.A. (Hons). *After the Flood - The early post-flood history of Europe traced back to Noah.* New Wine Press. West Sussex, England. 1995.

Dino-era sex riddle solved by new fossil find. Contact: Dave Unwin. University of Leicester Press Office. Jan. 20, 2011. (www2.le.ac.uk)

Du serpent ou dragon volant, grand et merveilleux, apparu et veu par un chacun, sur la ville de Paris, le mercredi XVIII. Febvrier 1579, depuis deux heures apres midijusques au soir. Paris, J. d'Ongoys, (s.d.), 14 p. B.M. Amiens, fonds Masson, 3647 (5).

Gessneri, Conradi. *Historia Animalia. Liber V. QVI. Est De Serpentibus.* Ex officina Typographica Ioannis Wecheli, Impensis Roberti Cambieri. 1586.

Evans, Dyfed Lloyd. *Welsh Legends and Folk-tales.* ebook. First Kindle edition. June 2012.

Fabri, Felix. *Voyage en Egypte de Felix Fabri, 1483.* Institut Francais D'Archaeologie, Caire,Orientale du Caire. 1975.

Goertzen, John. M.S., M.A. *The Rhamphorhynchoid Pterosaur Scaphognathus crassirostris: A "Living Fossil" Until the 17th Century.* 587 W. Randall, #304, Coopersville, MI. 49404. Grand Rapids Baptist Seminary. M.S., Rutgers University. 09/26/1998. (Adapted from a paper presented at the 1998 International Conference on Creation, Geneva, PA).

Goertzen, John. M.S., M.A. *The Bible and Pterosaurs: Archaeological and Linguistic Studies of Jurassic Animals that Lived Recently.* An Article for the 1998 Midwestern Evangelical Theological Society Conference held at GRBS, Grand Rapids, MI.

Herodotus. *The History of Herodotus. Vol 1.* English translation by G. C. Macaulay. Kessinger Publishing. June 1, 2004.

Josephus, Flavius. *The Works of Flavius Josephus.* Translated by William Whiston, A.M., Ed. Auburn and Buffalo. John E. Beardsley. 1895.

The Journal of Père Jacques Marquette. Professor Jim Matthews. Illinois Wesleyan Univesity. 1998. (http://sun.iwu.edu)

Le Blanc, Vincent. *Les voyages fameux du sieur Vincent Le Blanc, marseillois, qu'il a faits depuis l'aage de douze ans iusques à soixante, aux quatre parties du monde: à scavoir aux Indes orientales & occidentales, en Perse & Pegu; aux royaumes de Fez, de Maroc, & de Guiné e, & dans toute l'Afrique interieure, depuis le cap de Bonne Esperance iusques en Alexandrie, par les terres de Monomotapa, du Preste Iean & de l'Egypte; aux isles de la Mediterranée, & aux principales prouinces de l'Europe, &c.* Publisher: A Paris: Chez Gervais Clovsier au Palais, sur les degrez de la Saincte Chappelle. 1648.

Mandeville, John. *The Travels of Sir John Mandeville. The version of the Cotton Manuscript in modern spelling.* Macmillan and Co., 1900; Series: The Library of English Classics.

McCrindle, J. W. *Ancient India As Described By Megasthenes and Arrian.* (Fragment. XII. Strabo, XV. i. 37, — p. 703. *Of some Wild Beasts of India.*) 1876-1870.

Native Languages of the Americas Online Resources. Laura Redish, Director. Orrin Lewis, Tribal Coordinator. (www.native-languages.org/animikii.htm).

Peters, David. *The Pterosaur Heresies. The myth of the bat-wing pterosaur.* July 17, 2011. https://pterosaurheresies.wordpress.com/2012/01/14/how-did-pteranodon-walk.

Philostratus, Flavius. *The Life of Apollonius of Tyana.*

Pliny the Elder (Secundus, Plinius). *Natural History.* c 77 - 79.

Sinclair, Sir John, Bart. *A Statistical Account of Scotland, Volume VI.* Edinburgh. 1793.

Steele, Robert. *The Project Gutenberg EBook of Mediaeval Lore from Bartholomew Anglicus.* September, 2004. [EBook #6493]. Edition 10. (www.gutenberg.org).

Steele, Robert. *Mediaeval Lore from Bartholomew Anglicus.* London: Alexander Moring (The King's Classics), 1893/1905.

Vallee, Jacques and Aubeck, Chris. *Wonders In The Sky - Unexplained Aerial Objects from Antiquity to Modern Times and their Impact on Human Culture, History, and Belief.* Published by the Penguin Group. 2009.

Chapter 6 - Monsters of the Deep

Adomnán (of Iona). *The Life of Columba*. 7th Century. CELT online at University College, Cork, Ireland. 2011. (www.ucc.ie/celt).

Anglicus, Bartholomaeus. *De Proprietatibus Rerum*. 1240 AD.

Chorvinsky, Mark. Nessie and Other Lake Monsters. *"Champ" of Lake Champlain*. Strange Magazine. 11772 Parklawn Dr. Rockville, MD 20852. (www.strangemag.com).

Clark, Jerome. *Unexplained!: Strange Sightings, Incredible Occurrences & Puzzling Physical Phenomena*. The Seeker Series. Visible Ink Press; 2nd ed. January 1, 1999.

Coleman, Loren and Huyghe, Patrick. *Field Guide to Lake Monsters, Sea Serpents, and Other Mystery Denizens of the Deep*. Penguin. 2003.

Driver, Rebecca. *Australia's Aborigines ... Did They See Dinosaurs?* Dec. 1, 1998. Answers in Genesis online article. Accessed Oct. 19, 2013. (www.answersingenesis.org/articles/cm/v21/n1/australias-aborigines).

Ellis, Richard. *Monsters of the Sea*. Globe Pequot, 2006.

Fox, William A. *Dragon Sideplates from York Factory, A New Twist on an Old Tail*. Manitoba Archaeological Journal Volume 2. Number 2. 1992.

Hetherington, M. F. *History of Polk County, Florida: Narrative and Biographical*. The Record Company. St. Augustine. 1928. (Reprinted by Mickler House, 1971).

Heuvelmans, Bernard. *In the Wake of the Sea-Serpents*. Translated from the French by Richard Garnett. Hill and Wang. New York. 1968.

Josselyn, John. *An Account of Two Voyages to New England - Made during the years 1638, 1663*. Boston. William Veazie. Riverside, Cambridge. Printed by H. O. Houghton & Co. 1865.

Magnus, Olaus. *Description of the Northern peoples, Rome 1555*. Edited by Peter Foote and John Granlund. Translated by Peter Fisher. Illustrated Edition. Hakluyt Society. 1998.

Magnus, Olaus. *Historia de gentibus septentrionalibus, earumque diversis statibus, conditionibus, moribus, ritibus, superstitionibus, disciplinis, exercitiis, regimine, victu, bellis, structuris, instrumentis, ac mineris metallicis, & rebus mirabilibus, necnon uniuersis pene animalibus in Septentrione degentibus, eorum natura.* Rome. 1555.

McCullough, Joseph A. *Myths and Legends: Dragonslayers from Beowulf to St. George.* Osprey Publishing Ltd. 2013.

McKee, Christopher. *Edward Preble: A Naval Biography, 1761-1807.* Naval Institute Press. 1996.

Oudemans, Antoon Cornelis. *The Great Sea Serpent.* Originally Published in 1892. Reprinted as: A. C. Oudemans. *Loren Coleman Presents The Great Sea Serpent.* Cosimo Inc. 2009.

People's Daily Online. *'Tianchi monster' caught on film.* Source: Xinhua's Jilin provincial bureau. September 10, 2007. (http://english.people.com.cn/90001/90781/90879/6258937.html).

Plattsburgh Republican. Vol. IX. No. 17. Printed by A. C. Flagg. July 24, 1819.
Reinstedt, Randall A. *Shipwrecks and Sea Monsters of California's Central Coast.* Ghost Town Publications. Seventh printing. 1975.

Schmidt, Franz Herrmann. *Prehistoric Monsters in Jungles of the Amazon. Amazing Narrative of an Explorer, Who Describes a Saurian That was Unhurt by Volleys of Bullets from Elephant Rifles.* Fort Wayne, Indiana, Weekly Sentinel, Feb. 8, 1911. Originally published by the New York Herald.
(www.strangeark.com) Historical Reprints section.

Scientific American, 49:3, 1883. "A Bolivian Saurian."

Steele, Robert. *Mediaeval Lore from Bartholomew Anglicus.* Project Gutenberg. 2004. (www.gutenberg.org).

Sydney Morning Herald, The. *China's 'Loch Ness Monster' resurfaces.* July 16, 2003. Reuters.
(www.smh.com.au/articles/2003/07/15/1058035005776.html).

Wide World Magazine, The. *An Illustrated Monthly of True Narrative, Travel, Customs, and Sport.* Vol XII. October 1903 to March 1904. London. George Newnes, LTD. 1904. Southampton St. Strand. The University of Michigan Libraries. (Google eBook)

Wilson, Fred A. *Some Annals of Nahant.*
Boston. Wright & Potter Printing Company. 1928.

Chapter 7 - Modern Accounts

Arment, Chad. *An Account of a North American Bipedal Reptile from Wyoming.* BioFortean Review. August 2008, No. 19. (www.strangeark.com).

Arment, Chad. (Editor). *Cryptozoology and the Investigation of Lesser-Known Mystery Animals.* Landisville, PA: Coachwhip Publications. June 5, 2006.

Clark, Jerome. *Unexplained!: Strange Sightings, Incredible Occurrences & Puzzling Physical Phenomena.* The Seeker Series. Visible Ink Press; 2nd ed. January 1, 1999.

Driver, Rebecca. *Australia's Aborigines ... Did They See Dinosaurs?*
Creation Ex Nihilo magazine. Volume 21, Issue 1. Published December 1998.

Eberhart, George M. *Mysterious Creatures: A Guide to Cryptozoology.* Vol 1. ABC-CLIO Inc. Santa Barbara, CA. 2002.

Geelong Advertiser and Squatters' Advocate. *Wonderful Discovery of a New Animal.* (Vic.: 1845 - 1847) (Vic.: National Library of Australia). 2 July 1845.

Gilroy, Rex and Heather. *Burrunjor! The Search for Australia's Living Tyrannosaurus.* Uru Publications. Katoomba, NSW. Australia. December 1, 2011.

Gilroy, Rex and Heather. *Out of the Dreamtime The Search for Australasia's Unknown Animals.* Uru Publications. Katoomba, NSW. Australia. September 1, 2006.

Hagenbeck, Carl. *Beasts and Men, Being Carl Hagenbeck's Experiences for Half a Century Among Wild Animals.* Longmans, Green, 1911.

Heuvelmans, Bernard. *On the Track of Unknown Animals.* 1958.

Heuvelmans, Bernard. *Lingering Pterodactyls, Part 2.*
Strange Magazine (17). pp. 18-21, 56-57. 1996.

Hughes, Joseph Edward. *Eighteen Years on Lake Bangweulu*. The Field. 1933.

Izzard, Ralph. *The Hunt for the Buru*. Craven Street Publishing. (1951) 2001.

Kasai Rex, Burrunjor, And Mini-T-Rex: Evidence of Surviving Carnivorous Dinosaurs? Part 2. [*Beware of Burrunjors In The Bush*. By Rex Gilroy]. http://thecryptozoologist.webs.com. Posted on May 30, 2012.

Kryptozoologie Online. *Kongamato*. Published Sept. 18, 2005. (www.kryptozoologie-online.de/enzyklopadie/enzyklopadie/kongamato.html)

Last Dinosaur, The. Monster Quest. Season 3, Episode 18. Producer: Jared Christie. History Channel. Aired: June 24, 2009.

Ley, Willy. *Willy Ley's Exotic Zoology*. 1959. Bonanza Books. Reprint. 1987.

Mackal, Roy P. *A Living Dinosaur: In Search of Mokele-mbembe*. Brill Archive. 1987.

Matthew, William Diller. *Dinosaurs With Special Reference to the American Museum Collections*. New York. American Museum of Natural History. 1915. (www.gutenberg.org)

McFarlane, Andrew. *The Lake Leelanau Monster*. August 31, 2011. (www.leelanau.com/blog/the-lake-leelanau-monster).

Melland, Frank Hulme. *In Witch-bound Africa: An Account of the Primitive Kaonde Tribe & Their Beliefs*. Seeley, Service & Company, Limited. 1923.

Millais, John Guille. *Far Away Up the Nile*. Longmans, Green. 1924.

Natural History Museum, London. *The Dino Directory*. (www.nhm.ac.uk/nature-online/life/dinosaurs-other-extinct-creatures/dino-directory/parasaurolophus.html)

Nature, "Giant Bird in New Guinea". (Nov. 25, 1875), V. 13. (www.strangeark.com/reprints/ngbird.html)

Norman, David. *The Illustrated Encyclopedia of Dinosaurs*. Crescent Books. New York. Salamander Books Ltd. 1985.

Peters, David. *The Pterosaur Heresies. How Did Pteranodon Walk?* Jan. 14, 2012. https://pterosaurheresies.wordpress.com/2012/01/14/how-did-pteranodon-walk.

Peters, David. *The Pterosaur Heresies. At Least Two Flat-Footed Pteranodon Specimens.* Nov. 23, 2011. *https://pterosaurheresies.wordpress.com/2011/11/23/at-least-two-flat-footed-pteranodon-specimens*

Proyart, Abbe (Liévain-Bonaventure). *Histoire de Loango, Kakongo, et Autres Royaumes d'Afrique; Rédigée d'après les Mémoires des Préfets Apostoliques de la Mission française; enrichie d'une Carte utile aux Navigateurs.*
Pre-1801 Imprint Collection (Library of Congress), DLC.

Proyart, Abbé Lievain Bonaventure. *History of Loango, Kakonga, and other Kingdoms in Africa.* 1776. Translated by John Pinkerton. *A General Collection of the Best and Most Interesting Voyages and Travels in all Parts of the World: Volume 16.* 1914.

Shuker, Karl P. *In Search Of Prehistoric Survivors: Do Giant 'Extinct' Creatures Still Exist?* Blandford Press. 1996.

"The Flap of Pteradactyloid Wings". Strange Magazine. Issue 7.
11772 Parklawn Dr. Rockville, MD 20852.

Strickler, Lon. *Cryptid Encounter on Lake Leelanau.* Article dated November 5, 2012. Phantoms and Monsters / PM Network. 2013.
(www.phantomsandmonsters.com/2012/11/cryptid-encounter-on-lake-leelanau.html).

Unknown Explorers - Online Resources. *Leelanau.* 2006.
(www.unknownexplorers.com/leelanau.php).

Wavell, Stewart. *The lost world of the East: an adventurous quest in the Malayan hinterland.* London. Souvenir Press. 1958.

Weston, Paula. *The Platypus Still More Questions Than Answers for Evolutionists.* Answers in Genesis. March 1, 2002.
(www.answersingenesis.org/articles/cm/v24/n2/platypus#b1f1).

Woetzel, David. *The Fiery Flying Serpent.*
Creation Research Society Quarterly. Volume 42, Number 4, Winter 2006.

Whitcomb, Jonathan D. *Live Pterosaurs in America: Not extinct, flying creatures of cryptozoology that some call pterodactyls or flying dinosaurs or prehistoric birds.* CreateSpace Independent Publishing Platform. November 2, 2011.

Whitcomb, Jonathan D. *Live Pterosaur Media Center.*
4503 Walnut Ave., Long Beach, CA. 90807. (www.livepterosaur.com).

Whitcomb, Jonathan D. *Reports of Living Pterosaurs in the Southwest Pacific. Creation Research Society Quarterly.* Volume 45, Number 3, Winter 2009.

Chapter 8 - Dragon Art

Abrahams, Ishmael. *Kachina Bridge Dinosaur Petroglyph - Still Good Evidence.* March 18, 2011.
(https://answersingenesis.org/dinosaurs/humans/kachina-bridge-dinosaur-petroglyph)

Childress, David Hatcher. *The Lost Cities of North and Central America.*
Lost Cities Series. Adventures Unlimited Press. 1992.

Di Peso, Charles C., 1953. The Clay Figurines of Acambaro, Guanajuato, Mexico. *American Antiquity* 18(4). Published by the Society for American Archaeology.

McIntosh, Andy. *Utah's Testimony to Catastrophe.* May 8, 2007.
(https://answersingenesis.org/geology/natural-features/utahs-testimony-to-catastrophe)

Meyboom, Paul G.P. *The Nile Mosaic of Palestrina: Early Evidence of Egyptian Religion in Italy.* Leiden: E.J. Brill, 1995.

Nelson, Vance. *Untold Secrets of Planet Earth - Discovery Series - Amazon Expedition.* Untold Secrets of Planet Earth Publishing Company, Inc. 1st Ed. 2015.

Nelson, Vance. *Untold Secrets of Planet Earth - Dire Dragons.*
Untold Secrets of Planet Earth Publishing Company, Inc. 2nd Ed. 2013.

Sjögren, Bengt. *Berömda vidunder.*
Settern. 1980. ISBN 91-7586-023-6

Appendix A - Living Fossils

Denton, Michael. *Evolution: A Theory in Crisis.*
London. Burnett Books, Ltd. 1985.

Zimmer, Carl. *Insects Ascendant.*
Scientific American. Vol. 14. November 1993.

Appendix C - Biblical Dinosaurs

Goertzen, John. *The Bible and Pterosaurs.* Grand Rapids Baptist Seminary. M.S., Rutgers University. An Article for the 1998 Midwestern Evangelical Theological Society Conference held at GRBS, Grand Rapids, MI.

Chapter heading graphic references:

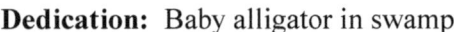

Dedication: Baby alligator in swamp
Table of Contents: Stegosaurus stenops skeleton
Preface: Nautilus
Introduction: Orthoceras

1: Opposing views: Charles Darwin, Phillip Morris, Hugh Ross.
2: Geologic Evidence of a Catastrophe: Wulingyan, China.
3: Eastern Historic Dragons: Ming Dynasty roof tile - "dragon guardian".
4: Western Historic Dragons: Artistic rendition of a French stone carving from the Royal Chateau of Blois (~1500 AD).
The original dragon sculpture portrays features that are remarkably similar to a plateosaurus. Notice how the 'spit' is different in appearance to the fire surrounding the dragon. If carved from an eyewitness description, this may be additional evidence that a 'fire breathing' dragon excreted chemicals that caused burns (like fire) and not actual fiery flames (as discussed in chapter 3, under the section entitled "Fire!", and also in chapter 4, under the section entitled "Dragon Slayers").
5: Flying Fiery Serpents and Thunderbirds: Pterosaurs in flight.
6: Monsters of the Deep: Elasmosaurus platyurus (homage to Charles R. Knight).
Note that the neck has been found to be not as flexible as shown in Knight's painting.
7: Modern Accounts: Binoculars and old compass.
8: Dragon Art: Tang Dynasty bronze dragon (carrying a "pearl" in its mouth).
Afterward: Ant in amber.

A: Living Fossils: Armadillo lizard.
B: Toxins & Bioluminescence: Giant pangolin (*M. gigantea*).[1]
C: Biblical Dragons: Bible with magnifying glass.
D: Corrections and Notes: Roman (ballista-looking) catapult.[2]

References: Geology/Archaeology tools.
Graphic references: Drafting compass.
Index: Trilobite (An index fossil!)

---

1. Pangolin copied from plate 150 of the *Handbook of the Mammals of the World - Volume 2.* Illustrated by Toni Llobet. Pub: Lynx.
2. See Edwin Tunis. *Weapons, A pictoral History.* Johns Hopkins University Press. 1999.

Index

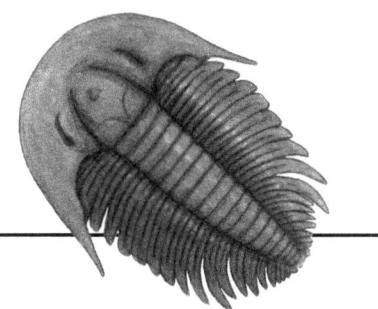

Beard: 86, 87, 96, 97, 207

Bioluminescent: 41, 69, 157, 159, 160, 162, 184, 199, 200

Bone: xii, 19, 21, 22, 36, 37, 43–47, 94, 99, 100, 115, 147, 203

Burial / Buried: 18–21, 23, 24, 28, 93, 94, 164

Camouflage: 62–66, 145

Cave / Cavern: 20, 2`, 29, 30, 33, 36, 59, 65, 71–74, 76, 77, 83, 87, 88, 91, 94, 96, 99, 104, 113, 116, 150, 152, 153, 184

Ch'ih Muh: 75 (see dragontite)

Charles Darwin / Darwinian: xi, xii, xiii, 2, 3, 4, 6, 10, 12, 15–18, 28, 39, 129, 145, 193, 212, 230

Cosmology: 12, 16

Dragon Horse: 35, 54–58, 141

Dragon Rearer: 54, 55

Dragontite: 74–76, 96

Elephant: 25, 30, 44, 45, 59–61, 71–75, 88, 97, 98, 135, 136, 142, 143, 152, 153, 155–157, 184, 185, 203

Eye: 8, 20, 30, 32, 35, 36, 38, 41, 56, 58, 61, 69, 73, 74, 85, 87, 92, 97–99, 105, 116, 117, 119, 124, 126–128, 130, 132, 134, 136, 140, 141, 145, 150, 161, 173, 174, 184, 190, 198, 202, 204

Eyebrows: 35, 36, 97

Eyewitness: xii, 47, 64, 69, 86, 88, 90, 103, 104, 108, 109, 112, 114, 117, 118, 121, 123, 124, 132–134, 141–143, 145, 153, 154, 158, 159, 161–163, 185, 230

Face: 82, 87, 163, 204

Fire: xii, 9, 29, 32, 37, 58, 61, 76–79, 82, 92, 95, 96, 98, 99, 108, 109, 111, 120, 125, 134, 137, 149, 162, 184, 198, 199, 203, 204, 208, 230

Flood / Flooding: x, 4, 7, 9, 10, 13, 18, 19, 21–28, 48, 57, 60, 94, 95, 105, 157

Fly / Flight / Flying: xiii, 25, 29, 33, 34, 36, 39, 41, 42, 52, 62, 68, 69, 75, 76, 79, 81, 91, 92, 95, 96, 100, 101–112, 157–162, 175, 191, 199, 204, 205, 207

Fossil: x, xii, xiii, 7, 17–28, 32, 36, 38, 43, 45–47, 56, 67–69, 76, 89, 90, 109, 112, 144, 145, 147, 148, 158, 163, 167, 175, 176, 179, 183–197

Geology / Geologic: 4, 7, 9, 10, 15, 17, 22–28, 74, 75, 185

Glow(ing): 41, 128, 159, 199

Hair(y): 29, 31, 35, 38, 39, 55, 56, 59, 61, 62, 82, 86, 107, 110 (haire), 116, 117, 161, 184, 185, 204, 207

Horn: 29, 31–35, 38–41, 43, 47, 51, 56, 59, 64, 67, 82, 87, 108, 136–138, 152, 153, 155–157, 166, 176, 198

Hugh Ross: 9, 12, 15

Kiao (lung): 33–39, 84, 86, 140

Lips: 45–47

Macro Evolution: 10–12, 15–18, 28, 145, 185, 193

Marco Polo: 29, 30, 34, 53, 54, 92, 137, 153, 206

Medicine: 30, 43, 44, 52, 101, 184

Micro Evolution: 10, 145

Nāga(s): xiii, 59, 60, 76, 78, 108, 156

Neck: 32, 35, 36, 47, 55, 59, 69, 70, 84–86, 88, 90, 92, 96, 97, 98, 101, 104, 106, 113, 114, 116, 117, 119, 126, 127, 130, 132, 136, 137, 139, 140, 144, 145, 147, 153, 154, 156, 158, 161, 166, 167–170, 178, 182, 184, 204, 208, 209, 230

Necking: 166–168, 170

Nose: 33, 45–47, 85, 111, 127, 137, 148, 163, 186, 203

Old Earth / OE: xii, 3–7, 9, 12, 14, 15, 22, 183

Progressive Creation(ist / ism): 3, 5–7, 9, 10, 12–16, 28

Saliva: 36, 52, 53, 58, 76, 128

Scales: xii, 29, 31–35, 52, 55, 56, 62, 76, 85–89, 97, 107, 109, 116, 128, 131, 144, 151, 153, 156, 184, 204

Serpent / Serpentine: xiii, 8, 29–31, 33, 35, 39, 56, 61, 62, 66, 67, 68, 70–76, 78, 79, 81–85, 88–90, 92–94, 99–124, 126–133, 138, 139, 147, 152, 156, 160, 165, 166, 168–170, 178, 184, 187, 199, 201, 202, 204–206, 208

Swallow (bird): 34, 53

Swallow (eat): 30, 31, 34, 35, 73, 88, 116, 202

Tiger: xii, 30–37, 42, 43, 50, 54, 72, 80, 87, 184

Tissue: xii, 19, 21, 22, 138

Uniformitarianism: 3, 4, 12

Vision / sight: 35, 37, 58, 59, 78, 85, 93, 99, 102, 110, 121, 122, 124–126, 137, 141, 146, 150, 154, 184, 203

Water: xiii, 4, 9–11, 19, 20, 23–26, 29–32, 34–40, 42, 43, 48, 50–53, 55, 56, 58, 59, 64, 65, 72, 77, 78, 80, 82, 88, 89, 92–94, 99, 105, 108, 113–128, 130–138, 140–142, 144–148, 151, 153–156, 165, 184, 187, 188, 190, 198, 202, 203, 205, 208

Well (water): 36, 37, 48–50, 60, 65, 83, 201

White ring: 35, 85, 86, 140

Wing: 19, 29, 33, 35, 38, 39, 55, 56, 67, 68, 82, 85, 87, 90–92, 95, 100, 101, 104, 105, 107–111, 141, 157–163, 174, 181, 191, 206

Young Earth / YE: x - xii, 3, 4, 5, 11, 12, 15, 16, 18, 21, 27, 28

www.ingramcontent.com/pod-product-compliance
Lightning Source LLC
Chambersburg PA
CBHW061925290426
44113CB00024B/2825